Art Nouveau
in
Munich

Masters of Jugendstil

*from the Stadtmuseum, Munich,
and other
Public and Private Collections*

Edited and with an introduction by
Kathryn Bloom Hiesinger

Prestel

in association with the Philadelphia Museum of Art

This book was published in conjunction with the exhibition
"Art Nouveau in Munich: Masters of Jugendstil"
Philadelphia Museum of Art
September 25 – November 27, 1988
Los Angeles County Museum of Art
December 22, 1988 – February 19, 1989
The Saint Louis Art Museum
March 30 – May 28, 1989
Stadtmuseum, Munich
June – July 1989

The exhibition was supported by The Pew Charitable Trusts, the
National Endowment for the Arts, Lufthansa German Airlines, and
the Bayerische Vereinsbank AG. Additional support for the catalogue
was provided by Merck Fink & Co and the Vereinigte Werkstätten für
Kunst im Handwerk AG, Munich.

Translations from the German: John William Gabriel, with Michael Foster,
Hanna Kunz, and Eileen Martin

Cover
Gertraud von Schnellenbühel, Candelabra, c. 1910 (no. 141)

Frontispiece
Hans Eduard von Berlepsch-Valendas, Bookcase, 1899 (no. 16)

Prestel-Verlag
Mandlstrasse 26
D-8000 Munich 40
Federal Republic of Germany

Softcover edition not available to the trade

Distributed in the USA and Canada by
te Neues Publishing Company,
15 East 76 Street, New York, NY 10021, USA

Distributed in the United Kingdom, Ireland and the rest of the world with the
exception of continental Europe, USA, Canada and Japan by
Thames and Hudson Limited,
30-34 Bloomsbury Street, London WC1 B3 QP, England

Composition by Fertigsatz GmbH, Munich
Color separations by Repro Dörfel, Munich
Printing by Karl Wenschow-Francis Druck GmbH, Munich
Binding by Conzella, Pfarrkirchen

Printed in the Federal Republic of Germany

ISBN 3-7913-0881-5

German Edition ISBN 3-7913-0887-4

Contents

Lenders to the Exhibition

Architektursammlung der Technischen Universität, Munich
Bayerische Staatsbibliothek, Munich
Bremer Landesmuseum/Focke-Museum, Bremen
Bröhan-Museum, Berlin
The Danish Museum of Decorative Art, Copenhagen
Gewerbemuseum der LGA im GNM, Nuremberg
Hessisches Landesmuseum, Darmstadt
Kaiser Wilhelm Museum, Krefeld
Kunsthalle, Bremen
Museen der Stadt, Sammlungen der Städtischen Galerie, Regensburg
Museum für Kunsthandwerk, Frankfurt
Museum für Kunst und Gewerbe, Hamburg
Museum of Fine Arts, Boston
The Museum of Modern Art, New York
Philadelphia Museum of Art
Schleswig-Holsteinisches Landesmuseum, Schleswig
Staatliche Graphische Sammlung, Munich
Staatliche Kunstsammlungen, Museum für Kunsthandwerk, Dresden
Staatliche Museen Preussischer Kulturbesitz, Kunstbibliothek, Berlin
Staatliche Museen Preussischer Kulturbesitz, Kunstgewerbemuseum, Berlin
Staatliche Porzellan-Manufaktur Nymphenburg, Munich
Städtische Galerie im Lenbachhaus, Munich
Stadtmuseum, Munich
Vereinigte Werkstätten für Kunst im Handwerk AG, Munich
Württembergisches Landesmuseum, Stuttgart

K. Barlow Ltd., London
Prof. Dr. Tilmann Buddensieg, Sinzig
Dr. Beate Dry von Zezschwitz, Munich
Wolfgang Ehrlich
Dr. Tauchner, Munich
and ten anonymous lenders

Preface

In the years immediately surrounding 1900, the Philadelphia Museum of Art (then the Pennsylvania Museum and School of Industrial Art) expressed its enthusiasm for modern decorative arts in a variety of ways, purchasing contemporary objects in ceramics and glass at the Paris exposition of 1900 and the St. Louis world's fair of 1904, encouraging its students to work in the new styles of decoration, and – in 1905 – publishing its quarterly *Bulletin* in a new, "pretentious" format with an elegant cover designed by a student, which can only be described as a charming exercise in Art Nouveau. The Museum's acquisitions extended to the work of Louis Comfort Tiffany, Taxile Doat, and Emile Gallé, but the only German examples purchased at these exhibitions were those of the royal porcelain manufactory in Berlin. Philadelphia had the opportunity to see a variety of contemporary German achievements in interior decoration and furnishings at first hand when a large suite of rooms from the German section of the St. Louis exposition was acquired by the Wanamaker stores and put on display. Despite these early ventures, many of the major artists and innovations of Jugendstil remain little known in the United States. This exhibition of work from Munich, where Jugendstil first began in Germany, now expands the context created by several recent exhibitions devoted to the decorative arts of Vienna, Paris, and Berlin in the early years of this century.

Organized by Kathryn Bloom Hiesinger with her customary zeal and thorough scholarship, *Art Nouveau in Munich: Masters of Jugendstil* is the first survey of this remarkable movement to be shown in the United States, and we are delighted that it will also be seen in Los Angeles and St. Louis. Originally inspired by the rich collections of Jugendstil in the Stadtmuseum, Munich, the exhibition owes much to the enthusiasm and generosity of two successive directors, Dr. Christoph Stölzl and Dr. Wolfgang Till, and of the chief curator Dr. Hans Ottomeyer, who has been an extraordinarily helpful and congenial colleague over the past four years. We are deeply grateful to the Stadtmuseum for its very handsome loans, which form the core around which the exhibition developed, and to the many public institutions and private collectors whose interest in the exhibition prompted them to part with important works of art, most of which have never been seen before by the public in this country. It is a matter of much satisfaction that the exhibition will conclude its tour at the Stadtmuseum itself.

Many members of the staff of the Philadelphia Museum of Art have worked together toward the realization of the exhibition, and the departments of the registrar, packing, special exhibitions, and conservation have made special contributions in their careful planning for the transportation and handling of objects in a wide variety of mediums. George H. Marcus, Head of Publications, in collaboration with the editorial and production staff of Prestel Verlag, has overseen every stage of the evolution of this handsome volume, which presents the first overview in English of the artists who created Munich Jugendstil.

A project of this complexity could not have been realized without crucial funding from the National Endowment for the Arts and The Pew Charitable Trusts. We are delighted that the project was of interest to several German companies, and most gratefully acknowledge the contributions of the Bayerische Vereinsbank AG and Merck Finck and Co. Lufthansa German Airlines provided substantial support for the cost of transporting works of art between the United States and the Federal Republic of Germany. We are grateful to Timotheus R. Pohl and Prinz Franz von Bayern for their help and good counsel, and to Goethe-House New York for its support of a scholarly symposium. It is particularly pleasing to have had assistance from the Vereinigte Werkstätten für Kunst im Handwerk AG in Munich, which was founded ninety years ago by several of the artists represented in this exhibition.

Anne d'Harnoncourt

The George D. Widener Director

Acknowledgments

This exhibition and catalogue demonstrate the importance of Munich as one of the world's most advanced centers of decorative arts and design in the years around 1900. At this time, a remarkable group of artists, many trained as painters and sculptors, abandoned their previous careers to design objects for everyday use and illustrations for the new periodicals that so often published their work. It is around these artists and the applied art of great originality they created that this undertaking is centered.

Without the cooperation of the Stadtmuseum, Munich, and in particular of its chief curator Dr. Hans Ottomeyer, this could not have been achieved. The Stadtmuseum boasts the richest collection of this little-known material and has lent generously of it. We are profoundly indebted to Dr. Ottomeyer for his help in coordinating all aspects of the Stadtmuseum loan; to Dr. Christoph Stölzl and Dr. Wolfgang Till, the two successive directors of the Stadtmuseum who encouraged it; and to the conservation department of the Stadtmuseum, in particular to its head, Angela Hückel, who prepared the objects for travel.

We would particularly like to thank the contributing authors, who provided new and often unpublished information as well as advice about these outstanding Munich artists. In addition, the following have offered valuable suggestions and thoughtful advice: Theresia Arndt, Emilie Arndt-Meislinger, Kenneth Barlow, Ingeborg Becker, Konrad O. Bernheimer, Elisabeth Bornfleth, Tilmann Buddensieg, Adolfo S. Cavallo, Barry Friedman, Manfred Galaske, Leni Gerg, Glasmalerei Gustav van Treeck, Munich, Goethe House New York, Goethe-Institut, Munich, Hans-Ulrich Haedeke, Richard Harprath, Carl Benno Heller, Georg Himmelheber, Matthias Klein, Ruth Malhotra, Gerhard Martin, Eva Moser, Barbara Mundt, Klaus Naudé, Winfried Nerdinger, Juergen Ohlau, Gianni Pirrone, Maritheres Preysing, Axel von Saldern, Gisela Scheffler, Heike Schröder, Staatliche Porzellan-Manufaktur Nymphenburg, Benjamin C. Stone, Carl Strehlke, Christina Thon, Frank Trommler, Robert Venturi, Vereinigte Werkstätten für Kunst im Handwerk AG, Munich, Gabriel P. Weisberg, Larry L. Wellman, Hans Wichmann, Siegfried Wichmann, Albrecht Widmann, and David van Zanten.

The production of this catalogue depended on the combined efforts of Prestel Verlag, Munich, and the departments of publications and European decorative arts at the Philadelphia Museum of Art. Our warmest thanks are owed to George H. Marcus and Peter Stepan, who coordinated the various aspects of the publication in Philadelphia and Munich, respectively; Michael Foster, who with skill, elegance, and patience, edited this book under pressure; Franz Mees, who provided its design and layout; Jennifer Johnson, Elizabeth Janus, Beth Anne Weidler, Helen Neithammer, Anne Sims, and Anne LeBourgeois, who worked on the bibliography in various stages; and Susanne Immerheiser and Ulrich Hiesinger, who provided translations of various research materials.

Of the other departmental staffs at the Philadelphia Museum of Art who worked enthusiastically on this project, we would particularly like to thank Lilah Mittelstaedt and Sherry Hiatt of the library, who mastered the art of building a Munich research library by loan, as well as Barbara Sevy; Graydon Wood, for special photography; Grace Eleazer, Martha Small, and Irene Taurins of the registrar's office; and Marigene Butler, Cor van Horne, Olaf Unsoeld, Randall Couch, Andrew Lins, Melissa Meighan, and Rae Beaubien of the department of conservation, who contributed in their areas of expertise both treatments and valuable advice; and Suzanne F. Wells, who coordinated the exhibition.

Melanie Ingalls worked on a slide-video program for the exhibition, and Cleo Nichols and his assistant Eyal Ungar designed the installation, which David Wolfe realized in Philadelphia. Christina Melk-Haen undertook a range of responsibilities in Munich, from gathering the photographs of the artists, to pursuing elusive information and people, verifying bibliographical citations, and providing the documents that are published herewith in the Appendix. Julia H. M. Smith in London also provided research materials.

Finally, we are indebted to Donna Corbin in the Museum's Department of European Decorative Arts, who skillfully accomplished the enormous task of compiling and checking the catalogue information and bibliography, and coordinated the myriad aspects of the exhibition and catalogue with her customary grace and efficiency. K.B.H.

Introduction

Kathryn Bloom Hiesinger

It is ironic that the Art Nouveau movement in Munich, which so accurately predicted the course of modern design, should have been so neglected in the literature on modern art.[1] Boasting that it had more artists per inhabitant than any other city,[2] Munich in the 1890s offered a heady maelstrom of conflicting artistic tendencies, ranging from the "official" neoclassicism of the Bavarian government, with its historicizing affection for the styles of ancient Greece and eighteenth-century Germany, to the anti-historicist, expressive, and visionary new art of utilitarian objects that in 1896 burst upon the city known as "the Athens on the Isar." In that year appeared the first decisive examples of Art Nouveau: the embroideries of Hermann Obrist, including the abrupt and powerful "whiplash" design, as it instantly became known (fig. 1),[3] which soon inspired the architecture of the Hof-Atelier Elvira by August Endell, with its gigantic abstract relief decoration utterly defying definition by contemporary critics (fig. 2); and the tapestries of Otto Eckmann, which were hailed as "the freshest product[s] of the new movement" (see no. 30).[4] The same year also saw the founding in Munich of *Jugend* (Youth), an avant-garde periodical of art and literature that gave its name to the new movement ("Jugendstil," or Style of Youth) and whose innovative typography and illustrations were said to have "introduced a new line with regard to book illustration" (fig. 3).[5]

However, even as they combined advanced thinking with self-appointed purposefulness, the leading artists of the Munich Jugendstil were themselves divided between expressive and rational styles that were related to, but independent of, the international Art Nouveau movements in France and Belgium, and the Arts and Crafts movement in England. The dominant stylistic characteristic of Art Nouveau on the Continent was its ornamental use of curving lines, frequently associated with natural forms such as the stems of plants and flowers. It could be seen in all forms of architecture and the applied arts. In England, where Art Nouveau never made any real headway, the stylistic vocabulary of the Arts and Crafts movement persisted in rectilinear, solid, simple, and unornamented decorative designs.

It is in the mix of these two styles in Munich, where they were oriented toward a more restrictive, specifically German culture, that the aesthetics of the modern machine-made product were founded. Based on abstract forms, both freely curved and cubic, and, unlike either of the related Continental or English styles, unapologetic about its use of mechanized production techniques, the Munich movement affected the look of smoothness, sparse detail, and sometimes brutal simplification that has had a lasting effect on twentieth-century industrial design.

The issue of nationalism stood at the heart of the new movement and was evident even at the first Jugendstil exhibition at the Munich Glaspalast in 1897 (fig. 4). The program published by the committee members of the exhibition's

1 There have been no scientific publications on this subject as a whole. *Kandinsky in Munich* (Princeton, 1979, and the related exhibitions [New York and Munich, 1982]), with its exemplary scholarship by Peg Weiss, dealt with one aspect of the movement in the limited context of Kandinsky's early work. *München 1869-1958: Aufbruch zur modernen Kunst* (Munich, 1958) included Jugendstil material within a wide chronological and stylistic context, as did *Bayern Kunst und Kultur* (Munich, Stadtmuseum, 1972). Material specific to the Munich movement is included in such general Jugendstil studies as Fritz Schmalenbach, *Jugendstil: Ein Beitrag zu Theorie und Geschichte der Flächenkunst* (Würzburg, 1934); Friedrich Ahlers-Hestermann, *Stilwende: Aufbruch der Jugend um 1900* (Berlin, 1941); and Stephan Tschudi Madsen, *Sources of Art Nouveau* (New York, 1955). Other contributions to the literature on the subject include exhibition catalogues dealing with individual Munich artists, such as Endell (Munich, 1977), Obrist (Munich, *Hermann Obrist,* 1968), and Riemerschmid (Nerdinger, ed., 1982).

2 Leopold Gmelin, ed., *German Artistical Handicraft at the Time of the Worlds-Exhibition in Chicago 1893* (Munich, 1893), p. 45.

3 Georg Fuchs, "Hermann Obrist," *Pan,* vol. 1, no. 5 (1896), p. 324.

4 Peter Jessen, "Scherrebek," *Kunstgewerbeblatt,* n. s., vol. 9 (1898), p. 154.

5 Peter Jessen, "Book Industry," in Paris, Exposition Universelle 1900, *Official Catalogue: Exhibition of the German Empire* (Berlin, 1900), p. 77.

Figure 1 Hermann Obrist, *Whiplash*, c. 1895. Wool with silk embroidery, 47 x 72¹/₄" (119 x 183 cm). Stadtmuseum, Munich

decorative arts section, who included the artists Hans Eduard von Berlepsch-Valendas, Obrist, and Richard Riemerschmid, stated its tenets: "It...places the main emphasis on *originality of invention* and on *the perfect artistic and technical execution* of such artistic objects as fulfill the *requirements of our modern life*....It excludes everything that appears as a thoughtless and false copy or imitation of past and foreign styles, that is not abreast of the latest developments in modern technology."[6] Directly following the 1897 Glaspalast exhibition, all of the committee members of the decorative arts section (with the exception of Berlepsch-Valendas, who was replaced by F.A.O. Krüger) regrouped as the board of a new organization set up to produce and market the designs of the movement. This organization, the Vereinigte Werkstätten für Kunst im Handwerk (United Workshops for Art in Handicraft), has existed continuously since then. Designs provided either by outside artists or in-house designers and approved by the board members, were to be made in the company's factories and workshops, and sold through their retail offices. The aims of the Vereinigte Werkstätten, published together with an appeal for new members by the board on January 1, 1898, bear witness to the remarkably modern business sense of these artists, whose concerns were economic and nationalistic, as well as aesthetic:

Experience over the last few years here in Germany and abroad has shown that ever larger sections of the purchasing public would gladly espouse the new, individual direction in the arts and crafts if they had more and better opportunities to see such new objects of interior decoration and if prices were not higher than those of generally available merchandise in the well-known styles. Those familiar with the situation also know that a considerable number of artists have created individual, beautiful, and functional designs in all areas of the applied arts, but are not in a position to have them carried out or to find customers for them. Furthermore, we know that enough craftsmen and manufacturers exist in Germany who possess both the technical ability to satisfy every artistic demand and the desire to carry out new designs, but who are unable to take the commercial risk of manufacturing pieces in large numbers....And the merchants, who are naturally interested in continually offering new and good wares, are in the difficult position of not knowing where the new is manufactured and in what quantities. Because the artists cannot find craftsmen to execute their designs, and because the craftsmen and manufacturers have no opportunity of exhibiting, and

6 Abtheilung für Kleinkunst der VII. Internationalen Kunst-Ausstellung im Kgl. Glaspalaste zu München, *Programm* (Munich, Feb. 24, 1897), n. p.; see Appendix "Documents."

7 *Der Ausschuss für Kunst im Handwerk München* (Munich, Jan. 1, 1898), n. p.; see Appendix "Documents."

8 Most recently in Nerdinger, ed., 1982, p. 16, and Heike Schröder, "Bernhard Pankok (1872-1943): Ein Lehrer der Reformzeit," in *Adolf G. Schneck 1883-1971* (Stuttgart, 1983), p. 21.

9 William Morris, "The Beauty of Life," in *William Morris,* ed. G. D. H. Cole (London, 1948), p. 564.

10 Hermann Muthesius, "Kunst und Maschine," *Dekorative Kunst,* vol. 10 (1902), p. 142.

11 C. R. Ashbee, *School and Guild of Handicraft: Statement of its Nature and Purpose* (Whitechapel, 1888), n. p.

Figure 2 August Endell, Facade of Hof-
Atelier Elvira, Munich, 1897-98

Figure 3 Ludwig von Zumbusch (German,
1861-1927), Cover for *Jugend*, 1896.
Lithograph, 23¹/₂ x 16¹/₄″ (59.5 x 41.4 cm).
Stadtmuseum, Munich

prospective purchasers and connoisseurs, none of seeing, buying, or ordering, the new is created sporadically and sold individually and expensively, whereas supply and demand in the new arts and crafts have long since been regulated satisfactorily in our neighboring countries. That is why the German market is flooded with foreign products of this kind of applied art.[7]

Scholars have tended to describe the Vereinigte Werkstätten as a German version of one of the English Arts and Crafts organizations, specifically, either Morris and Company, established by William Morris and others in 1861, or C. R. Ashbee's Guild of Handicraft, founded in 1888.[8] However, while the English Arts and Crafts movement was unquestionably its most valued guide in design reform and in setting aesthetic standards of simplicity, fitness, and propriety, the Vereinigte Werkstätten shared none of the Socialist concerns for the craftsman and the process of his work that were so fundamental to the British movement. The fallacy of the crusade launched by John Ruskin and William Morris to create an "art made by the people and for the people, a joy to the maker and the user"[9] was described by Hermann Muthesius, a Prussian architect, critic, and civil servant then attached to the German embassy in London, in the Munich periodical *Dekorative Kunst:* "Wherever today hand-craft is elevated to an ideal, one has to assume that unnatural economic conditions prevail. And immediately there comes to mind the peculiar cultural image that William Morris and the English artist-socialists have given us of an 'art of the people for the people' which, in the end, produced such expensive things that at the very most only the upper ten thousand could consider buying them."[10]

Even less comparable was Ashbee's Guild of Handicraft, a commune dedicated to the preservation of craft techniques in accordance with a social and economic philosophy "adapted from the practice of medieval Italy" (as Ashbee himself put it in his statement of purpose published in 1888).[11] This small, cooperative society, working out designs for public sale and continuing the guild values of the past, bore no resemblance in its ideals and little in its practices to the Vereinigte Werkstätten.

Not only did the Vereinigte Werkstätten für Kunst im Handwerk make no special virtue of handwork, despite its name; it also made no particular distinction between craft and machine production, placing the highest value on qual-

Figure 4   Room arranged by the architect Theodor Fischer for the "VII. Internationale Kunstausstellung" at the Munich Glaspalast, 1897, with paintings by Richard Riemerschmid, chair by Bernhard Pankok, and *portière* and frieze by August Endell.

ity, irrespective of technical means. This, and the idea of cooperation between artist, craftsman, and commercial manufacturer in economic and national self-interest, put the founders of the Vereinigte Werkstätten at the very forefront of European thinking about the nature and purpose of design, foreshadowing in a specific way programs of the Deutscher Werkbund, founded in Munich in 1907, and later the Bauhaus. In fact, the Werkbund included such members of the Vereinigte Werkstätten as Peter Behrens, Bernhard Pankok, Bruno Paul, and Riemerschmid, while Endell and Obrist were two of the three candidates (Walter Gropius, a pupil of Behrens, was the third) recommended to succeed Henry van de Velde as director of what was to become the Bauhaus in Weimar.[12]

While the Vereinigte Werkstätten did produce objects largely by hand on special commission – such as Pankok's vitrine for the Villa Obrist (no. 67), which was crafted according to traditional techniques, with solid board construction and carved decoration – the simple and rational furniture designed by Riemerschmid and others for the workshops lent itself to machine production with only a certain amount of hand finish. Even furniture that Obrist commissioned from Riemerschmid (nos. 95-98) was designed for inexpensive manufacture by machine, with thin, veneered boards and simple joints that allowed easy assembly.[13] In his important study *The English House*, published in 1904-5, Muthesius regarded English furniture as "still at a somewhat primitive stage" in its insistent use of solid wood by comparison with the use of lighter and cheaper veneers in Germany.[14] It was mechanization, which greatly lessened production costs and increased the demand for furniture at substantially lower prices, that gave Riemerschmid and the Vereinigte Werkstätten their reputation for popular "middle-class" designs and accounted for the later success of Riemerschmid's program of *Maschinenmöbel* (machine-made furniture) with its standardized components for the Dresdner Werkstätten für Handwerkskunst (Dresden Workshops for Arts and Crafts; see nos. 125-26). In fact, by the late 1890s the furniture trade in Munich was already highly mechanized, judging from such surviving examples as the bookcase designed by Berlepsch-Valendas and made by the firm of Richard Braun from inexpensive pine boards, veneered with oak and elm and decorated with die-stamped and hand-punched metal mounts (no. 16).[15] A decade later, in *Das Kunstgewerbe in München*, Bruno Rauecker listed a large number of woodworking machines employed by other high quality furniture firms, such as those of Possenbacher and of Ballin.[16] The metalwares of the Vereinigte Werkstätten could also be produced by machine, as their shapes sometimes clearly expressed, a practice the workshops shared, as Rauecker duly reported,[17] with two of the most important independent metalsmiths in Munich, Reinhold Kirsch and Steinicken & Lohr.

In its organization and degree of mechanization the Vereinigte Werkstätten seemed a miracle of modernism to contemporary critics and, by association, Munich a capital of art industry. In 1898, the first year of the workshops' existence, *Dekorative Kunst* already remarked with pride that "whoever walks through the extensive collections of Berlin... will ask themselves how it is... that Munich is the leading city in Germany in artistic things... and has the best artistic intelligence in Germany... the success of last year's [Glaspalast] exhibition leading to the organization of the Vereinigte Werkstätten."[18]

For Joseph Lux, writing in 1908 in *Das neue Kunstgewerbe in Deutschland*, even after the establishment of the other workshops in Dresden, Munich was still the "first city where modern applied art in Germany received organized management through the founding of the Vereinigte Werkstätten."[19] Werner Sombart, author of *Der moderne Kapitalismus*, noted at the time: "What makes the Vereinigte Werkstätten so interesting is that... they created an organization and publicized the manufacture of 'artistic' applied arts on the basis of a modern industrial business organization and... modern technology."[20]

At the end of its first year, the Vereinigte Werkstätten employed fifty workers; by 1907 there were six hundred. With its branch offices in Hamburg, Bremen, and Berlin, the workshops were "capable of erecting houses and furnishing them completely, supported by a great number of machines, including all those... necessary for carpentry."[21] For Sombart, "the organization of the Vereinigte Werkstätten confirms my opinion that today the highest demands of artistic inspiration in the arts and crafts exclude handwork."[22]

In 1899, however, it was not so much technique, but the scale and variety of its products – designed and manufactured within a single organization – that made the Vereinigte Werkstätten impressive:

12 Toronto, Art Gallery of Ontario, *50 Years Bauhaus* (Dec. 6, 1969-Feb. 1, 1970), p. 26.

13 I would like to thank Olaf Unsoeld at the Philadelphia Museum of Art, who kindly examined this furniture for me in Munich.

14 Hermann Muthesius, *The English House*, ed. Dennis Sharp (London, 1979), p. 198.

15 I am grateful to Cor van Horne and Andrew Lins at the Philadelphia Museum of Art, who gave me much valuable technical advice.

16 Bruno Rauecker, *Das Kunstgewerbe in München* (Stuttgart, 1911), p. 27.

17 Ibid., p. 26.

18 "Vereinigte Werkstätten für Kunst im Handwerk, München," *Dekorative Kunst*, vol. 2 (1898), p. 137.

19 Joseph Lux, *Das neue Kunstgewerbe in Deutschland* (Leipzig, 1908), p. 120.

20 Quoted in Rauecker, 1911, p. 30.

21 Ibid., p. 29.

22 Ibid., p. 30.

Figure 5 The carpentry workshop at the Vereinigte Werkstätten für Kunst im Handwerk, Munich. c. 1910

It is hardly a year since the workshops were founded.... Here, a many-sided activity is developing to reshape all our commodities; nothing is considered too small to be given artistic charm and a new, practical shape...the carpenter's shop has become one of the busiest in Munich; patinated metals have already had to be moved to another building, as has machine embroidery, in which many [women] are occupied with the production of inexpensive embroideries, bringing artistry to this often misused technique. In the drawing studio young people are busy preparing various designs, there for the furnishing of rooms, here for the cabins of a modern steamer. Everywhere there are sketches for all kinds of applied art, whether of clay or glass, bronze or iron...and thus a picture emerges of an undertaking that, in spite of its variety, is permeated by a single idea; a picture we are hardly likely to see again [fig. 5].[23]

By comparison, the now better known workshops in Vienna, the Wiener Werkstätte, not founded until 1903, were a throwback to the handcraft traditions and ideas of the old pioneers of the English Arts and Crafts movement. Indeed, in the work program of the Wiener Werkstätte, Josef Hoffmann wrote: "Our aim is to create an island of tranquillity in our own country, which, amid the joyful hum of arts and crafts, would be welcome to anyone who professes faith in Ruskin and Morris."[24] The Vereinigte Werkstätten in Munich was no such island of tranquillity, and Lux, an admirer of both organizations, noted the difference: "While the artistic group in Vienna developed a monumental style in architecture, painting, sculpture, and the so-called minor arts...the Munich artists of the Vereinigte Werkstätten...tried to solve practical everyday needs. They had the courage to tackle everything...from completely furnished houses to the artistic arrangement of cemeteries."[25]

The style most closely associated with the Vereinigte Werkstätten was a kind of rational functionalism in which honesty of construction, truth to materials, and simplicity of form were the standards. As early as 1897, Leopold Gmelin, editor of *Kunst und Handwerk,* described this side of Munich Jugendstil in a review of the Glaspalast exhibition: "Two principles characterize the modern direction of applied art: first...simplicity of construction; secondly, the association with the plant and animal world.... Hand in hand with simplicity

23 "Neues aus den Vereinigten Werkstätten für Kunst im Handwerk München," *Dekorative Kunst,* vol. 3 (1899), p. 145.

24 Josef Hoffmann, "The Workprogram of the Wiener Werkstätte 1903," in Vienna and New York, Galerie Metropol, *Josef Hoffmann: Architect and Designer 1870-1956* (1981), pp. 7-8.

25 Lux, 1908, p. 124.

26 Leopold Gmelin, "Die Kleinkunst auf der Kunstausstellung zu München 1897," *Kunst und Handwerk,* vol. 47 (1897-98), p. 19.

27 Hermann Obrist, "Hat das Publikum ein Interesse daran, selber das Kunstgewerbe zu heben?" in *Neue Möglichkeiten in der Bildenden Kunst* (Leipzig, 1903), p. 53.

28 Richard Graul, "Deutschland," in Richard Graul, ed., *Die Krisis im Kunstgewerbe* (Leipzig, 1901), p. 40.

29 Including, for example, "Die 'Guild and School of Handicraft' in London," *Dekorative Kunst,* vol. 2 (1898), p. 41 ff., and "Benson's Elektrische Beleuchtungskörper," *Dekorative Kunst,* vol. 7 (1901), p. 105 ff.

30 M. H. Baillie Scott, "On the Choice of Simple Furniture," *The Studio,* vol. 10, no. 47 (Feb. 1897), pp. 152-57.

31 Hermann Muthesius, "Englische und Kontinentale Nutzkunst," *Kunst und Handwerk,* vol. 49 (1898-99), p. 321.

32 Munich, Königlicher Glaspalast, VII. Internationale Kunstausstellung, *Illustrirter Katalog* (June 1-end Oct. 1897), nos. 26-29.

33 Munich, Königlicher Glaspalast, Münchener Jahres-Ausstellung, *Offizieller Katalog* (1898), nos. 1898-1924.

34 Ibid., no. 2236.

35 Munich, Königlicher Glaspalast, Münchener Jahres-Ausstellung, *Offizieller Katalog* (1899), no. 2303.

Figure 6 Charles Rennie Mackintosh (Scottish, 1868-1928), Cabinet, 1897-98. Maple and metal, height 92¹/₂″ (235 cm). K. Barlow Ltd., London

of construction goes a preference for modest materials. Just as no doubt is left as to what a thing is made of, so its structure is rendered wholly transparent."²⁶

The aesthetic standards of simplicity and propriety were at first identified generally with the English Arts and Crafts movement and known in Munich as the "Neo-English style."²⁷ In 1901, Richard Graul, director of the Kunstgewerbe-Museum in Leipzig, spoke of the "artistic Anglomania" in Germany: evident in "lighter and plainer shapes in furniture, the English style has pleaded for simplicity in the name of common sense."²⁸ The principal apologist for the contemporary English Arts and Crafts movement in Germany was Muthesius, who, writing from London, published articles on a variety of English topics;²⁹ his monumental, three-volume book, *The English House,* is still the definitive study of British domestic architecture of the period. As Muthesius pointed out, the progressive English art journal *The Studio,* founded in 1893 and the source of such articles as M. H. Baillie Scott's 1897 essay "On the Choice of Simple Furniture,"³⁰ was widely read in Germany: "One day a tastefully laid-out periodical, *The Studio,* appeared, which through its reasonable price was accessible to everyone and which opened up to the Continental world the horizon onto a new art.... The situation changed at a stroke. No visitor to Germany can enter a store without English merchandise being praised above everything else. 'English taste' has become commonplace... today, English is the 'latest.'"³¹ British works were shown in Munich. The Munich Secession exhibition of 1896 included a retrospective collection of the work of Walter Crane; at the Glaspalast exhibition of 1897, the firm of Bernheimer exhibited "English furniture";³² while at the Glaspalast exhibitions of 1898 and 1899 furniture and objects by Ashbee,³³ C. F. A. Voysey,³⁴ and C. R. Mackintosh were shown. The Mackintosh piece, a cabinet, was produced for, and exhibited by, the Munich publisher Hugo Brückmann,³⁵ who also commissioned a dining room from Mackintosh at the same time (fig. 6).

Of the Munich artists who exhibited at the Glaspalast and designed for the Vereinigte Werkstätten, Riemerschmid led those on the side of simplicity and functionalism. Bode described his dresser (see no. 85) in 1897 as "spare" in profile, "unpretentious...and therefore most suited to the modern room."³⁶ Lux credited him as the earliest among artists of the new movement "to show a concern for simplicity and constructional logic,"³⁷ an opinion shared by Muthesius, who wrote that "of the leaders of the German arts and crafts movement, Richard Riemerschmid was the first to achieve clarity."³⁸ Early critics of Riemerschmid's work tended to identify his plain, largely undecorated style as "English." In reviewing the Glaspalast exhibition of 1898 Georg Fuchs wrote: "It is to be welcomed that our artists, first and foremost Richard Riemerschmid, aim to design plain and practical furniture for the middle class at reasonable prices and in good taste, like the English";³⁹ and a *Dekorative Kunst* article of the same year noted that the "elegant, simple shapes" of Riemerschmid's lighting fixtures "still show the superiority of their English models."⁴⁰

However, with Riemerschmid's dazzlingly inventive Music Room furniture for the Dresden exhibition of 1899 (see nos. 92-93), for which there were no artistic precedents, his work was suddenly recognized as "original." Paul Schultze-Naumburg praised Riemerschmid's "practical sense" and his resolution of the "problem of functionalism [by] original ideas of construction which, in his hands, become lines of decoration."⁴¹ Combining the freely curved lines associated with Art Nouveau with simple rectilinear profiles,

36 Wilhelm Bode, "Künstler im Kunsthandwerk, II: Die Abteilung der Kleinkunst in den internationalen Ausstellungen zu München und Dresden 1897," *Pan* (1897), p. 113.

37 Lux, 1908, p. 144.

38 Hermann Muthesius, "Die Kunst Richard Riemerschmids," *Die Kunst,* vol. 10 (1904), p. 249.

39 Georg Fuchs, "Angewandte Kunst im Glaspalaste 1898," *Deutsche Kunst und Dekoration,* vol. 5 (1899-1900), p. 34.

40 "Vereinigte Werkstätten," cited above, p. 138.

41 Paul Schultze-Naumburg, "Die Dresdener Kunstausstellung," *Dekorative Kunst,* vol. 3 (1899), p. 91.

Figure 7   Bernhard Pankok, Bench, 1898. Oak, length 92⁷/₈" (236 cm). Stadtmuseum, Munich

Riemerschmid's Music Room chairs are today considered classics of modern design, remaining variously in production in English and American versions. By the turn of the century, Riemerschmid's style of utilitarian simplicity, to which Pankok and Paul also frequently subscribed, had become identified as *the* original progressive style of the Munich movement. According to Graul, "The experiments made by a number of Munich artists... were carried out with the declared intention of creating furniture and utensils for the German home.... Everyone had the same ambition, to be simple, to seek good taste not in exaggerated decoration, but in good proportions.... [Of these artists] Bernhard Pankok, Bruno Paul, and Richard Riemerschmid showed the greatest daring and originality in their modern inventions. All of them create from the depths of their soul according to modern principles individually discovered... they distinguish themselves in several new ways... especially in the promotion of a middle-class style."[42]

This utilitarian style was perceived not only as original, but also as distinctively German. Behrens, later recognized as a pioneer of modern industrial design, was singled out at the Glaspalast exhibition of 1899 as the "most German" artist exhibiting there on account of his dining room ensemble of table, embroidered cloth, ceramics, glasses, and carpet, which was described as "calm and simple" in shape, with a "restrained" decoration "impossible anywhere but in Germany."[43] At the Paris Exposition Universelle of 1900 the interiors by Pankok and Paul were judged by some as much in national terms as on their design merits: "Pankok's and Paul's rooms are somehow thoroughly German.... Paul's rooms exude a genuinely German *Gemütlichkeit* [cosy atmosphere].... It is Pankok's and Paul's special achievement to have reawakened joy in the individually shaped detail, which is a truly German characteristic."[44] In contrast to progressive interiors elsewhere, particularly in England, with their light-colored and white walls, the dark color schemes of the German Neo-Renaissance persisted here, much to the despair of one foreign critic who found these German rooms not cosy, but "somber" and "melancholy."[45] Of all the Munich artists, Riemerschmid was judged "most representative of the German character," his work, as Lux described it, distinguished by "homeliness, honesty, and a somewhat staid" character and his furniture "plain, practical, and sturdy in nature."[46] Other critics agreed. Paul Johannes Rée, librarian and secretary of the Bayerisches Gewerbemuseum in Nuremberg, wrote that Riemerschmid's art was "deeply rooted in the German

Figure 8   Emile Gallé (French, 1846-1904), Vase, c. 1900. Mold-blown glass with "marquetry" and carved decoration, height 8¹/₈" (20.5 cm). Philadelphia Museum of Art. Gift of John T. Morris

42   Graul, ed., 1901, pp. 43-44.

43   Julius Meier-Graefe, "Peter Behrens," *Dekorative Kunst,* vol. 5 (1900), p. 3.

44   "Die Vereinigte Werkstätten auf der Pariser Weltausstellung," *Dekorative Kunst,* vol. 6 (1900), p. 270.

45   Gabriel Mourey, "Round the Exhibition, III: 'German Decorative Art,'" *The Studio,* vol. 21, no. 91 (Oct. 1901), p. 49.

46   Lux, 1908, p. 144.

47   Paul Johannes Rée, "Die Wiedergeburt unserer bürgerlichen Wohnungskunst," *Der Sämann: Monatsschrift für Pädagogische Reform,* vol. 11 (1906), p. 81.

Figure 9   Henry van de Velde (Belgian, 1863-1957), Plate, 1903-4. Porcelain, diameter 10½″ (26.7 cm). Philadelphia Museum of Art, Purchased: Funds given in memory of Sophie E. Pennebaker

Figure 10   Hermann Obrist, Vase, c. 1901. Limestone, height 17¾″ (45 cm). Stadtmuseum, Munich

48   Muthesius, 1904, p. 283.

49   Eduard Heyck, ed., *Moderne Kultur: Ein Handbuch der Lebensbildung und des guten Geschmacks,* vol. 1 (Stuttgart, 1907), p. 422.

50   Julius Meier-Graefe, "Floral-Linear," *Dekorative Kunst,* vol. 4 (1899), p. 169.

51   Graul, ed., 1901, p. 43.

52   Otto Eckmann, *Neue Formen: Dekorative Entwürfe für die Praxis* (Berlin, 1897), Foreword.

53   Munich, 1897, nos. 35-54.

54   "Kleine Nachrichten: Emile Gallé in Nancy," *Kunst und Handwerk,* vol. 47 (1897-98), p. 70.

55   Munich, Internationale Kunst-Ausstellung . . . "Secession," *Offizieller Katalog* (1899), pp. 43-45, nos. 540-64.

56   August Endell, *Um die Schönheit: Eine Paraphrase über die Münchener Kunstausstellungen 1896* (Munich, 1896), p. 13.

57   August Endell, "Formkunst," *Dekorative Kunst,* vol. 1 (1898), p. 280.

soil"[47] and Muthesius acclaimed Riemerschmid's "natural modesty, simplicity, and ingenuity. Here is middle-class art of general validity, here is folk art. It is worthy of this name because it is modest and German."[48]

After the turn of the century, traditionalism sometimes went hand in hand with nationalism, so that as long as the aesthetic of simplicity was maintained, the new national style could legitimately return to the roots of national tradition. Riemerschmid and the designer Adelbert Niemeyer drew praise for their ceramic designs, "plain sets with tasteful borders" that seemed to "recall those good old traditions . . . at the time of the Empire."[49]

The other side of the movement in Munich, an alternative to the functional simplicity of artists such as Riemerschmid, was an expressive, ornamental style first identified in 1899 by Julius Meier-Graefe, editor of the art journals *Pan* (Berlin) and *Dekorative Kunst* (Munich). He divided this style into "floral" and "linear" idioms – a distinction that has persisted in the literature on the subject and is frequently misapplied to the period as a whole. According to Meier-Graefe: "A single issue dominates the applied arts; its discussion is becoming fiercer each day, threatening to divide the artists into two enemy camps. It concerns the character, or rather the elements, of ornament. One group insists that the elements can be found only in nature, that plants or other natural forms suffice for every kind of surface ornament, provided they are stylized by an expert hand. The others will hear nothing of nature; they maintain that anything reminiscent of plants or other natural forms should be eschewed and that salvation lies only in the abstract line."[50]

The distinction made by Meier-Graefe between the floral and the linear followed national lines, with the "floral" artists, committed to nature as the source of their inspiration, on the side of such French Art Nouveau figures as the furniture- and glassmaker Emile Gallé (fig. 8), and the "linearists," exploiting line as a free agent, on the side of the Belgian Art Nouveau architect and designer Henry van de Velde (fig. 9). Of the artists in Munich who first showed work in the decorative arts section of the Glaspalast exhibition in 1897, Eckmann was seen to epitomize the floral style – "the floral world to which Otto Eckmann gave the most individual shape"[51] – and it was to Nature that Eckmann dedicated his book of ornamental designs, *Neue Formen,* published in the same year: "These designs are neither borrowed from old masters nor stolen from living ones; they originate from all-encompassing Nature . . . a never ending source [of inspiration]."[52] Gallé himself exhibited twenty pieces of glass at the 1897 exhibition,[53] and was the only artist to receive a medal for decorative arts there.[54]

The linear or abstract idiom was developed independently of van de Velde (whose work was first shown in Munich at the Secession exhibition of 1899)[55] by the young architect August Endell, both in his writings and in his most famous work, the Hof-Atelier Elvira, a Munich photography studio of 1897-98 that was decorated with a gigantic free-form plaster relief (fig. 2). In his critical pamphlet *Um die Schönheit* (no. 33) Endell proclaimed "there is no greater error than the belief that the painstaking imitation of nature is art,"[56] and in an article on "Formkunst" (literally, form art), Endell went on to describe "*Formkunst,* which bubbles up out of the human soul through forms that are like nothing known, that represent nothing, and symbolize nothing, that work through freely invented forms, as music does through free tones."[57] This proclamation of expressionism, of the primacy of the sensual, reflects the aesthetic theories of the psychologist-philosopher Theodor Lipps, who is thought to have influenced an entire generation of Munich artists in developing toward abstraction, among them, Wassily Kandinsky and Paul Klee.[58]

Obrist, whose exhibition of embroideries in 1896 was said to herald "the birth of a new applied art" in Munich (see nos. 57-58),[59] stood between the "floral" and the "linear." His sculptures, designs for fountains, tombs, and urns (fig. 10), and certain of his textiles were largely nonrepresentational and expressive, as Georg Fuchs wrote when reviewing Obrist's exhibition of embroideries for *Pan*: "These embroideries are not intended to 'mean' anything, to say anything.... They involve themselves in our feelings."[60] Endell credited Obrist and his "free, organically invented" embroideries with his conversion to the practice of architecture and design.[61] Obrist, like Endell, viewed aesthetics through psychology: "Art offers intensified emotions, art is heightened life.... If we trustingly followed our feelings and thoughts...we would see that we can find everywhere this essence of all that is art."[62] However, most of Obrist's work in the applied arts was based on recognizable organic or natural forms, such as his famous cyclamen embroidery, which he transformed into a powerfully expressive, ornamental motif (fig. 1), dubbed the "whiplash" (*Peitschenhieb*) by Fuchs.[63] In fact, Obrist had begun as a student of the natural sciences, drew from nature after he became an artist in the late 1880s, and introduced summer drawing and painting classes in the country as part of the curriculum of the school of art and design, the Lehr- und Versuch-Ateliers für Angewandte und Freie Kunst, that he founded with the painter Wilhelm von Debschitz in Munich in 1902 (fig. 11).[64] Like the French Art Nouveau artists (whose work Obrist's never resembled), he began with nature: "Only three things exist for the creative spirit. Here am I, there is nature, that is the object I shall decorate";[65] and his use of natural forms in his embroideries and furniture won him praise at the 1897 Glaspalast exhibition: "Obrist has shown how deeply he enters into the spirit of...the plant world and how firmly he adapts the shapes of nature to his chosen techniques."[66]

Obrist and Endell, who embraced the, for them, higher truth of "heightened life" and *Formkunst,* were sometimes regarded, particularly by later critics,[67] as exemplars of unbridled imagination and artistic freedom, of a glorification of artistic personality at the expense of restraint and economy in the use of form and materials. The critic for *Dekorative Kunst* argued in 1899 that this expressionism was removed from the making of utilitarian objects: Endell "goes his own special way, arriving at areas of shapes that are strange both to past and present sensibilities. He always thinks and, transferring his thinking into fine lines and the psychology of these lines, produces forms in his own way."[68] Other critics, such as W. Fred, complained that the new movement in Munich suffered from the aestheticism of those of its artists who were painters and sculptors, who had no training in the applied arts. Their designs showed the "dangers of 'artist's furniture'.... The United Workshops in Munich furnish the most exact examples of the style of furniture as made by painters. Lines without any constructive meaning result from clever whims. Nothing is considered but the decorative element."[69]

The artist most castigated (and admired) for his expressiveness was Pankok, a painter by training, but the son of a furniture maker (figs. 7, 12). Muthesius complained "of the new phenomenon in furniture...an impetuous progress toward risky experiments...sometimes in complete contradiction to the dictates of usefulness. The Munich painter Pankok has exhibited a chair that has only one leg at the back, instead of two, and that therefore becomes positively

Figure 11   Hermann Obrist and Wilhelm von Debschitz in Obrist's studio, 1902

58 On Lipps, see Weiss, 1979, pp. 34, 159-60, n. 29, 170, n. 73.

59 Munich, *Hermann Obrist,* 1968, n. p.

60 Fuchs, "Hermann Obrist," cited above, p. 324.

61 "The starting point of my work was the embroidery of Hermann Obrist, in which for the first time I got to know free, organically invented, not externally composed forms," from *Berliner Architekturwelt* (1902), cited in Munich, 1977, p. 12.

62 Hermann Obrist, "Wozu über Kunst schreiben?" *Dekorative Kunst,* vol. 5 (1900), pp. 189-90.

63 Fuchs, "Hermann Obrist," cited above, p. 324.

64 Munich, *Hermann Obrist,* 1968, n. p.

65 Fuchs, "Hermann Obrist," cited above, p. 319.

66 Gmelin, "Kleinkunst," 1897-98, p. 26.

67 See, for example, Richard Hamann and Jost Hermand, *Stilkunst um 1900* (Berlin, 1967), p. 252ff.

68 "Neues aus den Vereinigten Werkstätten," cited above, p. 146.

69 W. Fred, "Interiors and Furniture at the Paris Exhibition," *The Artist,* vol. 29 (Sept. 1900), pp. 9-10.

70 Muthesius, "Nutzkunst," cited above, p. 326.

71 Hermann Obrist, "Zweckmässig oder phantasievoll?" (1901), quoted in Stuttgart, Württembergisches Landesmuseum, Altes Schloss, *Bernhard Pankok, 1872-1943: Kunsthandwerk – Malerei – Graphik – Architektur – Bühnenausstattungen* (May 24-July 29, 1973), p. 8.

72 "Zu der Nachricht von dem Verkauf der deutschen Räume in St. Louis," *Kunst und Handwerk,* vol. 55 (1904-5), p. 227.

Figure 12   Bernhard Pankok, Cabinet, 1902. Mahogany, height 80" (203 cm). Staatliche Museen Preussischer Kulturbesitz, Kunstgewerbemuseum, Berlin

73 One Italian critic noted Basile's northern style (Enrico Thovez, "Nord o sud? nell'indirizzo decorativo," *L'Arte Decorativa Moderna*, vol. 1, no. 9 [1902], p. 283) and another raised the issue of nationalism with regard to Basile and the modern movement (R. Savarese, "Arte nuova italiana: Il movimento moderno in Sicilia," *L'Arte Decorativa Moderna*, vol. 1, no. 9 [1902], pp. 257–77).

74 Milan, Palazzo della Permanente, *Mostra del Liberty Italiano* (Dec. 1972–Feb. 1973), no. 383.

75 I am grateful to Prof. Arch. Gianni Pirrone, who has charge of the Basile and Ducrot material at the university of Palermo and who kindly answered my questions about Basile and the Ducrot production. Prof. Pirrone is himself preparing a study of Basile's unpublished notes for a history of contemporary architecture.

76 Bode, "Künstler im Kunsthandwerk," cited above, p. 112.

77 See R. Davis Benn, "The Paris Exhibition," *The Cabinet Maker & Art Furnisher* (Dec. 1900), p. 150, and Irving K. Pond, "German Arts and Crafts at St. Louis," *The Architectural Record*, vol. 17, no. 1 (Feb. 1905), pp. 121–22.

78 Otto Schulze-Köln, "Jugendstil-Sünden," *Kunst und Handwerk*, vol. 52 (1901), p. 201.

79 Schmalenbach, *Jugendstil*, cited above, p. 12.

life-endangering at even the slightest sideways movement of the sitter."[70] An ardent supporter of Pankok, Obrist described him as "the absolute antipode to the whole group of functionalist artists; they act on each other like fire and water...owing to his inexhaustibly fertile gift for invention, which... receives its nourishment from the equally inexhaustible fountain of plant, animal, and human life."[71]

The leading artists of the Munich Jugendstil, both functionalist and expressive, showed their work at the great international exhibitions in Paris (1900), Turin (1902), and St. Louis (1904) to acclaim by foreign critics. For their permanent collection, the Danish Museum of Decorative Art in Copenhagen purchased an elaborately carved armchair by Pankok shown at the Paris exhibition and sold from Meier-Graefe's shop there, La Maison Moderne (no. 63). The largest single purchase of German material was made by the American merchant John Wanamaker following the St. Louis exhibition of 1904: for display in his Philadelphia store he acquired twenty-one German interiors (see fig. 13), presumably including that designed by Bruno Paul (see no. 75) and made by the Vereinigte Werkstätten.[72] None of this material appears to have survived.

The simple, functional furniture designed by Riemerschmid for the Vereinigte Werkstätten was imitated by the young Sicilian architect Ernesto Basile, who around 1900 produced a version of Riemerschmid's mahogany armchair of 1897 for the furnishings of the Grand Hôtel Villa Igea in Palermo. Basile's furniture was made by the Palermo firm of Carlo Golia (later, Ducrot), which exhibited a study designed by Basile at the Turin exhibition of 1902 (fig. 14), its chairs again based on a well-known Riemerschmid/Vereinigte Werkstätten model, the 1898 chair from the Otto residence.[73] Ducrot may also have been responsible for a rather faithful version of Riemerschmid's chair for Obrist (no. 97) that has been attributed to Basile.[74] There are few surviving documents that attest to direct contacts between Basile and any Munich artists. However, the Ducrot library did include the early numbers of *Dekorative Kunst,* where so many of the Vereinigte Werkstätten pieces were published, and moreover, Basile planned to include a treatise on the "Munich School" as part of a larger study of contemporary architecture.[75]

Given the heterogeneous stylistic nature of the Munich movement, the question arises as to how far the term "Jugendstil" can be stretched if it is to retain an analyzable meaning. At first, the new movement was described simply as "modern" or "new," as Wilhelm Bode, director of the Berlin museums, did when he identified the accomplishments of the Glaspalast exhibition of 1897 as a "new trend" in Munich.[76] Foreign publications sometimes called it "the new art," a direct translation of "l'Art Nouveau," the name that Siegfried Bing had given to his shop (and critics to the style of the objects shown there) when it opened in Paris in December 1895.[77] However, as the movement spread beyond Munich it soon became known as Jugendstil, after the magazine *Jugend,* which had been founded by Georg Hirth in 1896. One contemporary critic considered the association of "youth" (*Jugend*) with novelty to be appropriate to the new style, and "far more poetic and profound than the usual highfaluting terms 'modern style' or 'the modern movement.'"[78] The word Jugendstil was apparently already in use by 1899,[79] and by 1901 Muthesius was employing it in a pejorative sense to describe the ornamental side of the new movement:

In almost all magazines concerned with the new movement, as if by agreement, a feeling of uneasiness was voiced with regard to what the educated *commis voyageur* in

Figure 13   John Wanamaker's store in Philadelphia, c. 1910, installed with wood-work and furniture by Hermann Billing (German, 1867-1946), purchased from the Louisiana Purchase Exhibition, St. Louis, 1904

Germany calls 'Jugendstil' and in Austria 'Secessionstil'.... This is a sign that one side of the new cause was about to deteriorate to the point of ridiculousness.... Its products are not practical.... It is superficial elements that dominate the new prod-ucts, whether it be the characteristic swinging lines ... or the ornamentation that covers the new wallpapers, textiles, and carpets. No wonder that the public is begin-ning to consider these the essence of the new fashion, and unthinkingly labels it 'Jugend- or Secessionstil.'"[80]

At about the same time, and in much the same way, "Jugendstil sins" (*Jugendstil-Sünden*) were being laid at the feet of unprincipled manufacturers who quickly popularized the new style in inferior products that they called "Jugendstil": "Meanwhile the weeds spring up, overwhelming the young seeds that had promised, albeit prematurely, a strong and superior fruit. The deed fades, the word remains and promotes the weeds that are shooting up in speculative manufacturing circles and go by the name of 'Jugendstil prod-ucts.'"[81] By 1907 the catalogues of the Dresdner Werkstätten, which marketed so many of Riemerschmid's designs, were using the word Jugendstil exclu-sively in connection with the ornamental, expressive side of the movement, and contrasting it with the rational style promoted by the workshops: "Tired of too rich and too numerous ornaments ... people are asking for simple, calm, almost plain styles. Simplicity is the watch word.... This is even true of the social circles that had taken a liking to the gaudy showpieces of cheap markets, to the empty pomp of ornaments, or to the cascades of the so-called 'Jugendstil.'"[82] Yet however much Jugendstil had fallen into disfavor by the end of the Munich movement, there were still those who recognized in it a source of an advanced "machine" style, among them Rauecker, writing in 1911 on the applied arts in Munich: "The essence of machine production is exact duplication ... smooth, undecorated shapes are the province of the machine. Without doubt, this newly developing style, which has its origins in Jugendstil forms, will be of great influence in the creation of an artistic machine produc-tion."[83]

Figure 14 Ernesto Basile (Italian, 1857-1932), Study, Esposizione Internazionale, Turin, 1902.

From the two sides of the Munich movement, the expressive and the rational, came both the notion of abstract form as the basis of the aesthetics of product design and the ideas, put into practice by the Vereinigte Werkstätten, that the product could be independent of its designer and rely with propriety on machine techniques. And while the Munich movement only rarely cast its objects in the geometrical mold so specific to the twentieth-century image of standardized industrial design, its affection for smooth, simple, unornamented shapes influenced the development of the modern machine-made product.

Munich Jugendstil was not one movement, but at least two, and these were not sequential, as has often been suggested, but simultaneous. One movement was concerned largely with decoration and individual expression, the other with functionalism and rational standards. Although related to the international Art Nouveau and Arts and Crafts movements, Munich, in the work of her best artists, was remarkably impervious to outside influences, as Pevsner has suggested.[84] Under the common name "Jugendstil," at least in the early years of the movement, these two distinct traditions could occasionally amalgamate in a single style that, while possessing national overtones, displayed a universal, modern identity.

80 Hermann Muthesius, "Neues Ornament und neue Kunst," *Die Kunst,* vol. 4 (1901), p. 350.

81 Schulze-Köln, "Jugendstil-Sünden," cited above, p. 201.

82 Dresdner Werkstätten für Handwerkskunst, *Dresdner Kleingerät* (Dresden, 1907), n. p.

83 Rauecker, 1911, p. 18.

84 Nikolaus Pevsner, *Pioneers of Modern Design* (New York, 1949), p. 63.

Contributing Authors

B.D.v.Z.   Beate Dry von Zezschwitz, Munich

G.D.   Graham Dry, Munich

E.v.D.   Elisabeth von Dücker, Museum der Arbeit, Hamburg

M.F.   Michael Foster, Munich

N.G.   Norbert Götz, Stadtmuseum, Munich

S.G.   Sonja Günther, Berlin

J.H.v.W.   Joachim Heusinger von Waldegg, Staatliche Akademie der Bildenden Künste, Karlsruhe

K.B.H.   Kathryn Bloom Hiesinger, Philadelphia Museum of Art

R.J.   Rüdiger Joppien, Museum für Kunst und Gewerbe, Hamburg

B.-V.K.   Birgit-Verena Karnapp, Architektursammlung der Technischen Universität, Munich

U.K   Udo Kultermann, Washington University, St. Louis

C.M.-H.   Christina Melk-Haen, Munich

G.M   Gisela Moeller, Württembergisches Landesmuseum, Stuttgart

R.N   Reto Niggl, Munich

H.O.   Hans Ottomeyer, Stadtmuseum, Munich (with Michaela Rammert-Götz)

G.R.   Günter Reinheckel, Staatliche Kunstsammlungen, Museum für Kunsthandwerk, Dresden

H.R.   Heide Marie Roeder, Stuttgart

B.S.   Brigitte Streicher, Freiburg

C.S.   Clelia Segieth, Munich

C.S.v.W.S.   Clementine Schack von Wittenau Simitzis, Stadtmuseum, Munich

Chr.S.   Christina Schroeter, Frankfurt

E.S.   Ernst Schäll, Laupheim

H.S.g.E.   Helga Schmoll gen. Eisenwerth, Munich

G.W.   Gerhard P. Woeckel, Munich

P.W.   Peg Weiss, Syracuse University

W.W.   Wilhelm Weber, Mainz

B.Z.   Beate Ziegert, Cornell University, Ithaca

Catalogue

Friedrich Adler

1878-1942 (?)

A native of Laupheim in the southwestern German province of Württemberg, Adler came of a Jewish family of artisans and tradespeople who had settled there in the eighteenth century. From 1894 to 1898 he studied at the Kunstgewerbeschule in Munich, obtaining a grounding in the applied arts. After two years working independently he became the first student to enroll in OBRIST's and DEBSCHITZ's Lehr- und Versuch-Ateliers für Angewandte und Freie Kunst, where he was later to teach.

His work began to appear in 1897-98 in such prestigious art journals as *Kunst und Handwerk* and *Deutsche Kunst und Dekoration* – designs for textiles, ivory carving, leather goods, and metalwork, which were produced both by hand and industrially. Utility and decorative pewter objects were made to his designs in Nuremberg, by Orion and by Walter Scherf & Co. (under the trademarks Isis and Osiris), and in Munich by Reinemann and Lichtinger. Early in his career he also began a long association with the Peter Bruckmann silver company in Heilbronn, for whose products Adler frequently executed the prototypes himself. Adler's furniture designs too were soon widely acclaimed, and he was commissioned to design the entrance hall of the Württemberg Landes-Gruppe exhibit at the international exhibition of decorative art in Turin in 1902. Contributions to this and many other national and international exhibitions firmly established his reputation.

Until 1907, when he accepted a teaching post at the Landesgewerbeschule (later Landeskunstschule) in Hamburg, Adler's designs were stylistically affiliated with Munich Jugendstil, particularly as practiced by his teacher, Obrist, though he was able to forge these influences into a highly original style. After he arrived in Hamburg he began to adopt the more stringent line of Viennese Jugendstil, probably through the example of his fellow faculty member at the Landesgewerbeschule Carl Otto Czeschka. How highly regarded Adler was as an artist and teacher is shown by his nomination as head of the master course at the Bayerisches Gewerbemuseum in Nuremberg, where young master artisans received

Friedrich Adler, c. 1935

advanced training in design and drawing under his direction from 1910 to 1913. His predecessors in this post were BEHRENS, RIEMERSCHMID, and HAUSTEIN.

Adler's synagogue design for the Deutscher Werkbund exhibition in Cologne in 1914 brought him special recognition. Its architectural style, and that of his ceremonial objects for synagogue and household use also exhibited there, was closer to Expressionism than to Art Nouveau. The specialist journals were unanimous in their praise, writing that Adler's work was "up to the best Werkbund standard, in both inspiration and design."

In 1933 the Nazis rescinded Adler's teaching permit and forced him to retire. Under the auspices of the Hamburger Jüdischer Kulturbund, however, he was able to continue giving lectures and courses on a private basis, and a number of his writings from this period have survived. On July 11, 1942, Adler was deported to Auschwitz. The date of his death is not known.

References

Schäll, 1980; Schäll, 1981.　　　　　　　E.S.

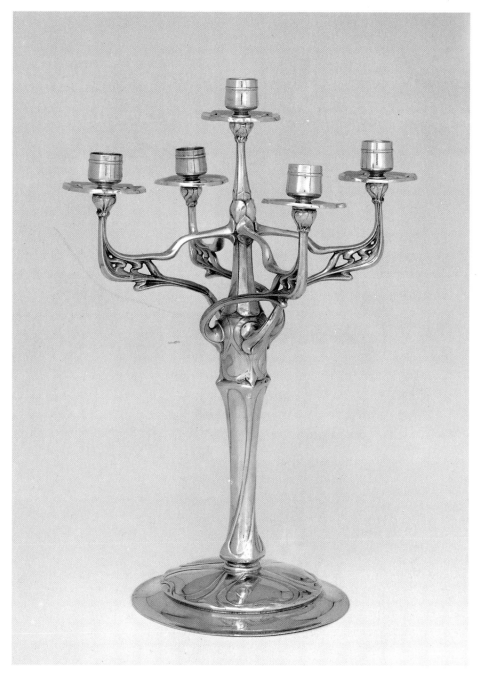

1 Candelabra, 1901

Made by Walter Scherf & Co., Nuremberg
(established 1899)
Pewter, height 16¹/₈″ (41 cm)
Mark: OSIRIS 600
Collection of Wolfgang Ehrlich, West Germany

References

Kunst und Handwerk, vol. 52 (1901–2), p. 118,
figs. 194, 195; Woeckel, 1968, no. 12; Karlsruhe,
1978, p. 239, no. 32; Nuremberg, 1980, p. 174,
no. 190; Schäll, 1980, p. 29, no. 19; Pese, 1980,
pp. 224, no. 600, 350–51, no. 104; Schäll, 1981,
pp. 56–57; Heskett, 1986, p. 55.

The candelabra, which relates to a Baroque form and belongs stylistically to
Adler's vegetal, or plant-inspired, phase
(from 1899 to 1902), is undoubtedly his
finest achievement in this field. Its four
branches emerge in sinuous curves from
the gentle, spiraling ribbed shaft, which
sits on a round base with heart-shaped
decoration. The central shaft tapers upward from a calyx and ends, like the four
arms, in a stylized bud. The shaft and
base recall earlier designs by the artist, for
example, a kerosene lamp and goblet illustrated in the 1898–99 and 1900–1901
volumes of *Kunst und Handwerk* (p. 161,
fig. 230, and p. 24, fig. 33, respectively).
The candelabra was sold under the Scherf
company's Osiris trademark and was
number 600 in its line. Adler's metal candelabras, which include three-, four-, and
five-candle versions, were either polished
or gilded; the example in Karlsruhe
(Landesmuseum) still bears slight traces
of gilding.

   In 1904 and 1905, a few years after he
designed this candelabra, Adler was to
design others in a quite different style, influenced by his studies at the Debschitz
School. These were manufactured by
Georg Friedrich Schmitt's company in
Nuremberg and by Reinemann and Lichtinger in Munich.   E.S.

2 Sugar Box, 1905

Chased silver, 5³/₄ x 5⁵/₈ x 5⁵/₈″ (14.6 x 14.3 x
14.3 cm)
Mark: A 05
Bremer Landesmuseum/Focke-Museum,
Bremen. 8121

References
Kunst und Handwerk, vol. 56 (1905-6), p. 351,
no. 759 (ill.); Schäll, 1980, p. 28, fig. 15.

While both the mark "A 05" (for Adler
1905) and contemporary reports give
Adler as the designer of this unusual sugar
box with abstracted natural decoration,
the name of the manufacturer has not
been recorded. The Nuremberg goldsmith firm of J.C. Wich, whose proprietor was Oskar Dessart, has been suggested, since the high quality of its craftsmanship would seem to indicate that it
was made by the same company that
made the splendid bowl by Adler now
preserved in that city's Gewerbemuseum
(see Darmstadt, 1976-77, vol. 2, pp. 128-
30). However, *Kunst und Handwerk* illustrated the box in 1906 as a "piece in
chased silver from the Debschitz School"
and the possibility that it was made at
the school in Munich should not be dis-
counted, especially since it was shown at
the Nuremberg "Bayerische Jubiläums-
Landes-Ausstellung" in 1906 in a room
designed by Adler and devoted to the
Debschitz School. It was purchased immediately afterward by the Bremen
museum.   E.S.

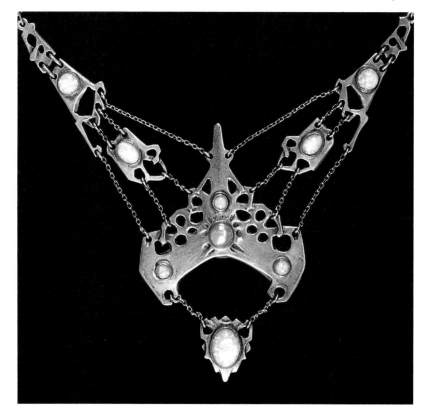

3 Chair, 1902

Made by Versuchs- und Lehrwerkstätten für
Handwerkskunst of the Kunstgewerbeschule,
Stuttgart (established 1902)
Stained oak, height 36½" (92.5 cm)
K. Barlow Ltd., London

References

Gmelin, 1901-2, p. 301, fig. 488 (in Turin); W.
Fred, "The International Exhibition of Modern
Decorative Art at Turin: The German Section,"
The Studio, vol. 27, no. 117 (Dec. 1902), p. 196 (as
B. Paul); *Die Kunst,* vol. 6 (1902), p. 449; *Deko-
rative Kunst,* vol. 10 (1902), p. 449 (in Turin);
Fuchs, 1902-3, p. 60 (ill.); Waltraut ter Jung, in
Schwäbische Zeitung (Laupheim), Aug. 2, 1982.

By 1902 Adler, though still a student at
the Debschitz School in Munich, was already a recognized artist and designer. In
that year, at the age of twenty-four, he
was invited, along with such well-known
artists as BEHRENS, BERLEPSCH-VALENDAS,
and J. M. Olbrich, to design interiors for
the 1902 international exhibition of decorative art in Turin.

The noble simplicity of the entrance
hall that Adler designed stood in pleasant
contrast to some of the other, overdecorated interiors in the exhibition. Among
its furnishings was this graceful oak chair,
sparingly decorated with plant-derived
ornament; in spite of its simple, conventional construction, which recalls the
style of the Biedermeier period, the design is of great beauty and elegance.

E. S.

4 Necklace, 1905

Made by Lehr- und Versuch-Ateliers für
Angewandte und Freie Kunst, Munich
(established 1902)
Silver, opals, and pearl; length 20" (50.8 cm)
Private collection

References

Deutsche Kunst und Dekoration, vol. 17 (1905-6),
p. 391 (ill.); Schäll, 1980, p. 28, no. 17; Schäll,
1981, p. 61, no. 23.

Jugendstil saw a revival of exquisite fashion accessories, and many artists, including Adler, turned to the design of
jewelry. Like all of his jewelry, this hammered silver necklace is a one-off creation, in contrast to his pewter and brass
objects, which were produced in workshops and foundries. Adler's jewelry was
usually designed and made for friends and
relatives only, and considering this, it is
remarkable how much attention the
pieces received in specialist art journals; as
early as 1901 a number of them were illustrated in *Kunst und Handwerk* in its report on the fiftieth anniversary of the
Bayerischer Kunstgewerbeverein.

The harmonious composition of this
necklace, with its web of delicate chains,
seems self-assured and convincing, and its
skillful design takes full advantage of the
properties of its materials. Each element
relates naturally to the next, climaxing in
a richly ornamented, central pendant
adorned with opals and a pearl, from

which a large opal in a triangular setting
held by two short lengths of chain is suspended.

E. S.

in Hamburg, under the direction of Alexander Schönauer.

Like the rest of Adler's early jewelry, this necklace is strongly influenced by OBRIST. The delicate design of the central ornament recalls the roots of a tree, its parts uniting in a convex cartouche set with a Zircon in the center. A triangle, decorated with a pearl, hangs from the main ornament by two small chains, while the double chain is held by a rectangular plate on each side and a finely shaped clasp, each set with a pearl.   E.S.

6 Brooch, c. 1907

Gold and amethyst, 1¹/₈ x 1¹/₈″ (2.8 x 2.8 cm)
Private collection

Reference
E. W. Bredt, "Friedrich Adler," *Kunstgewerbeblatt,* n. s., vol. 21 (1910), p. 147 (ill.).

The geometrical brooch, designed at the end of Adler's Munich period, was made either in Munich by the Lehr- und Versuch-Ateliers für Angewandte und Freie Kunst or under the direction of Alexander Schönauer in the metal workshops of the Hamburg Staatliche Kunstgewerbeschule. It is notable for the pierced decoration of its corners, with Jugendstil forms that recall Baroque ornament. Based on ancient jewelry design, it is a work of restrained elegance and stylishness.

Published as the work of Adler in *Kunstgewerbeblatt* in 1910, the brooch was illustrated there together with other pieces of his jewelry. In the accompanying text, the Munich art historian E. W. Bredt wrote that Adler "on no account belongs among the sentimentalists and fantasists.... He attempts to meet firmly the continual challenges presented to the artist by materials, techniques, and the present day. A critical examiner of the works of previous ages, he knows how to extract from them what is valid and valuable; yet his concern is with the present – he sees his path *in front* of him, not behind."   E.S.

5 Necklace, c. 1906

Made by Lehr- und Versuch-Ateliers für Angewandte und Freie Kunst, Munich (established 1902)
Silver, pearls, and Zircon; length 15¹/₂″ (39.4 cm)
Marks: 800, crown, and moon
Private collection

Reference
Die Kunst, vol. 14 (1906), p. 344 (ill.).

A considerable amount of jewelry designed by Adler has survived. Some of these one-off pieces were made by professional goldsmiths, but most were executed, like this one, in the metal workshops of the Debschitz School in Munich or, after 1907, at the Kunstgewerbeschule

Peter Behrens

1868–1940

Born in Hamburg, Behrens attended the Altona Realgymnasium and then studied art in Karlsruhe from 1885 to 1887, followed by private lessons with the painter Ferdinand Brütt in Düsseldorf. In fall 1889 he moved to Munich, where he studied privately with the painter Hugo Kotschenreiter, but in 1892 left to continue his studies independently. His work at this time was in an Impressionist style, but from 1895 it became increasingly decorative. In 1892 Behrens was one of the founders of the Munich Secession, and the following year he helped initiate another artists' group, the Freie Vereinigung Münchener Künstler.

By 1897 Behrens had decided to give up painting altogether. Encouraged by the reform movements in all fields of art, he turned to applied art, with his color woodcuts between 1896 and 1898 marking this transitional period (see nos. 7-9). Behrens became one of the main protagonists of Munich Jugendstil, and was among the first to join the Vereinigte Werkstätten für Kunst im Handwerk. In 1898 he made his first contribution to the applied art section of the annual Glaspalast exhibition.

Initially, most of his designs were for works in two dimensions – carpets, wallpaper, and textiles, bookbindings and illustrations, endpapers and monograms, supplemented by drawings for jewelry, stained-glass windows, and furniture fittings. His first furniture design, a child's bed for the son of his friend Dr. Walter Harlan, dates from the fall of 1898. As a designer of ornament he relied largely on a simple, tensely sinuous line that reveals the influence of the Belgian designer Henry van de Velde. A dining room ensemble shown at the 1899 Glaspalast exhibition marked the culmination of Behrens's Munich years.

In 1899 he accepted the invitation of Grand Duke Ernst Ludwig of Hesse-Nassau to join the reinstituted artists' colony in Darmstadt. At its first exhibition in 1901 Behrens made his architectural debut with a house he had designed for himself, including its furnishings and interior decoration. In 1903 Behrens became director of the Düsseldorf Kunstgewerbeschule, where he introduced thoroughgoing reforms that soon made it the leading

Peter Behrens, 1901. Photograph by Wilhelm Weimer

school of applied art in Germany. In his own design work, the linearity of the Darmstadt period gave way to a formal geometric vocabulary. Behrens developed his own, highly original system of proportions, and began an involvement with the art of Antiquity that was to have far-reaching consequences.

From 1907 to 1914 Behrens served as artistic adviser to the Allgemeine Elektricitäts-Gesellschaft (AEG) in Berlin, designing the company's monumental factory buildings, its product lines, and advertising – a comprehensive effort that created the AEG image. Among those who worked in his office around 1910 were Walter Gropius, Le Corbusier, and Mies van der Rohe.

From 1922 to 1936 Behrens headed the Meisterschule für Architektur at the Akademie der Bildenden Künste in Vienna, then went to Berlin, where in 1936 he assumed the directorship of the Meisteratelier für Baukunst at the Prussian academy of arts.

References

Meier-Graefe, 1898; Carstanjen, 1898; Meier-Graefe, 1900; Hoeber, 1913; Cremers, 1928; Kaiserslautern, 1966-67; Stanford O. Anderson, "Peter Behrens and the New Architecture of Germany 1900-1914" (diss., Columbia University, 1968); Nuremberg, 1980; Guglielmo Bilancioni, *Il primo Behrens: Origini del moderno in architettura* (Florence, 1981); Windsor, 1981; Buddensieg, 1984; Gisela Moeller, "Der frühe Behrens: Zu seinen kunstgewerblichen Anfängen in München und Darmstadt," *Wallraf-Richartz-Jahrbuch,* vol. 44 (1984), pp. 259-84; Tilmann Buddensieg, "Peter Behrens," in Wolfgang Ribbe and Wolfgang Schäche, eds., *Baumeister – Architekten – Stadtplaner: Biographien zur baulichen Entwicklung Berlins* (Berlin, 1987), pp. 341-64; Gisela Moeller, "Peter Behrens in Düsseldorf: Die Jahre von 1903 bis 1907" (diss., Universität Bonn, 1988). G.M.

7 Storm (Eagle), 1897

Color woodcut, 19¹/₂ x 25¹/₂″ (49.5 x 65 cm)
Signature: PB (intertwined) (lower left)
Staatliche Museen Preussischer Kulturbesitz,
Kunstbibliothek, Berlin. 50050 (gr)

References

Gmelin, "Kunsthandwerk," 1897-98, p. 373,
no. 557 (ill. in Glaspalast); *Kunstgewerbeblatt,* n. s.,
vol. 9 (1898), p. 43; Otto Julius Bierbaum, "Moderne Holzschnitte," *Ver Sacrum,* vol. 1 (Oct.
1898), pp. 7-8; Meier-Graefe, 1898, p. 73; *Dekorative Kunst,* vol. 1 (1898), p. 46 (ill.); Carstanjen, 1898, pp. 118-19; William Ritter, "L'Art décoratif aux dernières expositions de Vienne," *Art
et Décoration,* vol. 4 (1898), p. 36 (ill.); Munich,
1898, p. 164, no. 1934; *Dekorative Kunst,* vol. 2
(1898), pp. 241 (ill.), 244 (ill. in Dülfer room);
Krefeld, 1898, no. 127; *Deutsche Kunst und Dekoration,* vol. 3 (1898-99), p. 33 (ill. in Glaspalast);
Hofmann, 1898-99, p. 43 (ill. in Glaspalast);
Dresden, 1899, p. 57, no. 826; Franz Blei, "Peter
Behrens – A German Artist," *The Studio,* vol. 21
(1901), p. 237 (ill.); Hoeber, 1913, pp. 5, 6, fig.3,
221; Munich, 1958, p. 168, no. 459; Kaiserslautern, 1966-67, pp. 41, no. 3, 55, fig. 9; Berlin,
1970-71, no. 165; Kadatz, 1977, p. 139; Spielmann, 1979, p. 60, no. 78; Nuremberg, 1980,
p. 48, no. 33; S. Wichmann, 1980, pp. 108-9,
no. 248; Windsor, 1981, pp. 8-9.

The woodcuts of Behrens, wrote Otto
Julius Bierbaum in 1898, manifest "a decorative talent of unassuming grandeur, an
austere and noble sense of style, the likes
of which are found in no other German
artist working in this field at the present
time." Behrens was not concerned in his
graphic art to produce an effect of veri-
similitude. Although *Storm* has a figurative motif and describes something ob-
servable in the real world, both motif and
event have been divested of their original,
objective meaning. The eagle dominating
the composition with its enormous
wings, the windswept clouds, flashing
waves, and storm-tossed trees – all are
reduced to a pattern of ornamental lines
in an attempt to express the intrinsic nature
of movement itself. In the image of the
eagle, Zarathustra's favorite creature, one
can probably recognize one of Behrens's
early references to Nietzsche.   G.M.

8 Butterflies on Water Lilies, 1897

Color woodcut, 19¹/₄ x 24³/₄″ (48.9 x 63 cm)
Signatures: PB (intertwined) (lower center),
Peter Behrens (lower right)
Museum of Fine Arts, Boston. Fund in memory
of Horatio Greenough Curtis. 1985.247

References

Meier-Graefe, 1898, pp. 73-74; Carstanjen, 1898,
pp. 118-19; Munich, 1898, p. 164, no. 1935; Krefeld, 1898, no. 128; Octave Maus, "Les Industries
d'art au Salon de la Libre Esthétique," *Art et Décoration,* vol. 5 (1899), p. 103 (ill.); Dresden, 1899,
p. 57, no. 827; Kurt Breysig, "Das Haus Peter
Behrens," *Deutsche Kunst und Dekoration,* vol. 9
(1901-2), p. 167 (ill. in Room of a Lady); Hoeber,
1913, pp. 5-6, 221; Frankfurt, 1955, p. 13, no. 51;
Schmutzler, 1962, p. 295, fig. 328; Kaiserslautern, 1966-67, pp. 41, no. 6, 55, fig. 10; Berlin, 1970-71, no. 164; Berlin, 1972, p. 126,
no. 15; Brussels, 1977, p. 261, no. 619; Kadatz,
1977, pp. 12, 18, fig. 5, 139; Hans Hofstätter,
"Die Bildwelt im Jugendstil," in Bott, ed., 1977,
p. 64, fig. 21; Nuremberg, 1980, p. 48, no. 34,
fig. 34; Windsor, 1981, pp. 8-9, 13, n. 6.

In his earliest prints, *Pine Forest, Dry
Flowers,* and *Brook* (no. 9), Behrens still

paid great attention to the rendering of details. By contrast, in *Butterflies on Water Lilies* he achieved a design of lucid simplicity, exploiting fully the planar, decorative effects offered by the woodcut medium. Julius Meier-Graefe recognized this when he wrote in 1898: "The ornament is contained in the most concrete form. The framework of the design is almost geometric, circumscribed by a circle, with six dark-green leaves on a blue-gray ground that are basically ellipses. The white flower in the middle is an arrangement of the same elliptical motifs, and the two butterflies, which, significantly, are fluttering in a circle around the flower, are delightful ornaments in their own right." Behrens created the woodcut for a portfolio of prints that Meier-Graefe planned to issue under the title *Germinal*.

G.M.

9 Brook, 1898

Color woodcut, 15¹⁵/₁₆ x 20⁵/₈″ (38.9 x 52.3 cm)
Signature: PB (intertwined) (lower left)
Staatliche Museen Preussischer Kulturbesitz,
Kunstbibliothek, Berlin. 5842, 11

References

Munich, 1958, pp. 168, no. 458, 273; Paris, 1960–61, p. 284, no. 792; Schmutzler, 1962, pp. 199, 206, fig. 205; Roger-H. Guerrand, *L'Art Nouveau en Europe* (Paris, 1965), ill. facing p. 100; Kaiserslautern, 1966–67, p. 41, no. 8, fig. 11; Berlin, 1970–71, no. 163; Kadatz, 1977, p. 140; Brussels, 1977, p. 261, no. 618; Munich, *Kandinsky*, 1982, p. 253, no. 194; New York, 1982, p. 174, no. 141; Bouillon, 1985, pp. 165, 237; Masini, 1984, p. 182, fig. 492.

Along with ECKMANN, Behrens was one of the masters of the modern color woodcut, a medium in which the two artists worked quite independently of one another. Like the great Japanese printmakers, he prepared each impression by hand, applying colors to the block and printing without the aid of mechanical means. "I consider this important," he wrote to his friend Friedrich Deneken on May 12, 1898, "because there is much greater charm achieved with this technique than by printing with a press, which destroys the texture of the paper and does not permit variations in pressure in different areas of the sheet. Admittedly, I cannot produce more than a few prints each day that conform fully to my standards, which means that the total edition of any one print will never exceed twenty." Behrens's color woodcuts are remarkable for their large size, and the quiet, subdued colors used to establish the tonal values of the planes lend them an unmistakable aura.

G.M.

antly than *Storm* (no. 7) or *Butterflies on Water Lilies* (no. 8), this color woodcut illustrates the artist's endeavor to communicate deep emotion by means of tense and vital line. The motif has been reduced to a decorative, abstract pattern. As Carstanjen pointed out, Behrens was not concerned "with expressing the sensuousness of a kiss with realistic fidelity or by painterly means. The heads and their objective quality have been subordinated to the crucial issue – a purely decorative evocation of ecstasy and confusion by means of lines and planes alone" (Carstanjen, 1898, p. 119). A smaller version of the print, shown here, was published in the October 1899 issue of *Dekorative Kunst*. Behrens went on to design several vignettes for *Pan*, whose contributors included his friends the writers and critics Otto Julius Bierbaum, Franz Blei, Richard Dehmel, Otto Erich Hartleben, and Julius Meier-Graefe.   G.M.

10 The Kiss, 1899

Color woodcut, 10³/₄ x 8¹/₂" (27.3 x 21.8 cm)
Signature: PB (intertwined) (lower center)
Philadelphia Museum of Art. Gift of Mr. and
Mrs. Robert Walker. 1976-78-1

References

Meier-Graefe, 1900, p. 3, ill. facing p. 4; Hoeber, 1913, pp. 5-6, 221; Frankfurt, 1955, p. 13, no. 52; Ewald Rathke, *Jugendstil* (Mannheim, 1958), fig. 11; Munich, 1958, p. 168, no. 457; Seling, ed., 1959, p. 145, no. 111, ill. facing p. 161; New York, 1960, frontispiece, p. 83; Paris, 1960-61, p. 20, no. 21; Hamburg, 1963, p. 68, no. 649; Hans H. Hofstätter, *Geschichte der Europäischen Jugendstilmalerei* (Cologne, 1963), p. 177, fig. 27; Munich, 1964, p. 25, no. 22; Spielmann, 1965, pp. 5, fig. 5, 20; Bremen, Kunsthalle Bremen, *Europäischer Jugendstil* (May 16-July 18, 1965), pp. 69, 155, 230; Kaiserslautern, 1966-67, pp. 41, no. 9, 55, fig. 6; Brussels, Kursaal D'Ostende, *Europa 1900* (June 3-Sept. 30, 1967), p. 78, no. 623; Hamann and Hermand, 1967, pp. 272-73; Hans Adolf Halbey, "Buch-Illustration um 1900 und die Darmstädter Künstlerkolonie," *Kunst in Hessen und am Mittelrhein,* vol. 7 (1967), p. 70, no. 12; Hamburg, 1968, p. 17, fig. 1; Munich, 1969-70, (ill.); Jost Hermand, ed., *Jugendstil* (Darmstadt, 1971), p. 19; Berlin, 1972, p. 126, no. 16, fig. 65; Hofstätter, 1973, p. 139; Darmstadt, 1976-77, vol. 4, pp. 17, no. 28, 19; Brussels, 1977, pp. 261, no. 620, 263; Kadatz, 1977, pp. 12, 17, fig. 4, 140; Gasser, ed., 1977, pp. 80-81; Spielmann, 1979, p. 61, no. 80; Nuremberg, 1980, p. 49, no. 36a, figs. 36a, b; Windsor, 1981, pp. 9-10; Munich, *Kandinsky,* 1982, pp. 232, no. 136, 233; New York, 1982, p. 164, no. 126; Bouillon, 1985, pp. 125, 237; Bielefeld, 1986, pp. 62, fig. 17, 63, no. 158.

Commissioned by the lavish Berlin art journal *Pan* in August 1898, *The Kiss* was included in the November issue of the magazine together with an important essay by Friedrich Carstanjen on Behrens's Munich period. Even more poign-

11 Glasses, 1898

Made by Benedikt von Poschinger, Oberzwieselau (active 1880-1919)
Clear blown glass, heights a) liqueur 3³/₄″
(9.6 cm), b) Madeira 4¹/₄″ (11 cm), c) wine 6⁷/₈″
(17.5 cm), d) red wine 5³/₈″ (13.6 cm), e) Champagne 8¹/₄″ (21 cm), f) red wine 6¹/₈″ (15.5 cm),
g) beer 5¹/₄″ (13.1 cm), h) Rhine wine 8¹/₁₆″
(20.5 cm), i) Bordeaux 4⁷/₈″ (12.4 cm), j) rummer
8¹/₈″ (20.6 cm)
Collection of Prof. Dr. Tilmann Buddensieg,
Sinzig

References

Munich, Glaspalast, 1899, p. 169, no. 2243;
Georg Fuchs, "Die Darmstädter Künstler-
Kolonie," *Über Land und Meer,* no. 4 (1899), p. 70
(ill.); Meier-Graefe, 1900, pp. 18-19 (ills.); *Velhagen und Klasings Monatshefte,* vol. 1 (1903-4),
p. 128 (ill.); Heyck, ed., 1907, pl. 73; Hoeber,
1913, pp. 7-8, fig. 5; Paris, 1960-61, p. 283,
no. 789; Munich, 1964, p. 93, nos. 717-18,
fig. 49; Kaiserslautern, 1966-67, p. 55, fig. 40;
Pevsner, 1968, p. 172 (as Riemerschmid); *An-
zeiger des Germanischen Nationalmuseums* (1969),
pp. 235, fig. 26, 236; Christel Mosel, *Kunsthandwerk im Umbruch: Jugendstil und Zwanziger Jahre*
(Hanover, 1971), p. 8, no. 8; Schack, 1971,
pp. 51, 236-38, fig. 46; Munich, Die Neue
Sammlung, *Eine Auswahl aus dem Besitz des
Museums* (Munich, 1972), fig. 29; Munich, Stadtmuseum, 1972, pp. 529, no. 2164, 220, fig. 245;
Bott, ed., 1973, pp. 29, no. 8, 35; Helga Hil-
schenz, *Das Glas des Jugendstils: Katalog der Sammlung Hentrich im Kunstmuseum Düsseldorf* (Munich,
1973), p. 105, no. 37; Zurich, 1975, p. 26, no. 10;
Darmstadt, 1976-77, vol. 4, p. 13, no. 15; Brussels, 1977, p. 242, no. 561; Nuremberg, 1980,
pp. 60-61, no. 69; Prague, 1980, pp. 39, no. 13,
123; Darmstadt, Hessisches Landesmuseum,
Jugendstil: Kunst um 1900 (1982), p. 26, no. 13;
H. Wichmann, 1985, p. 133; Bielefeld, 1986,
no. 173.

Displayed in 1899 as part of his dining
room ensemble for the Munich Glaspalast
exhibition, Behrens's first set of table
glasses stood in the greatest conceivable
contrast to the complex and elaborately
ornamented tableware then in common
use. It included no decanters or pitchers,
consisting solely of twelve glasses of varying sizes. Still more innovative was Behrens's exclusion of all decoration, engraved, faceted, or otherwise. A sweeping contour varied slightly from glass to
glass, describing graceful negative forms
in space – that was their sole decoration,
and the source of their timeless elegance.
The lucid design also met the demands of
functionality, for it was both well adapted
to the nature of the material and inexpensive to produce. With his first glassware,
Behrens created designs of lasting beauty
and compelling simplicity. Exclusive distribution rights in the set were held by
Kunstsalon Keller & Reiner of Berlin.

G.M.

12 *Der Bunte Vogel,* 1898

Published by Schuster & Loeffler, Berlin
Printed by Otto von Holten, Berlin
Printed book, 5¹/₂ x 4¹/₂″ (13.9 x 11.3 cm)
Staatliche Museen Preussischer Kulturbesitz,
Kunstbibliothek, Berlin. 5133.4

References

L'Art Décoratif (1899), no. 6, facing p. 272;
Munich, Glaspalast, 1899, p. 198, no. 2871;
Zeitschrift für Bücherfreunde, 2nd year, vol. 2
(Mar. 1899), pp. 532-33; *Dekorative Kunst,* vol. 3
(1899), ill. facing p. 240; Meier-Graefe, 1900,
cover and p. 25 (ill.); Otto Grautoff, *Die Entwicklung der modernen Buchkunst in Deutschland* (Leipzig, 1901), p. 81; Hoeber, 1913, pp. 6-7, fig. 4,
221; Ahlers-Hestermann, 1956, p. 117, fig. 26;
Seling, ed., 1959, fig. 158; New York, 1960,
pp. 36, 164, no. 31; Georg Kurt Schauer, *Deutsche
Buchkunst 1890 bis 1960* (Hamburg, 1963), vol. 2,
pl. 6; Hamburg, 1963, p. 68, nos. 651-53;
Kaiserslautern, 1966-67, pp. 42, no. 18, 55,
fig. 23; Munich, 1969-70, p. 39, no. 36; Berlin,
1972, p. 149, no. 288, fig. 133; Hofstätter, 1973,
p. 138; Darmstadt, 1976-77, vol. 5, p. 209,
no. 34; Kadatz, 1977, pp. 19, fig. 6, 140; Spielmann, 1979, p. 65, nos. 90a, b; Nuremberg,
1980, p. 51, no. 43; Bouillon, 1985, pp. 125, 237.

After entrusting the design of his first
calendar *Der Bunte Vogel* (The Colorful
Bird) of 1897 to Félix Vallotton and Emil
Rudolf Weiss, Otto Julius Bierbaum
turned to Behrens in 1898 for the second
number. For the cover motif, Behrens
chose a stylized peacock with its tail
feathers extended to encompass the lettering. Inside the volume he excluded large
illustrations completely and limited himself to ornamental vignettes and head-
pieces.
   Behrens was one of the foremost German book designers and typographers at
the turn of the century. In addition to his
work for Bierbaum, a major accomplish-
ment of his Munich period was the 1897

cover design for the Fischer-Verlag edition of the works of Otto Erich Hartleben, an early example of the serial principle as applied to book design. In 1899
Behrens created the famous Insel-Verlag
mark, which is still used by the publisher
in a slightly modified form.   G.M.

13 Dinner Plate, 1898

Made by Villeroy & Boch, Mettlach (established
1836)
Glazed stoneware with painted decoration,
diameter 10¹/₄″ (26 cm)
Mark: factory mark
Collection of Dr. Tauchner, Munich

References

Munich, Glaspalast, 1899, p. 169, no. 2243;
Georg Fuchs, "Die Darmstädter Künstler-
Kolonie," *Über Land und Meer,* no. 4 (1899), p. 70
(ill.); Georg Fuchs, "Angewandte Kunst in der
Secession zu München 1899," *Deutsche Kunst und
Dekoration,* vol. 5 (1899-1900), p. 20; Meier-
Graefe, 1900, pp. 3, 18-19 (ills.); *Dekorative
Kunst,* vol. 13 (1905), p. 298 (ill.); Heyck, ed.,
1907, pls. 53, 73; Kaiserslautern, 1966-67, pp. 45,
no. 68, 55, fig. 34; Darmstadt, 1976-77, vol. 4,
p. 10, no. 8; Brussels, 1977, p. 176, no. 324;
Nuremberg, 1980, p. 59, no. 67a.

For a dining room set displayed at the
Munich Glaspalast exhibition of 1899,
Behrens designed his first ceramics, a
five-piece service to which this dinner
plate belonged. The room included a
massive, round table supported on six
legs manufactured by the Vereinigte
Werkstätten für Kunst im Handwerk. All
parts of the ensemble were given stylistic
unity by means of a swirling, involuted
linear ornament that was repeated in the
pattern of the carpet, in the embroidery of
tablecloth and napkins, in the blue underglaze painting on the large revolving
stoneware tray in the center of the table,
and in the soup, dinner, and dessert
plates. Behrens's masterpiece won the
highest accolades from critics of the day.
Writing in *Deutsche Kunst und Dekoration,*
Georg Fuchs, for example, praised it as
"one of the most mature and accomplished creations in the modern vein yet
to emerge in Germany."   G.M.

Hans Eduard
von Berlepsch-Valendas
1849-1921

Little is known of the life of Berlepsch-Valendas, and very little of his work has survived. Yet he was a major figure of Munich Jugendstil and stood at the center of the movement, as his own writings and contemporary texts about him demonstrate. Berlepsch's friend Raymond Unwin, the British Garden City reformer, compared him to William Morris; as with Morris, Berlepsch's chief concern was to improve the quality of life through art – hence his support of the Arts and Crafts and the Garden City movements.

Born in St. Gallen, Switzerland, Berlepsch studied architecture from 1868 to 1871 at the Zurich polytechnic, where he was taught by the German architect and critic Gottfried Semper, who had a lasting influence on him. After passing his exams, he moved to Frankfurt but gave up the architectural profession in 1875 in order to study painting at the Academy in Munich. He was dissatisfied with the traditional academic training offered there, however, and left in 1879, but he was soon an established figure in the city's artistic circles. In 1895 he became a regular member of the Munich Secession, having participated in its exhibition in Vienna the previous year.

Shortly after his move to Munich, Berlepsch had joined the Bayerischer Kunstgewerbeverein and, in 1876, published an important book on the "I. Deutsche Kunstgewerbe-Ausstellung," but he himself did not produce his first designs – for furniture in his and his sister's apartments – until the 1880s. Berlepsch was among the first German writers to emphasize both the equality of the decorative and the fine arts and the need to reform design education. In his introduction to the first issue of Alexander Koch's *Deutsche Kunst und Dekoration,* Berlepsch praised the 1897 Munich Glaspalast exhibition for introducing to Germany the latest developments from Great Britain. Yet he stressed the need to create an independent German art based on the study of nature: "Teach young artists to gain knowledge from nature, not to memorize the ideas of others. Reject the easily achieved expression of superficially picturesque appearances."

From 1897 on, Berlepsch participated in the major exhibitions of decorative art, including those at the Munich Glaspalast

Hans Eduard von Berlepsch-Valendas, c. 1897-99

(1897, 1898, and 1899), the first Munich "Kunst im Handwerk" show in 1901, the Munich "I. Ausstellung der Münchener Vereinigung für Angewandte Kunst" (summer 1905), and those in Darmstadt (1898), Dresden (1899), and Vienna (1899). Berlepsch designed the Reichsdruckerei catalogue for the German section of the St. Louis world's fair in 1904 (the official catalogue was the work of BEHRENS) and was honored at Paris and Turin in 1900 and 1902 respectively.

Berlepsch's interest in reforming the decorative arts arose from his admiration of Japanese craftsmanship (he was introduced to the Japanese decorative arts as a jury member for the exhibition of metalwork in Nuremberg in 1885) and from his familiarity with the ideas of the British Arts and Crafts movement. Issues of *The Studio,* together with personal contacts and travels, kept Berlepsch abreast of developments in Britain. Walter Crane, with whom Berlepsch corresponded from the mid-1890s on, was among the first British designers he met, and it was Crane who drew his attention to others – C. R. Ashbee, for example, whom Berlepsch visited at Campden in 1906. He was fascinated by Ashbee's social and educational ideas, finding that the train-

ing in Ashbee's workshop corresponded exactly to his own ideals. He set up a small school of his own in his house in Planegg near Munich; its best-known pupil was PANKOK, a close friend who, under Berlepsch's influence, turned from painting to designing. World War I put an end to Berlepsch's productive career and left him financially and spiritually a broken man, and he died in 1921.

Art historians have tended to see Berlepsch as an old-fashioned artist, insufficiently innovative and too much indebted to historicism. Yet it is wrong to compare him with artists such as Pankok and RIEMERSCHMID – who were both a generation younger than he was – especially as their early work, from the late 1890s, is usually omitted from the comparison. In addition, the wide-ranging development of Berlepsch's own designs has been ignored. It is astonishing that an artist of the older generation should have become so deeply involved in the avant-garde of his time. Berlepsch's main achievement lay in the impact of his theoretical writings on younger artists. He was the first to take up and promote reform ideas, and he encouraged young artists who had yet to establish themselves. As a transitional figure, Berlepsch demonstrates that Munich Jugendstil did not break completely with the past, but rather grew out of a rich, earlier tradition.

References

H. E. von Berlepsch-Valendas, *Kunst und Kunstgewerbe auf der Münchner Ausstellung des Jahres 1876: Unserer Väter Werke* (Munich, 1876); Berlepsch-Valendas, "Umschwung," 1897-98; "Studio Talk: Munich," *The Studio,* vol. 12 (1898), pp. 194-95; Arthur Weese, "Hans Eduard von Berlepsch, München," *Deutsche Kunst und Dekoration,* vol. 3 (1898-1899), pp. 1-20; H. R., "Deutsche Kunst und Dekoration," *The Architectural Review,* vol. 5 (1898-99), pp. 263-66; William Ritter, "Hans Eduard von Berlepsch-Valendas," *Art et Décoration,* vol. 7 (1900), pp. 74-82; Berlepsch-Valendas, 1902; Unwin, 1922; Melk-Haen, 1988.   C. M.-H.

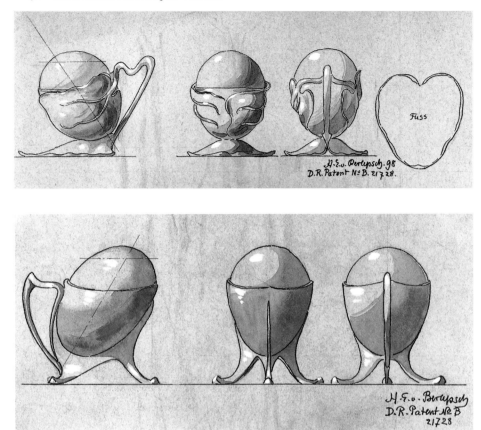

14 Designs for Egg Cups, 1898

Ink and watercolor on paper; a) 4 x 10³/₄″
(10 x 27.4 cm), b) 4 x 8³/₄″ (10 x 22.2 cm)
Signatures and inscriptions: a) H. E. v. Ber-
lepsch.98/D. R. Patent N° B. 21728 (lower
right); b) H. E. v. Berlepsch/D. R. Patent
N° B/21728 (lower right)
Private collection

Family tradition has it that Berlepsch-
Valendas was tired of eating eggs in the
usual way, with the egg standing upright
in the cup, so he designed cups in which
the egg lies at an angle, enabling a larger
hole to be made with the spoon. These
drawings show two versions of his egg-
cup design, on which Berlepsch took out
a patent (see no. 15). The unusual angled
form is identical in all versions, with
changes occurring only in the ornamentation. In addition to the Munich firm of
J. Winhart & Co., the Württembergische
Metallwarenfabrik in Geislingen-Steige
also requested permission to carry out the
design, but does not seem to have done so
(letter of February 2, 1898, to Berlepsch,
in the Berlepsch archive, Basel).

C. M.-H.

15 Egg Cup, 1898

Made by J. Winhart & Co., Munich (established
1883)
Tin alloy, 1⁷/₈ x 3³/₈ x 2³/₈″ (4.7 x 8.5 x 6 cm)
Mark: DRP 21728
Private collection

References

Gmelin, "Kleinkunst," 1897-98, pp. 422, no. 612
(ill.), 425 (ill.); Munich, 1898, p. 181, no. 2500;
Hofmann, 1898-99, pp. 46, 57 (ills.); Arthur
Weese, "Hans Eduard von Berlepsch, München,"
Deutsche Kunst und Dekoration, vol. 3 (1898-1899),
pp. 3 (ill.), 19.

When Berlepsch-Valendas's patented egg
cups were shown along with an egg
cooker at the 1898 Munich Glaspalast exhibition, the art critic Arthur Weese
hailed them as both "new and functional." Five of the cups remain in the
possession of the Berlepsch family, but
the accompanying cooker is lost. The
cups were made by J. Winhart & Co., the
firm that manufactured most of Berlepsch's metalwork, and in a letter of July
18, 1902, to his sister Goswine von
Berlepsch, the artist complained about
the fees they paid him: "The firm I work
for has achieved international renown
through my designs. They are producing
almost nothing but 'Berlepsch,' have
branches in Paris and New York, and I –
have nothing. Winhart has become a rich
man thanks to me, and I can only stand
and watch" (Stadtbibliothek, Winterthur,
R. Hunziker Bequest).   C. M.-H.

16 Bookcase, 1899

Made by Richard Braun, Munich (established 1897)
Oak, oak and elm veneer, brass, and steel; 99 x 39³/₈ x 22¹/₂″ (254 x 100 x 57 cm)
Private collection

References

Munich, Glaspalast, 1899, p. 180, no. 2378; C. F. Morawe, "Kunstgewerbe im Glaspalast zu München 1899," *Deutsche Kunst und Dekoration,* vol. 5 (1899-1900), pp. 20, 21 (ill.), 23 (ill.), 26; Leopold Gmelin, "Das Kunsthandwerk im Münchener Glaspalast," *Kunst und Handwerk,* vol. 50 (1899-1900), pp. 28, fig. 38, 29, fig. 39.

This bookcase was shown at the 1899 exhibition in the Munich Glaspalast as part of a suite of library furniture designed by Berlepsch-Valendas, and then remained in the artist's possession. The design illustrates his development toward simplicity and his emphasis on structure and the quality of materials. The dark, stained frame contrasts with lighter wooden panels, while the wood grain and metal fittings constitute the sole decoration. In his description of the library Morawe drew attention to the fine balance of the whole: "The only things of real value are Berlepsch's two small rooms.... They present a unified whole of great distinction from every angle.... The large chimney piece in the library has a fireplace of chased copper surrounded by glazed tiles that harmonize perfectly with the walnut [*sic*] panels of the otherwise black furniture."   C.M.-H.

17 Gate, c. 1900

Wrought iron and gilded metal, 34¼ x 40¾″
(87 x 103 cm)
Private collection

The gate is one of several pieces of metal-work created for the vestibule of Berlepsch-Valendas's house in Planegg near Munich, and was probably made by Kiefer & Co., Munich, who were responsible for much of the other metal-work in the house. Berlepsch was famous for his metal window grilles and gates. They are often founded in the study of nature and, as a passage in "Ansichten" (Opinions), Berlepsch's artistic credo of 1902, makes clear, he aimed at emulating the functionalism and beauty of nature: "What endless decorative possibilities for grilles of all kinds – whether the leading of stained glass or the trussing of iron or other metals – can be derived from the wing covers of butterflies, dragonflies, etc. Nothing, absolutely nothing in the world, is better constructed, and no combination of lines more beautiful" (Berlepsch-Valendas, 1902, p. 128).   C.M.-H.

18 Bowl, c. 1902

Made by J. Winhart & Co., Munich (established 1883)
Copper and bronze, height 7³/₄″ (19.5 cm)
K. Barlow Ltd., London

Reference
Berlepsch-Valendas, 1902, p. 137 (ill.).

Strong Japanese influence is seen in this bowl, and it is typical of the metalwork that Berlepsch-Valendas designed for J. Winhart & Co. Berlepsch often used flowers and animals in the design of handles, which were frequently made of a material different from that of the vessel itself. In Japanese metalwork Berlepsch admired the "intricate forms of animal depictions – dragons, toads, crabs, etc." and included these motifs in his own creations. He considered metalwork "among the most noble crafts" practiced by the Japanese, and saw the special quality of their art as deriving from the relationship of the Japanese people to nature and to tradition and from the equal status accorded to arts and crafts in Japan. For Berlepsch, Japanese art was "a true folk art. It demonstrates what a people can achieve when they are intimately familiar with the beauty of their surroundings, their flora and fauna" (Berlepsch-Valendas, *Japanische Kunst: Sonderdruck der Orientalischen Gesellschaft* [Munich, 1906], p. 26 ff.).   C.M.-H.

19 Vase, c. 1905

Made by Reinhold Merkelbach, Grenzhausen (established 1845)
Stoneware, colored and glazed, with slip-painted decoration, height 5⁷/₈″ (14.9 cm)
Marks: 1967 (impressed), cross within circle
Collection of Dr. Beate Dry von Zezschwitz, Munich

References
Merkelbach, 1905, pp. 110, no. 1967, 111, fig. 87; Mayreder, 1912, p. 385.

Although Berlepsch-Valendas exhibited ceramics as early as 1898, at the Munich Glaspalast, he was to produce few designs for this medium. Among the firms he did work for were Nymphenburg, Villeroy & Boch, and Merkelbach. The geometrical decoration of this Merkelbach vase (model number 1967) is typical of Berlepsch's late designs, which show the influence of RIEMERSCHMID and of Viennese artists. Berlepsch exhibited designs in Vienna on more than one occasion and wrote a number of articles for the Austrian periodical *Kunst und Kunsthandwerk*. Although he declined an invitation to exhibit with the Viennese Secession in 1900, he expressed his admiration for the group: "The little by-products of my work are not suitable for your distinguished exhibitions, all of which I have seen" (Archiv der Wiener Secession, Vienna).   C.M.-H.

Margarethe
von Brauchitsch
1865–1957

Although Margarethe von Brauchitsch (née von Abercron) was one of the most important German textile artists of the period, relatively little is known about her. Born in Frankenthal-Rügen, she was married briefly to a landscape photographer. She studied painting in Leipzig with the celebrated painter Max Klinger and, before the turn of the century, directed a school for painting in Halle. She also studied for a time with Koloman Moser in Vienna. As far as is known, none of her paintings has survived, and it is to be assumed that all her designs have been lost, too.

Brauchitsch apparently moved to Munich in 1898, as she was one of the founding members of the Vereinigte Werkstätten für Kunst im Handwerk in that year, and for a time managed its women's studio for ornamental design. From 1899 she participated regularly in the annual exhibitions at the Munich Glaspalast. According to the Munich directories, she resided continuously at Theresienstrasse 75/I, where later, as an independent proprietor, she headed a workshop in which sixteen women executed her embroidery designs on machines. "No piece that I could not have executed myself must leave my workshop," was her motto.

Brauchitsch participated in a number of international exhibitions, including those in Paris (1900) and Brussels (1910), as well as in national competitions. She was a member of the Münchner Verein für Angewandte Kunst, the Bayerischer Kunstgewerbeverein, and the Deutscher Werkbund. Her largest undertaking was a stage curtain for the Munich Schauspielhaus in 1901, a machine-made embroidery of abstract plant forms (destroyed in World War II, the curtain was recreated by Tatyana Ahlers-Hestermann in 1971 as a gift of the Riemerschmid family). She produced another curtain in the same technique for the Prinzregententheater in Munich.

The artist's versatility was demonstrated in designs for stained glass, wallpaper, and tiles, as well as textiles, and she is mentioned in contemporary literature as a designer of clothing for women and children. A specialty was her studio-made textile wall panels, including those

Margarethe von Brauchitsch, with faculty and students of the Debschitz School, 1914

commissioned for the steamship *Prinz Friedrich Wilhelm* in 1909. Her artistic activity came to an end with the outbreak of World War I.

References

Munich, Stadtmuseum, 1972, nos. 2115-16; Weiss, 1979, pp. 124-25; Niggl, 1980, p. 399.

G. W.

20 Cushion Covers, 1904-6

Linen with machine-embroidered decoration; a) 17$^{1}/_{4}$ x 22$^{5}/_{8}$″ (44 x 58 cm), b) 17$^{5}/_{8}$ x 24$^{3}/_{8}$″ (45 x 62 cm)
Signature: a) MvB
Private collection

References

Munich, Stadtmuseum, 1972, p. 526, nos. 2115-16; Gerhard P. Woeckel, "Münchens Kunst im Jugendstil: Kunsthandwerk um die Jahrhundertwende," *Weltkunst,* vol. 43, no. 15 (Aug. 1, 1973), p. 1205 [b]; Weiss, 1979, p. xiv, no. 111 [a].

The two cushion covers, with black and colored machine embroidery, must date from the period immediately after Brauchitsch's return to Munich from Vienna in 1903 or 1904, since they show a strict, Viennese geometry not evident in her earlier work. On the other hand, certain elements – the use of black with other colors, the clusters of black dots of various sizes, and the stylized leaf forms – are constant features of her designs.

The cushion covers, made of handspun and handwoven unbleached linen, are decorated with crank-handle machine embroidery. The geometric division of four large squares that are each divided by black outlines into four smaller squares in the first cover shown here is reminiscent of Moorish and Persian ceramic tiles, while the olive-green decoration within each square recalls Oriental linear ornament. The stylized floral and leaf motifs on the other pillow cover are related to Roman border decoration.

Brauchitsch was famous in Germany for her mastery of machine embroidery in the first decade of the century. In 1902 an article in *Dekorative Kunst* reported that she had turned exclusively to machine embroidery – in marked contrast to Berthe Ruchet, for example, who hand-embroidered OBRIST's designs in the pre-

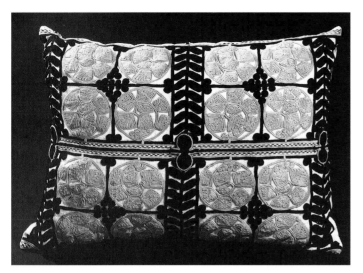

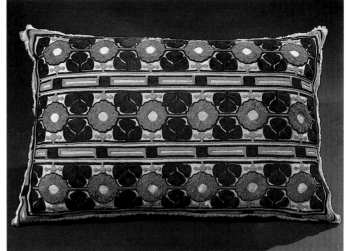

vious decade (see nos. 57-58, 60). A second *Dekorative Kunst* article pointed out in 1906 that many Brauchitsch designs were embroidered directly onto the fabric without the usual preliminary drawings. By 1909 most of her pieces were being executed by the Vereinigte Werkstätten für Kunst im Handwerk.   B.Z.

21 Pillow Cover, c. 1905

Linen with silk machine-embroidered decoration,
20 x 18⁷/₈″ (57 x 48 cm)
Mark: MvB (in rectangle) (upper right)
Stadtmuseum, Munich. 60/505

Reference
Heyck, ed., 1907, pp. 421-22, pl. 67.

Already well known to the readers of *Dekorative Kunst,* where a version of this embroidery was published in 1905 (vol. 13, p. 20), Brauchitsch was compared there to Koloman Moser and the Viennese artists with whom she had studied. Playing ornament off against background space, she extended the curved stems with stylized leaf clusters symmetrically from the four corners of the pillow cover to the center design of four circular blossoms. Strict organization of the surface pattern in this way was to become a characteristic of Brauchitsch's designs. The technique of her machine embroideries also recalls the work of Obrist, and she seems to have derived from him what one commentator called the "effectively nuanced layering of stitches" – threads that overlap or border the ornament – without attempting to imitate handwork in a design intended for machine manufacture.
          C.S.v.W.S.

Wilhelm von Debschitz
1871-1948

Debschitz is known less for his own designs (for furniture, lamps, and metal objects – only a few of which are documented in photographs) than for his outstanding activity as a teacher at the Munich Lehr- und Versuch-Ateliers für Angewandte und Freie Kunst, which he founded with OBRIST in 1902. Obrist had long been searching for someone to head the school, but, as he wrote in 1904, it was not until he "was fortunate enough to make the acquaintance of Wilhelm von Debschitz, a painter and interior decorator who had the crucial artistic, intellectual, and organizational skills needed for its success ... that we could begin ... to forge a curriculum from all that had developed out of years of opposition to the established type of instruction, out of a longing for naturalness, joyfulness, and insight, out of the experiments and technical skills of the modern movement."

In 1902, with six students, the two men began their courses in the Schwabing district of Munich. By 1904, when Obrist retired, leaving Debschitz to head the school alone, there was a student body of 146, and by 1913 the number had grown to 230. In his unpublished memoirs (copies in various private collections), Debschitz recalled having taught some two thousand students between 1902 and 1914. They came from all parts of Germany, from other European countries, even from overseas, to attend his courses. The school, which soon became known as the Debschitz School and obtained funding from the city of Munich and the state of Bavaria, became Germany's largest private educational institution in the field of art. It was also the most modern, thanks to liberal teaching methods in the fields of metalwork, textiles, ceramics, furniture, sculpture, graphic art, design, and the like, providing "free, individual, creative development of every talent under expert supervision."

Shortly before his death, Debschitz said that "this school was there for everyone who was dissatisfied with other methods of instruction." WERSIN, a former student and teacher at the Obrist-Debschitz School, summed up his impressions of the two men in a letter to the present writer in 1975: "Obrist was a genius, Debschitz was a temperament!"

Wilhelm von Debschitz, 1902

Under Debschitz's direction the school won many awards, including a number of gold medals, at important exhibitions in Nuremberg (1906), Munich (1908, 1912, and 1913), and Cologne ("Werkbund-Ausstellung," 1914). In putting Obrist's theories into practice, Debschitz was supported by universally gifted teachers, many of them former students: ADLER, Gertrud Kraut, REICHENBACH, Clara von Ruckteschell-Trueb, SCHMITHALS, Fritz Schmoll von Eisenwerth (who served as deputy director of the school in 1911, 1913, and 1914), Karl Schmoll von Eisenwerth, Hugo Steiner-Prag, Karl Thiemann, VIERTHALER, Wersin, and for a time even Paul Klee, who taught life drawing there in 1907. The school's famous alumni also included Ernst Ludwig Kirchner and Sophie Taeuber-Arp.

In 1914 Debschitz became director of the Kunstgewerbeschule in Hanover, a nationally accredited art school where he hoped to apply his teaching experience to even greater effect, though he initially retained contractual rights in the Munich workshops he had founded independently of the Debschitz School (Ateliers und Werkstätten für Angewandte Kunst Wilhelm von Debschitz und Hermann Lochner, renamed Gesellschaft für Angewandte Kunst m.b.H. in 1910). In the meantime, many public institutions had adopted the methods and facilities he had pioneered. The outbreak of war in August 1914 put a premature end to the reform efforts in both Munich and Hanover. Debschitz, suffering from asthma, had to leave the Hanover school and subsequently devoted himself to weaving. After World War II he worked at Lünen monastery, where he died in 1948.

References

Obrist, 1903; Obrist, 1904; Munich, 1976, p. 428; Schmoll, 1977; Linz, 1983, p. 10ff. (with bibliog.); Ziegert, 1985; Ziegert, 1986.   H.S.g.E.

H. Strauss
22 Bowls, 1906

Made by Sächsische Serpentinstein Gesellschaft
m. b. H., Zöblitz (Erzgebirge)
Serpentine stone; a) height 3″ (7.6 cm), b) height
3³/₄″ (9.5 cm)
Gewerbemuseum der LGA im GNM, Nuremberg. 8931, 8932

References

"Die Mitglieder der 'Lehr- und Versuch-Ateliers
für Angewandte und Freie Kunst, Wilhelm von
Debschitz, München' auf der Bayerischen
Jubiläums-Landesausstellung Nürnberg 1906,"
Die Kunst, vol. 14 (1906), p. 355 (ill.); Moritz
Otto von Lasser, "Ausstellung der Ateliers und
Werkstätten für Angewandte Kunst," *Kunst und
Handwerk,* vol. 58 (1907–8), p. 55, fig. 88;
Warlich, 1908, p. 237 (ill.).

These highly polished bowls with light-
colored geometric decoration share certain formal and ornamental features despite their differing shapes. They are the
only known extant pieces designed by
H. Strauss, a student at the Debschitz
School, and were exhibited in Nuremberg in 1906 and at the Debschitz School
exhibition in Munich in 1908.

Both designs carefully provide areas for
decoration: a broad straight band around
the top part of the larger bowl and the flat
shoulder of the bulbous, smaller one. The
decoration itself consists of fine lines that
create running geometric patterns con-
taining rectangular motifs. While they
may be similar to contemporary designs
in Vienna, the patterns as a whole must be
viewed as a specific result of Debschitz
School teaching. Similar decoration oc-
curs on the jewelry and textiles designed
at the school at this time, and a full exploitation of the creative possibilities of
line was part of the basic training offered
there.

The form of the bowls, too, bears witness to the teaching at an art school that
fostered ideals in design very different
from those espoused by other institutions
of the time. The metal, wood, glass, and
stone vessels made at the Debschitz
School between 1904 and 1908 all seem to
have low forms that recall both Roman
everyday utensils and some of C.R. Ashbee's work in England. These particular
bowls were admired by Lasser in 1908 as
"strong, ancient, and above all, highly
elegant, with all the charm of the material
developed."

Serpentine stone, with which Debschitz was probably familiar from his extensive travels in Italy (the stone comes
from Tuscany), was an uncommon material for vessels at the time, and its use at
the Debschitz School suggests personal
contact between Silesian-born Debschitz
and the Serpentinstein Gesellschaft, the
manufacturing company located in Silesia
which made these bowls.   B.Z.

23 Inkwell, 1906

Made by Lehr- und Versuch-Ateliers für
Angewandte und Freie Kunst, Munich
(established 1902)
Patinated bronze, 3 x 8³/₄ x 6³/₄″ (7.5 x 22 x
17 cm)
Württembergisches Landesmuseum, Stuttgart.
G6,333.

References

New York, 1960, pp. 114, 168, no. 72; Munich,
Stadtmuseum, 1972, p. 527, no. 2128; John Flem-
ing and Hugh Honour, *The Penguin Dictionary of
Decorative Arts* (London, 1977), p. 228.

Purchased by Stuttgart's Landesmuseum
from the Nuremberg exhibition of 1906,
the inkwell has heretofore been attributed
to Debschitz himself, but it is more likely
a product of his school. The "bold abstract forms" of its design show the influence of OBRIST's sculpture and of such
students of the school as Walter Haggenmacher and Max (Mauritius) Pfeiffer.
The same combination of flat front with a
curved shape rising toward the back can
be found in the work of these artists, and
the inkwell is particularly similar to one
by Haggenmacher that was published in
Deutsche Kunst und Dekoration in March
1906.

The inkwell is made of cast and patinated bronze, an important material at the
Debschitz School's metal workshop, one
of the first departments to be founded at
the school. Its overall form capitalizes on
the fluidity of the molten bronze, which
when being cast would flow easily into
complex, organically shaped molds.

B.Z.

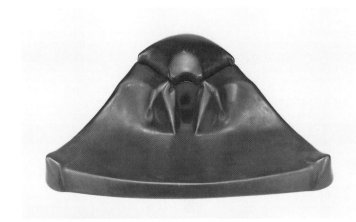

Julius Diez
1870–1954

Born in Nuremberg, Diez became one of the most characteristic, if least known, artists of Munich Jugendstil. Not easily categorized, his work, particularly of the early period, represents a variant of Munich Jugendstil, one that emerged directly from the later products of historical eclecticism.

Diez's training as a student of Ferdinand Barth and Rudolf von Seitz at the Munich Kunstgewerbeschule and Academy laid the foundations for an eclectic approach that is particularly evident in the pen and ink drawings he made for *Jugend*. His designs and caricatures soon made him one of the principal contributors to the magazine, but he had less luck with those he submitted to the Berlin journal *Pan,* only a few of which were published (now in the Museum für Kunst und Gewerbe, Hamburg). Diez's drawings for *Jugend* perfectly exemplify that journal's policy of stylistic pluralism and preference for the humorous in art and literature. Although his work was largely dominated by references to Classical art, the German Renaissance, Rococo, and Biedermeier – quite apart from Jugendstil motifs themselves – his contemporaries thought his style thoroughly modern, for it not only was witty and imaginative but also proved that historical styles could indeed be infused with new life, provided the artist was as personally confident as Diez.

In spite of their playful aestheticism, Diez's illustrations for *Jugend,* like his vignettes and ex libris, increasingly tended toward more stringent compositions and effects based on line and plane alone. Not surprisingly, his most modern designs were for posters, such as the pelican motif that won first prize in G. Wagner's 1898 competition for a poster to advertise his firm's Pelikan artists' colors. After becoming a teacher at the Kunstgewerbeschule in 1907, Diez influenced an entire generation of Munich poster designers.

Enormously versatile, Diez also designed typefaces and pewter objects, and developed prototypes for ceramic companies such as Villeroy & Boch. In the field of glassmaking, his work ranged from a revival of the German Primitives in the 1904 stained glass designs for Leipzig's city hall to the purest Jugendstil in a

Julius Diez, c. 1920

number of vessels produced by Poschinger from 1894 onward.

With a much-acclaimed frieze in the restaurant at the "München 1908" exhibition he embarked on a new career as a designer of large-scale murals. Working now in fresco, now in mosaics, he completed a number of projects, including murals for the spa in Wiesbaden, Nuremberg's railroad station, the city hall in Hanover, and the great hall of the university of Munich. At the same time Diez continued to produce paintings in a style whose free adaptations of Greek and Roman mythology recall the work of Böcklin. He underscored his belief in the continuing viability of easel painting by joining the Secession, of which he became president, albeit in 1925, when it had long become established and rather tame. That year, Diez accepted a position at the Munich Academy.

References

G. Hirth, "Jugendstil und Goethedenkmal," *Jugend,* vol. 5, no. 39 (1900), pp. 664–65; Habich, 1907, pp. 225–41; P. Westheim, "Diez-Vignetten," *Kunst und Handwerk,* vol. 60 (1909–10), pp. 361–72; F. von Ostini, "Julius Diez," *Deutsche Kunst und Dekoration,* vol. 25 (1909–10), pp. 3–

28; W. Zils, *Geistiges und künstlerisches München in Selbstbiographien* (Munich, 1913), p. 67; R. Braungart, "Kriegsgraphiken von Julius Diez," *Kunst und Handwerk,* vol. 67 (1915–16), pp. 1–16; Braungart, 1921; F. Schmalenbach, "Jugendstil: Ein Beitrag zur Theorie und Geschichte der Flächenkunst" (diss., Westfälische Wilhelms-Universität, Münster, 1934), pp. 19, 43, 99 ff.; P. Breuer, *Münchner Künstlerköpfe* (Munich, 1937), p. 136 ff.; Munich, Lenbachhaus, *Julius Diez: Sonderausstellung zum 70. Geburtstag des Künstlers* (1940); Munich, Stadtmuseum, *Die Münchner Secession und ihre Galerie* (July 10–Sept. 14, 1975), p. 44, fig. 20; Munich, 1976, pp. 37, 65, 67, 92, 131–32, 268, 430; Munich, Stadtmuseum, *Die Zwanziger Jahre in München* (1979), p. 506; G. P. Woeckel, "Glasfenster-Entwürfe des Münchner Jugendstilmalers Julius Diez (1870–1954)," *Weltkunst,* vol. 57, no. 15 (1987), p. 2025 ff., figs. 5, 6.   C.S.

24 Vase, 1900

Made by Ferdinand von Poschinger, Buchenau
(active c. 1900-1921)
Clear and colored glass with cut, enameled, and
gilded decoration, height 5″ (13.7 cm)
Mark: Ferd. von Poschinger Glashüttenwerke
Buchenau Bayern No. 117
Museen der Stadt, Sammlung der Städtischen
Galerie, Regensburg. 1958/67K

References

"Moderner deutscher Schmuck auf der Welt-
Ausstellung," *Deutsche Kunst und Dekoration,*
vol. 6 (1900), p. 518 (ill.); Gustav E. Pazaurek,
Moderne Gläser (Leipzig, 1902), pp. 78, 119;
Schack, 1971, p. 268, no. 106; Schack, 1976,
p. 265, fig. 195.

Diez's vase with a salamander was among
the glass made by the Poschinger factory
at Buchenau, near Zwiesel in the Bayerischer Wald, that was shown at the Paris
Exposition Universelle in 1900. *Deutsche
Kunst und Dekoration* described the collection as "highly successful and effective"
and it was awarded a silver medal. Apart
from Diez, Ferdinand K. B. von Poschinger, the cosmopolitan owner of the glass-
works, had commissioned such other
notable artists as Hans Christiansen and
Karl Schmoll von Eisenwerth to design
the exhibits. The versatility and international orientation of the long-established
factory, which was founded in 1629, are
particularly noticeable in the glass produced there around the turn of the century. Whereas many of the colored and
iridescent glasswares made by the firm
were in the style of Tiffany, the naturalistic decoration and flashed technique of
Diez's vase, combining colorless and blue
glass with gilded and enameled decoration, are more in the manner of such
French glassmakers as Gallé.   C.S.

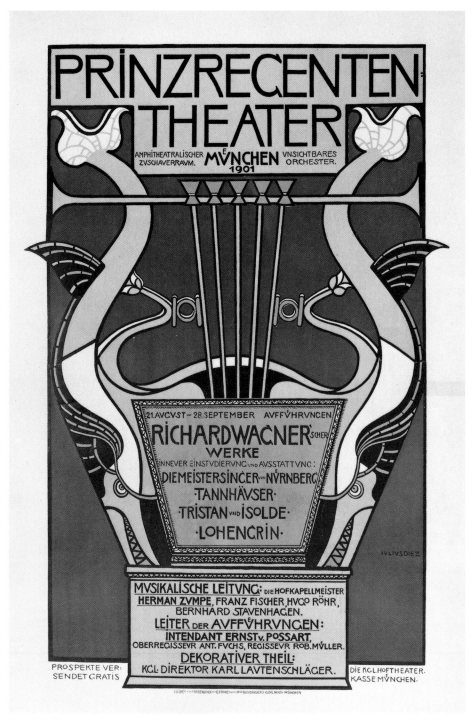

**25 Poster for Prinzregententheater,
1901**

Printed by G. Franz'sche Hofbuchdruckerei,
Munich
Color lithograph, 3 17/8 x 20 1/8″ (81 x 51 cm)
Signature: IVLIVSDIEZ (lower right)
Stadtmuseum, Munich. B 4/22

References

Suckale-Redlefsen, 1975, pp. 46–47, fig. 6;
Munich, 1975–76 (2nd ed., 1978), pp. 84, fig. 64,
85, 184, no. 77; Brussels, 1977, p. 280, no. 667;
Hollmann, et al., 1980, Part 1, p. 54, no. 582,
Part 2, pl. 43, no. 582; Munich, *Kandinsky*, 1982,
p. 196, no. 36; New York, 1982, p. 85, no. 2.

Diez designed this poster for the inau-
guration of the Prinzregententheater,
Munich's "second opera house," in 1901.
His image of a dolphin-sided lyre deliberately borrowed the most obvious symbols of official "Apollonian" neoclassicism as sponsored by the government of
Bavaria and its monarch, the Prince Regent Luitpold. Yet the image is so stylized, even caricatured by its strong linear
outline and flat planes of color, that it
places Diez well within the circle of modernist illustrators of *Jugend* to which he
belonged. For the inaugural season of the
Munich Künstlertheater in 1908–9, Diez,
along with the other *Jugend* artists ERLER
and HEINE, was invited to design sets,
Diez's being for a production of *Twelfth
Night*.   K. B. H. / C. S. v. W. S.

Otto Eckmann

1865-1902

The son of a Hamburg businessman, Eckmann finished a commercial apprenticeship before turning to art. He attended the Gewerbeschule in Hamburg, the Kunstgewerbeschule in Nuremberg, and then enrolled in 1885 at the Munich Academy. Several study trips and the bohemian life of Munich influenced the development of the young painter, whose early, naturalistic style soon gave way to Symbolism. His success at exhibitions from 1890 on rapidly established Eckmann's reputation, yet in November 1894 he auctioned all his paintings. His covering letter to the auctioneer ended with an ironic, "cordial farewell" to his paintings: "May we never meet again."

From then on Eckmann devoted himself entirely to applied art, within a short time creating designs for ceramics and jewelry, stained glass and tapestries, metal and silver objects, furniture, and even women's fashions (sketchbooks are preserved in the Kunstbibliothek, Berlin, Museum für Kunst und Gewerbe, Hamburg, and Kaiser Wilhelm Museum, Krefeld). But what made Eckmann famous overnight were his color woodcuts, for which he cut the blocks and even made some of the inks himself. He had been encouraged in this direction while still a painter, by Justus Brinkmann, director of the Hamburg Museum für Kunst und Gewerbe, who collected Japanese woodblock prints and made them available to young artists for study. Two of Eckmann's finest works in this medium, *Irises* (no. 26) of 1895 and *Night Heron* of 1896, appeared in *Pan,* for which he also designed ornamental borders and vignettes from 1895 to 1900. Eckmann was also one of the first contributors to *Jugend,* for which he designed five covers and a large number of illustrations and ornaments. Book covers, endpapers, and ex libris round off the list of his contributions to the art of book design.

As his early woodcuts showed, Eckmann was destined to be a master of form and line. His graceful and imaginative plant and animal motifs were derived from a close observation of nature, as indeed was all his work. Combining his talent for planar articulation with an unerring sense of color, Eckmann produced tapestry designs for the Kunstwebschule

Otto Eckmann. Portrait by Lovis Corinth, 1897. Kunsthalle, Hamburg

and blossom shapes, were controversial (see no. 27).

The year 1897 brought important changes for Eckmann. His friend Deneken, now director of the new Kaiser Wilhelm Museum in Krefeld, procured him commissions from textile manufacturers. Grand Duke Ernst Ludwig of Hesse asked him to design, furnish, and decorate the study in the Neue Palais, Darmstadt, and in the fall of 1897 Eckmann became instructor in ornamental painting at the Kunstgewerbeschule in Berlin, a city that provided many opportunities for work in the arts and crafts. In spite of the tuberculosis from which he had suffered for many years, Eckmann's creative drive remained unhampered. He continued to design outstanding carpets and wallpapers, a typeface that bears his name, and advertisements for many companies.

References

Gmelin, "Kleinkunst," 1897-98, p. 17 ff; Fedor von Zobeltitz, "Eckmannscher Buchschmuck," *Zeitschrift für Bücherfreunde,* vol. 1 (1897-98), p. 104 ff.; Otto Eckmann, "Zu meinen Bildern," in Simmen, 1982; Schlee, 1984. B.S.

at Scherrebek in northern Schleswig (now in Denmark), which was founded in 1896 to perpetuate the tradition of fine weaving. Thanks to his friendship with Friedrich Deneken, one of the school's founders, Eckmann became the first designer to have tapestries, including the famous *Five Swans* (no. 30), handwoven in the Scherrebek workshops.

Also highly successful were Eckmann's innovative works in metal, which were first shown at the 1897 Glaspalast exhibition in Munich. These objects – a kettle in hammered copper, a wrought-iron flower stand, ceiling and wall lamps in bronze, wrought-iron candlesticks and vase holders – were manufactured by the well-known Munich firm of Josef Zimmermann & Co. The candlesticks in particular, with their fantastically curved stem

SCHWERTLILIEN · HOLZSCHNITT VON OTTO ECKMANN   PAN

26 Irises, 1895

Color woodcut, 8¹/₂ x 5″ (21.5 x 12.5 cm)
Signature: OE (intertwined) (lower left)
Staatliche Museen Preussischer Kulturbesitz,
Kunstbibliothek, Berlin. 5119,6

References

Loubier, 1902, p. 314; Jean Loubier, *Die Neue Buchkunst* (Weimar, 1902), p. 147; Meyer, 1905, p. 150; Walter H. Damann, *Deutsche Schriftkünstler der Gegenwart, III: Otto Eckmann* (Hamburg, 1921), p. 417; Frankfurt, 1955, p. 13, no. 53; Ahlers-Hestermann, 1956, ill. facing p. 8; Munich, 1958, p. 175, no. 498; Hamburg, 1963, p. 64, no. 554; Karl August Reiser, *Deutsche Graphik von Leibl bis zur Gegenwart* (Reutlingen, 1964), p. 56; Spielmann, 1965, p. 19, no. 4; Hamburg, 1968, p. 19, fig. 3; Hofstätter, 1968, p. 135; Ingrid Dennerlein, ed., *Bildende Kunst, 1850-1914: Dokumentation aus Zeitschriften des Jugendstils*, vol. 1: *Pan: 1895-1900* (Berlin, 1970), p. 27, no. 512; Munich, Haus der Kunst, 1972, p. 112, no. 724; Mieczyslaw Wallis, *Jugendstil* (Munich, 1974), p. 183, no. 130; Volker Detlef Heydorn, *Maler in Hamburg 1886-1945,* vol. 1 (Hamburg, 1974), p. 67; Krefeld, 1977-78, no. 192; Spielmann, 1979, p. 371, no. 518; Jutta Thamer, *Zwischen Historismus und Jugendstil: Zur Ausstattung der Zeitschrift "Pan" (1895-1900)* (Frankfurt, 1980), p. 57; Prague, 1980, p. 26; S. Wichmann, 1980, p. 88; Simmen, 1982, pp. 22, no. 41b, 57, fig. 12; Krefeld, 1984, pp. 125, 129, 131, no. 10.

Published in the distinguished Berlin art journal *Pan* in 1895 (no. 3, facing page 158), *Irises* helped to bring fame quickly to the artist. The subject of irises had occupied Eckmann long before he turned to graphics and the applied arts, and there are numerous sketches and drawings that show a wide range of his studies of the plant. Irises were also incorporated as symbols in Eckmann's last painting, *The Four Ages of Man.*

This print was made under the impact of woodcuts by the Japanese artists Hokusai and Hiroshige, and the vertical format and extreme close-up view of the flowers derive from these models. In Aemil Fendler's foreword to Eckmann's *Neue Formen* of 1897, he explained: "We have rediscovered the way to nature via Japan. No longer does our present flourishing art rely upon past style, nor does it seek its motifs from the Renaissance or Rococo periods .... Gratefully, we must remember Japan, whose wonderful art, with its rare combination of the freshness of nature with the finest decorative taste and great stylistic assurance, first demonstrated the right path and opened the eyes of those who were able to see" (quoted by Siegfried Wichmann, "The Lily and Iris as European Picture Motifs in the Nineteenth and Early Twentieth Centuries," in Munich, Haus der Kunst, 1972, p. 110).   B.S.

27 "Narcissus" Candlestick, 1896–97

Made by Josef Zimmermann & Co., Munich
(established 1888)
Wrought iron, height 17¹/₈″ (43.5 cm)
Museum für Kunst und Gewerbe, Hamburg.
1912.223

References

Verkaufskatalog der Firma Zimmermann mit Werken von Otto Eckmann (Munich, 1896–97), no. 361; Henry Nocq, "A Munich," *Revue des Arts Décoratifs,* vol. 17 (1897), p. 328 (ill.); Wilhelm Bode, "Künstler im Kunsthandwerk, II: Die Abteilung der Kleinkunst in den Internationalen Ausstellungen zu München und Dresden 1897," *Pan,* vol. 3 (1897), pp. 114, 116 (ill.); Munich, 1897, p. 205, nos. 17–18; Gmelin, "Kleinkunst," 1897–98, pp. 22, fig. 18, 26; *Dekorative Kunst,* vol. 1 (1898), p. 13 (ill.); *Deutsche Kunst und Dekoration,* vol. 3 (1898–99), p. 128 (ill.); Hamburg, 1968, p. 37, fig. 28; Hamburg, Museum für Kunst und Gewerbe, *Hohe Kunst zwischen Biedermeier und Jugendstil: Historismus in Hamburg und Norddeutschland* (1977), p. 175, no. 280; Spielmann, 1979, p. 434, no. 607; Graham Dry, "Münchener Jugendstilleuchter um 1900: Aspekte des floralen und linearen Stils," *Weltkunst,* vol. 57, no. 15 (1987), pp. 2030–31.

The author of the article on modern lighting fixtures in the 1897–98 volume of *Dekorative Kunst* – probably the editor Julius Meier-Graefe himself – compared the development from kerosene lamp to gas and electric lighting to that from stagecoach to railroad car. Yet all three forms of lighting coexisted for a time at the end of the nineteenth century, and all three challenged designers. Although Germany had "not yet participated to any great extent in the creation of modern lighting fixtures" and "creative innovations [had] yet to emerge," several designers working in Germany, among them J. M. Olbrich, PAUL, RIEMERSCHMID, Henry van de Velde, and Eckmann, had shown considerable interest in that portable source of illumination, the candlestick.

Eckmann provided a number of designs for wrought-iron lighting fixtures for the Munich metalworking firm of Josef Zimmermann & Co., including candlesticks, candelabra, and even wall-mounted electric lamps. Work in wrought iron, such as hinges and cabinet fittings, music stands, flower pots, and, of course, candlesticks and lamps, was then especially popular in Munich and bore a close affinity to popular art. When Gmelin reviewed the 1897 Munich Glaspalast exhibition, which included the first examples of Eckmann's wrought-iron candlesticks, he was able to note the gratifying spread of such "democratic metals" as copper, pewter, and iron (Gmelin, "Kleinkunst," 1897–98, p. 19). Eckmann's designs for wrought-iron objects were singled out for praise: "Excep-

tionally convincing [are] the naturalistic wrought candlesticks by Otto Eckmann (executed by Zimmermann & Co.); certain parts, particularly the leaves and the undulations of their edges, are reproduced quite unsurpassably. One was initially taken aback by their somewhat large scale, but even in smaller versions the pieces would lose none of their beauty."

The fact that Eckmann's "Narcissus" candlesticks were frequently illustrated in contemporary publications indicates that they were considered a viable alternative to mass-produced items. Several candlesticks by Eckmann, with imaginative variations on the blossom motif, are known from reproductions, but apparently few

have survived. This one, and a companion piece in the Städtische Kunstsammlungen, Darmstadt, are thus highly significant as examples of the turn-of-the-century renascence in the applied arts.

R.J.

28 Flock of Gulls, 1896

Made by Kunstwebschule, Scherrebek
(established 1896)
Wool, 14⁷/₈ x 57¹/₂" (38 x 146 cm)
Museum für Kunst und Gewerbe, Hamburg.
1962/192

References

Vossische Zeitung, no. 95 (Feb. 26, 1897); Munich,
1897, p. 193, no. 13; Ernst Zimmermann,
"Scherrebeker Kunst-Webereien," *Kunst und
Handwerk,* vol. 47 (1897-98), p. 79, fig. 113;
Deutsche Kunst und Dekoration, vol. 1 (1897-98),
p. 3 (ill.); Justus Brinckmann, "Museum für
Kunst und Gewerbe, Hamburg: Bericht für das
Jahr 1897," *Jahrbuch der Hamburgischen Wissenschaftlichen Anstalten* (1898), p. 47; Peter Jessen,
"Scherrebek," *Kunstgewerbeblatt,* n. s., vol. 9
(1898), p. 154; *Liebhaberkünste,* vol. 7 (1898), p. 12
(ill.); *Liebhaberkünste,* vol. 8 (1899), p. 358;
Deutsche Kunst und Dekoration, vol. 4 (1899),
p. 496 (ill.); *Kunst und Kunsthandwerk,* vol. 2
(1899), p. 220; Dresden, 1899, p. 91, no. 1487;
Felix Poppenberg, "Das Kunstgewerbe auf der
Pariser Weltausstellung," in Hans Kraemer, *Das
19. Jahrhundert in Wort und Bild,* vol. 4 (Berlin,
1900), p. 242; A. L. Plehn, "Die Zimmerausstat-
tung auf den Ausstellungen in Berlin, München
und Dresden im Sommer 1899," *Kunstgewerbeblatt,* n. s., vol. 11 (1900), p. 22 (ill. in Dresden);
Krefeld, 1903, p. 6, no. 94; Schleswig, 1959,
no. 19; Hamburg, 1963, no. 19; *Jahrbuch der Hamburger Kunstsammlungen,* vol. 8 (1963), pp. 181,
182, fig. 2, 184; Gabriele Howaldt, "Bildteppiche
der Stilbewegung," *Kunst in Hessen und am Mittelrhein,* vol. 4 (1964), pp. 103, 120, fig. 51, 151;
Spielmann, 1965, p. 22, no. 15; Wolfgang
Scheffler, *Werke um 1900* (Berlin, 1966), p. 184,
fig. 273; Hamburg, 1968, pp. 26, fig. 13, 27;
Ernst Schlee, "'Möwenschwarm'-Bildteppiche
des Jugendstils," *Schleswig-Holstein,* vol. 26, no. 8
(1974), pp. 206-8; Spielmann, 1979, p. 417,
no. 584; Schlee, 1984, pp. 208, no. 29, 209,
fig. 29.

With the Scherrebek tapestries Eckmann
designed his first "useful objects – which
tapestries, too, were considered to be," as
Friedrich Deneken said (*Zweiter Bericht
des Städtischen Kaiser Wilhelm Museums in
Krefeld 1899-1904* [Krefeld, 1904], p. 43).
His work on *Flock of Gulls* must date toward the end of 1895, since the cartoon
was already available when the weaving
school was opened on February 18, 1896.
The tapestry was finished before Christ-
mas 1896 and was shown at the first public exhibition of Scherrebek work at Louis
Bock & Sohn in Hamburg. *Flock of Gulls*
is the first Scherrebek tapestry that was
not made as a compound weave with
multiple warps and wefts in layers, but as
conventional tapestry weave with one
warp, so that the color goes in a single
layer, a change from yardage to individual piece production. Both subject and
composition provided models for several
other Jugendstil tapestries. *Flock of Gulls*
is also a fine example of the strong effect
that can be achieved by dyeing wool
thread with vegetable dyes, a technique
well suited to Eckmann's sense of color.

B.S.

29 Three Swans on Dark Water, 1895

Color woodcut, 16³/₈ x 15¹/₄″ (41.5 x 38.8 cm)
Signature: OE (intertwined) (lower left)
Museum für Kunst und Gewerbe, Hamburg.
1895/121

References

Munich, 1897, p. 169, no. 2529; *Zeitschrift für Bücherfreunde,* vol. 1 (1897-98), p. 105; Krefeld, 1898, no. 138; Max Osborn, "Otto Eckmann, II: Seine kunstgewerbliche Tätigkeit," *Deutsche Kunst und Dekoration,* vol. 6 (1900), p. 314; Zimmermann, 1900, p. 311, ill. facing p. 312; E. Kulbe, "Otto Eckmann," *Gemeinnützige Polytechnische Monatsschrift* (1902), p. 84; "Otto Eckmann," *Vossische Zeitung,* no. 273, sup. no. 1 (June 14, 1902); Loubier, 1902, pp. 312, 314, ill. facing p. 316; Krefeld, 1903, pp. 2, 5, no. 6; Meyer, 1905, p. 150; Hirth, ed., 1908, p. 43, no. 356 (ill.); Julius Rodenberg, *In der Schmiede der Schrift: Karl Klingspor und sein Werk* (Berlin, 1940), p. 42; Frankfurt, 1955, p. 25, no. 236; Hamburg, Museum für Kunst und Gewerbe, *Bestiarium* (1962), p. 117, no. 57; Karl August Reiser, *Deutsche Graphik von Leibl bis zur Gegenwart* (Reutlingen, 1964), p. 56; Spielmann, 1965, cover, p. 19; Hamburg, 1968, p. 18, fig. 2; Berlin, 1970-71, pp. 67, 70, no. 131; Spielmann, 1977, pp. 7, 9; Brussels, 1977, p. 265, no. 628; Krefeld, 1977-78, no. 189; Spielmann, 1979, p. 369, no. 516d; Thomas Walters, ed., *Jugendstilgraphik* (Cologne, 1980), p. 145; Simmen, 1982, frontispiece, p. 22, nos. 39a, b; Krefeld, 1984, p. 131, no. 12.

According to Ernst Zimmermann, writing in 1900, the color woodcuts that Eckmann produced around 1895 "made him famous overnight. The first was *Black Swans* [*Three Swans on Dark Water*], the striking motif that was virtually forced upon him in his native city, where water and swans are an intrinsic part of the city's image. Here he was interested mainly in the play of lines created by the water, that never-ending confusion of twisting and crisscrossing lines, the attraction of which assumed ornamental significance for him for the first time." In the *Zeitschrift für Bücherfreunde* Eckmann himself was quoted as saying that *Three Swans on Dark Water* was his first color woodcut and "brought me unexpected success.... The main thing for me was that I was immediately asked to do ornamental work." Soon there was scarcely an exhibition of modern art that did not include this print, and numerous reports and commentaries speak of it with the highest praise. Writing in *Dekorative Kunst,* Karl Scheffler, for instance, who often strongly criticized Eckmann and his work, said that "the renowned woodcuts with the swans are very beautiful and endlessly delightful." Eckmann did another woodcut of swans on blue water the same year and his much celebrated tapestry in 1896-97 (no. 30).   B.S.

30 Five Swans, 1896-97

Made by Kunstwebschule, Scherrebek (established 1896)
Wool, 93⁵/₈ x 27¹/₂″ (238 x 70 cm)
Marks: OE (intertwined), factory mark (lower left)
Schleswig-Holsteinisches Landesmuseum, Schleswig. 1978/932

References

Vossische Zeitung, no. 95 (Feb. 26, 1897); L. Hagen, "Die Persönlichkeit des Künstlers im Kunstgewerbe," *Das Atelier: Organ für Kunst und Gewerbe,* vol. 7, no. 18 (1897), p. 2; Munich, 1897, p. 193, no. 15 (ill.); *Deutsche Kunst und Dekoration,* vol. 1 (1897-98), p. 2 (ill.); *Kunst und Handwerk,* vol. 47 (1897-98), p. 76 (ill.); *Möbel*

und Decoration (1898), p. 115; *Liebhaberkünste,* vol. 7 (1898), p. 14 (ill.); Emil Hannover, "Skaerbaek Taepper," *Kunstbladet,* vol. 1 (1898), p. 56; Peter Jessen, "Scherrebek," *Kunstgewerbeblatt,* n. s., vol. 9 (1898), pp. 154, 224; Justus Brinckmann, "Museum für Kunst und Gewerbe, Hamburg: Bericht für das Jahr 1897," *Jahrbuch der Hamburgischen Wissenschaftlichen Anstalten* (1898), pp. 45, 47, 174-75; *Deutsche Kunst und Dekoration,* vol. 3 (1898-99), p. 126 (ill. in interior); *Liebhaberkünste,* vol. 8 (1899), p. 358; Rosner, 1899, p. 143, fig. 129; Schumann, 1899, p. 517 (ill.); Dresden, 1899, p. 91, no. 1484; *Gewerbeblatt aus Württemberg,* vol. 52 (1900), p. 86; Felix Poppenberg, "Das Kunstgewerbe auf der Pariser Weltausstellung," in Hans Kraemer, *Das 19. Jahrhundert in Wort und Bild,* vol. 4 (Berlin, 1900), p. 242; Paul Schumann, "Das Kunstgewerbe auf der internationalen Kunst-Ausstellung zu Dresden Mai-Oktober 1901," *Deutsche Kunst und Dekoration,* vol. 8 (1901), p. 443 (ill. in interior); *Berliner Architekturwelt,* special issue no. 1 (Oct. 1901), p. 45; Felix Poppenberg, "Otto Eckmann," *Die Nation,* vol. 19, no. 28 (1902), p. 604; Hugo Schmerber, "Otto Eckmann," in Anton Bettelheim, ed., *Biographisches Jahrbuch und Deutscher Nekrolog,* vol. 7: *1902* (Berlin, 1905), p. 41; Krefeld, 1903; Meyer, 1905, p. 152; Frankfurt, 1955, p. 36, no. 363; Heinrich Kohlhaussen, *Geschichte des deutschen Kunsthandwerks* (Munich, 1955), p. 560, fig. 532; Ahlers-Hestermann, 1956, ill. facing p. 60; Ewald Rathke, *Jugendstil* (Mannheim, 1958), fig. 6; Baden-Baden, Staatliche Kunsthalle, *Aus der Zeit um 1900* (1958), no. 250; Hamburg, Museum für Kunst und Gewerbe, *Bestiarium* (1962), p. 116, no. 55; *Jahrbuch der Hamburger Kunstsammlungen,* vol. 8 (1963), p. 182, n. 3; Gabriele Howaldt, "Bildteppiche der Stilbewegung," *Kunst in Hessen und am Mittelrhein,* vol. 4 (1964), pp. 102, 119, fig. 50, 155; Maurice Rheims, *L'Art Nouveau ou le Style Jules Verne* (Paris, 1965), p. 318, no. 449; Spielmann, 1965, p. 22, no. 17; Rheims, 1966, p. 336, no. 449; Brussels, Kursaal D'Ostende, *Europa 1900* (June 3-Sept. 30, 1967), p. 73, no. 524; Hamburg, 1968, pp. 28, fig. 16, 29; Madeleine Jarry, *La Tapisserie des origines à nos jours* (Paris, 1968), p. 305; Mieczyslaw Wallis, *Jugendstil* (Munich, 1974), p. 78, no. 61; Volker Detlef Heydorn, *Maler in Hamburg 1896-1945* (Hamburg, 1974), p. 36; Brigitte Klesse and Hans Mayr, *Verborgene Schätze aus sieben Jahrhunderten* (Cologne, 1977), pp. 206-7; Spielmann, 1977, pp. 9, 24-25; Spielmann, 1979, p. 419, no. 587; S. Wichmann, 1980, pp. 280, 289, no. 765; Thérèse Thomas, "Ein Kännchen aus Steinzeug nach einer Otto-Eckmann-Arbeit," *Mettlacher Turm,* no. 16 (Dec. 1982), p. 6; Hamburg, 1983, pp. 118-19; Berlin, Berlinische Galerie and Akademie der Künste, *Berlin um 1900* (1984), p. 256, no. 866; Krefeld, 1984, pp. 27, 135, 137, no. 1; Masini, 1984, p. 176, no. 470.

The *Five Swans* tapestry was the most successful of all the works produced at Scherrebek. Justus Brinckmann, director of the Museum für Kunst und Gewerbe in Hamburg, noted in the *Jahrbuch der Hamburgischen Wissenschaftlichen Anstalten:* "The swan tapestry must be regarded as one of the finest pieces woven so far at Scherrebek, and we bought it immediately after Eckmann's cartoons were woven. It has since been copied many times." In the same year the tapestry was reproduced in virtually all the "modern" magazines, and barely a year later critics were referring to it as "the famous swan tapestry," the "freshest product of the new movement," and "the swan tapestry, which immediately became world famous." The work was described variously by critics; some saw it as simple naturalism, others as heraldic ornament. Felix Poppenberg, among others, pointed out the Japanese influence in 1902: "This is a good example of how a pupil of Japanese art can transpose natural motifs into a delightful play of colored surfaces and lines by suppressing the material process and concentrating entirely on the decorative."

As early as 1899 Heinrich Sperling made a parody of the *Five Swans* with his pug-dog and stork tapestry, also produced at Scherrebek. Eckmann was highly offended by these ironic copies and, after the ensuing differences of opinion, he left the Scherrebek weaving school. But demand for *Five Swans* continued and about one hundred examples of the tapestry were woven. B.S.

31 Moonlight on Water, 1896–97

Color woodcut, 12³/₈ x 5¹/₂″ (31.4 x 13.8 cm)
Signature: OE (intertwined) (lower left)
Kaiser Wilhelm Museum, Krefeld

References

Munich, 1897, p. 169, no. 2530; Krefeld, 1898, no. 140; Zimmermann, 1900, p. 311; E. Kulbe, "Otto Eckmann," *Gemeinnützige Polytechnische Monatsschrift* (1902), p. 84; "Otto Eckmann," *Vossische Zeitung*, no. 273, sup. no. 1 (June 14, 1902); Jean Loubier, *Die Neue Buchkunst* (Weimar, 1902), p. 147; Krefeld, 1903, p. 5, no. 10; Max Osborn, *Der Holzschnitt,* Sammlung Illustrierter Monographien, ed. Hanns von Zobeltitz, no. 16 (Bielefeld, 1905), p. 149; Hofstätter, 1968, p. 135; Krefeld, 1978, no. 195; Simmen, 1982, pp. 22, no. 44, 58, fig. 16; Krefeld, 1984, p. 131, no. 11.

This was probably Eckmann's last color woodcut. The theme of moonlight reflecting on water, light, and water also inspired him to produce other designs and sketches for prints (now divided between the Museum für Kunst und Gewerbe, Hamburg, and the Kunstbibliothek, Berlin). "Rippling water is a recurring motif in his ornamental vocabulary. It was important to him because it was so free, so untraditional and, as it were, so immaterial.... It left him completely free," explained Ernst Zimmermann. He made use of this freedom in *Moonlight on Water,* creating one of his most sensitive prints.

As in his other woodcuts the main features are the two-dimensional quality and the spareness of the drawing. In 1905 Max Osborn regretted that "Eckmann designed and printed only a small number of color woodcuts. Nevertheless, he may be regarded as the father of a whole group of young Munich woodcut artists who emerged around the turn of the century and whose works showed a decorative approach that owed much to him." B.S.

32 Arrival of Spring, c. 1897

Made by Kunstwebschule, Scherrebek (established 1896)
Wool, 130¹/₈ x 84¹/₂″ (331 x 215 cm)
Marks: OE (intertwined), factory mark (lower center)
Inscription: FANGET AN / SO RIEF DER LENZ IN DEN WALD (lower center)
Schleswig-Holsteinisches Landesmuseum, Schleswig. 1981/971

References

Peter Jessen, "Scherrebek," *Kunstgewerbeblatt,* n. s., vol. 9 (1898), pp. 154–55, 157 (ill.); *Deutsche Kunst und Dekoration,* vol. 2 (1898), p. 417; Krefeld, 1898, no. 72; Max Metzger, "Moderne Wandteppiche," *Möbel und Decoration* (1898), p. 116; Friedrich Deneken, *1. Bericht des Städtischen Kaiser Wilhelm-Museums in Krefeld 1897–1899* (1899), fig. 61 (in Krefeld); *Deutsche Kunst und Dekoration,* vol. 3 (1898–99), pp. 122 (ill.), 127; *Kieler Zeitung,* June 22, 1899; *Kunst und Handwerk,* vol. 50 (1899–1900), p. 284, fig. 452; *Dekorative Kunst,* vol. 7 (1901), pp. 80, 82 (ill); *Die Kunst,* vol. 4 (1901), p. 82; Turin, 1902, p. 34, no. 16; Hugo Schmerber, "Otto Eckmann," in Anton Bettelheim, ed., *Biographisches Jahrbuch und Deutscher Nekrolog,* vol. 7: *1902* (Berlin, 1905), p. 41; Gabriele Howaldt, "Bildteppiche der Stilbewegung," *Kunst in Hessen und am Mittelrhein,* vol. 4 (1964), pp. 103–4; Schleswig, Schleswig-Holsteinisches Landesmuseum, *Kunsthandwerk in Schleswig-Holstein: Bildteppiche seit 1900* (1974), pp. 40–42; Fanelli and Fanelli, 1976, no. 366; Schlee, 1984, pp. 178, 216, no. 39, 217, fig. 39.

The tapestry was presumably first shown at the Krefeld "Künstlerische Möbel und Geräte" exhibition in 1898. The subject, indicated by the quotation from Wagner's *Die Meistersinger von Nürnberg* about the arrival of spring in the forest, the unusually bright colors, and the very large size made it the brilliant centerpiece of many exhibitions of the period. In 1901 the critic of *Die Kunst* objected that "the placing of the figures in perspective, one behind the other, and the prominence of the frame are not quite in keeping with the flat surface effect expected in a tapestry," but there was generally positive agreement on Eckmann's use of color. As Peter Jessen wrote in *Kunstgewerbeblatt,* "The deeper and lighter tones of green and blue, laid side by side in broad flat areas, combine to full accord," and he went on to say aptly that "this is true wall decoration, not too slight to be considered on its own, but not laying claim to be a picture; in that sense it is similar in intent to earlier tapestries." The work's size and its consequent high price were possibly among the reasons that only some four versions were made, for according to Metzger, it took about four months to weave a tapestry as large as this one. At the Krefeld exhibition the tapestry was priced at 900 marks. B.S.

August Endell
1871-1925

Born in Berlin, Endell enrolled at Tübingen university in 1891 to study to become a teacher, but transferred the following year to Munich. By late 1892, however, he had decided on the career of a scholar, and began to take courses in philosophy, psychology, and aesthetics, with a minor in the history of German art and literature.

A meeting with OBRIST in the spring of 1896 completely altered the young scholar's life. He gave up his academic career and began to teach himself to draw and paint. By 1897 he was already among those young craftsmen and architects who, in the applied art section of the Munich Glaspalast exhibition, helped form the Jugendstil in Munich. In a room with furnishings by the Munich architect Theodor Fischer, Endell showed a carpet, a small tapestry, a *portière,* and four wall friezes in low relief.

His first furniture designs, done in the summer and fall of 1897, were for a standing desk and a bookcase. In 1899 Endell contributed inexpensive furniture, made by the Dresdner Werkstätten für Handwerkskunst, to the "Volksthümliche Ausstellung für Haus und Herd" in Dresden, and showed jewelry at the Secession exhibition in Munich. His design activity, which also involved drawings for furniture fittings, stained glass, and lamps, now expanded to include book design – for example, vignettes for the art journals *Pan* and *Dekorative Kunst.*

In 1896-97 Endell made his first foray into architecture, resulting in his Munich masterpiece, the Elvira photography studio, for which he created the famous facade with its bizarre "dragon" ornament (fig. 2) as well as the interiors. In 1898 he received a commission to design a sanatorium at Wyk on the island of Föhr. These years brought contacts with a number of poets, authors, and critics, including Stefan George, Lou Andreas-Salomé, Rainer Maria Rilke, and critic Georg Fuchs.

Together with Obrist, who exerted a strong influence on him, Endell was an eloquent advocate of the Jugendstil in Munich. In his early writings he outlined his ideas for a completely new approach to design, an art of forms stripped of all objective reference to nature, an expressive art of shapes and colors that would elicit strong emotional responses like the notes and chords in music. These aesthetic theories had a determining influence on Endell's designs for finely crafted objects and on his fantastic and expressive ornament.

In 1901 Endell moved to Berlin, where before the year was out, he had built the Buntes Theater for the writer and theater director Ernst von Wolzogen, a building that still belonged stylistically to the architecture of his Munich period. Yet soon Endell's penchant for elaborate ornamentation began to give way to increasingly straightforward and functional designs. Milestones of this transition included the Neumann Festsäle (1905-6), the Haus am Steinplatz (1906-7), villas in Berlin-Westend (1908, 1910), and the racetrack in Berlin-Mariendorf (1911-13). Endell's furniture and interior decoration underwent a similar development.

In 1904 Endell founded his own school, the Schule für Formkunst, which existed until 1914. In 1918 he succeeded Hans Poelzig as director of the Wroclaw (Breslau) Akademie für Kunst und Kunstgewerbe.

August Endell, 1918

References

Karl Scheffler, "August Endell," *Kunst und Künstler,* vol. 5, no. 8 (May 1907), pp. 314-24; Ernst Schur, "August Endell," *Dekorative Kunst,* vol. 18 (1910), pp. 375-79; Karl Scheffler, "Neue Arbeiten von August Endell," *Kunst und Künstler,* vol. 11 (1913), pp. 350-59; Karl Scheffler, *Die Architektur der Grosstadt* (Berlin, 1913), pp. 187-93; Karl Scheffler, *Die fetten und die mageren Jahre: Ein Arbeits- und Lebensbericht* (Leipzig, 1946), pp. 24-26; Ahlers-Hestermann, 1956, p. 36 ff.; Seling, ed., 1959, pp. 420-24; Eberhard Marx, "August Endell," in *Neue Deutsche Biographie,* vol. 4 (Berlin, 1959), pp. 490-91; Berlin, Akademie der Künste, *Poelzig, Endell, Moll und die Breslauer Kunstakademie 1911-1932* (1965); Peter Stressig, "August Endell," in *Karl Ernst Osthaus: Leben und Werk* (Recklinghausen, 1971), pp. 447-52; Reichel, 1974; Munich, 1977; Weiss, 1979, pp. 34-40; Tilmann Buddensieg, "Zur Frühzeit von August Endell: Seine Münchener Briefe an Kurt Breysig," in Justus Müller-Hofstede and Werner Spies, eds., *Festschrift für Eduard Trier zum 60. Geburtstag* (Berlin, 1981), pp. 223-50; Munich, 1985-86.   G.M.

33 *Um die Schönheit,* 1896

Published by Emil Franke, Munich
Printed pamphlet, 7⁷/₈ x 18¹/₂" (20 x 47 cm)
Bayerische Staatsbibliothek, Munich. Bavar.
1317 ˣᵗʳ (6

References

Endell, "Möglichkeiten," 1898, pp. 147–53;
Endell, "Formenschönheit," 1898, pp. 75–77;
August Endell, *Zauberland des Sichtbaren* (Berlin,
1928), p. 31; Berlin, Akademie der Künste, *Poelzig, Endell, Moll und die Breslauer Kunstakademie
1911-1932* (1965), p. 17; Munich, 1969–70, p. 44,
no. 76; Schaefer, 1971, pp. 402–3; Brussels, 1977,
p. 266, fig. 634; Munich, 1985–86, p. 28.

Decorated with a sensuous orchid splayed
abstractly across its title page, the critical
pamphlet *Um die Schönheit* (On Beauty)
brought Endell his first public recognition both as a critic and as an artist. Reviewing the Munich Secession exhibition
of 1896, Endell attacked the official art
of the day and outlined a revolutionary
theory of art based not on nature, but
on psychological aesthetics. In *Um die
Schönheit* Endell wrote: "He who has
once learned to give himself over completely to his visual impressions, without
associations and without afterthoughts,
who has once truly felt the effect of forms
and colors, will discover a never failing
source of extraordinary and unimagined
pleasure.... He who has not gone
through such an experience will never
understand art" (p. 11). As he exhorted
the public to stop thinking and start feeling, Endell's orchid and the free-form
plaster relief with which he decorated a
Munich photography studio, the Hof-
Atelier Elvira, in the same year announced him as a prophet of abstract
forms. Endell's Munich writings, which
had a stimulating effect on the young
Kandinsky, show him to be OBRIST's
equal as a pioneer of modern abstraction
and one of the most significant among
twentieth-century writers on art.

K.B.H./G.M.

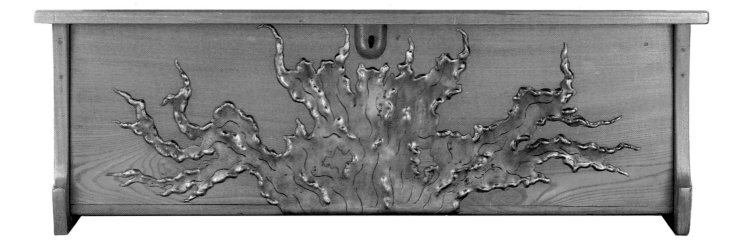

34 Chest, 1899

Made by Wenzel Till, Munich (established before
1897), and Reinhold Kirsch (royal Bavarian court
locksmith, active Munich from 1878)
Elm and galvanized iron, 17³/₄ x 53¹/₂ x 29³/₈"
(45 x 136 x 74 cm)
Stadtmuseum, Munich. 59/849

References

Endell, 1900, p. 315 (ill.); Schaefer, 1971, p. 404,
fig. 9; Munich, Stadtmuseum, 1972, p. 525,
no. 2098; Himmelheber, 1973, pp. 244, 248,
fig. 1071, 387, no. 1071; Reichel, 1974, pp. 113-
16; Munich, 1977, pp. 122, 138; Prague, 1980,
pp. 50, no. 57, 102; Munich, *Kandinsky*, 1982,
pp. 202, no. 52, 203; New York, 1982, p. 98,
no. 26; Ottomeyer, 1988, p. 113, no. 33.1.

This chest formed part of a suite of library
furniture (see also nos. 35-38) that was
commissioned from Endell by the poet
Henry von Heiseler in 1899, the year of
his marriage to Emilie von Thieme,
daughter of RIEMERSCHMID's patron (see
no. 111). The sides of the chest are decorated with engraved, parallel wavy lines
that appear in similar form on the side
panels of the bookshelf for which the
chest was designed as a base (no. 35). The
bizarre and fantastic shape of the galvanized iron ornament on the hinged
front of the chest recalls organic forms
without imitating anything found in nature.   H.O.

35 Bookshelf, 1899

Made by Wenzel Till, Munich (established before
1897)
Elm, 84⁵/₈ x 51¹/₄ x 15³/₄" (215 x 130 x 40 cm)
Stadtmuseum, Munich. 62/845

References

Endell, 1900, p. 315 (ill.); Paris, 1960-61,
no. 894; Schaefer, 1971, p. 404, fig. 9; Reichel,
1974, pp. 113-16; Munich, 1977, pp. 122, no. 1,
138; Ottomeyer, 1988, pp. 113-15, no. 33.2.

With its accompanying chest (no. 34), the
bookshelf belongs to the suite of library
furniture created for Henry von Heiseler.
Endell published the furniture in his 1900
article titled "Architektonische Erstlinge"
and described his efforts to create a new
system of ornamentation: "None of my
ornaments emerged from nature studies,
though of course, since nature is so rich in
forms, certain parallels were unavoidable.
However, my aim was never naturalistic
reproduction but solely the production of
a characteristic effect by freely invented
forms, conceived with this effect in
mind.... The goal, in a word, was an
aesthetic effect, not narration or instruction about plants and animals."   H.O.

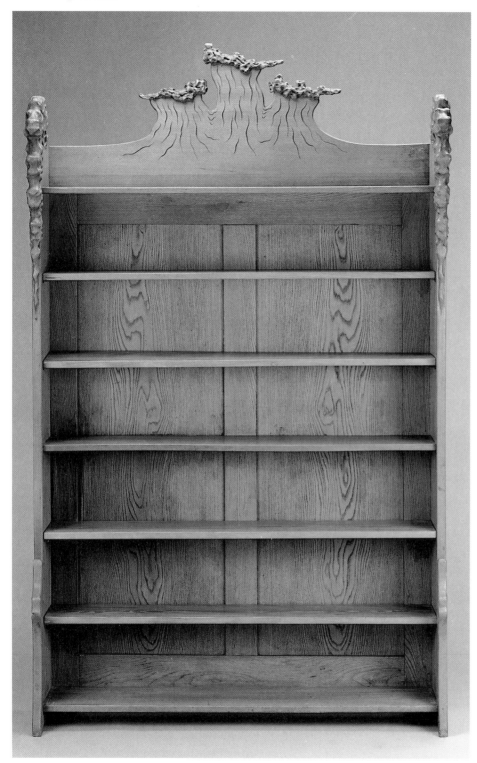

36 Bookcase, 1899

Made by Wenzel Till, Munich (established before 1897)
Elm, 70¹/₂ x 47¹/₂ x 11⁷/₈″ (179 x 120 x 30 cm)
Stadtmuseum, Munich. 75/1

References

Munich, 1958, p. 178, no. 514; Paris, 1960-61, p. 308, no. 894; Reichel, 1974, pp. 113-16; Munich, 1977, pp. 126, no. 3, 127, 138; Ottomeyer, 1988, pp. 113-15, no. 33.3.

This bookcase, also part of Heiseler's library furniture (see also nos. 34-35, 37-38), exists in three identical versions. It is richly ornamented with carvings in high relief on the sides, and decorated on the front at the top with a series of engraved agitated lines that swirl upward toward three plastic configurations suggestive of roots, sponges, or clouds. Such free association was part of Endell's intent, although he himself considered the shapes abstract, organic ornaments, as he wrote in 1898: "Knowledgeable people see quite clearly that we stand not only at the beginning of a new stylistic period, but at the inception of an entirely new art – the art of using forms that, although they signify nothing, represent nothing, and recall nothing, can move the human soul as profoundly and irresistibly as only the sounds of music have been able to do" (Endell, "Formenschönheit," 1898, p. 75).   H.O.

37 Table, 1899

Made by Wenzel Till, Munich (established before 1897)
Elm, 45¹/₄ x 38¹/₄ x 28³/₄″ (115 x 97 x 73 cm)
Private collection (on permanent loan to the Stadtmuseum, Munich)

References

Paris, 1960-61, p. 309, no. 196; Himmelheber, 1973, pp. 231, 387, no. 1073, fig. 1073; Munich, 1977, pp. 135, 139, no. 6; New York, 1982, p. 95, no. 19; S. Wichmann, *Jugendstil Floral,* 1984, p. 107, no. 233; S. Wichmann, 1984, p. 107, no. 223.

This table belongs to the library suite commissioned from Endell by Henry von Heiseler (see also nos. 34-36, 38). Its imaginative silhouettes and spare unornamented surfaces, so characteristic of Endell, are based on simple board construction. The irregular shapes of the horizontal surfaces, curiously reminiscent of stretched animal skins, together with the angled legs, create a bizarre play of lines based on the transformation of a few basic forms. Endell was schooled in the psychology of perception, and the formal puzzle posed by the table points to what he called "visual impressions without associations."   H.O.

38 Armchair, 1899

Made by Wenzel Till, Munich (established before 1897)
Elm, 41¹/₄ x 18⁷/₈ x 20¹/₂″ (105 x 48 x 52 cm)
Private collection

References

Endell, 1900, p. 315 (ill.); Munich, 1958, no. 512; Paris, 1960–61, p. 309, no. 197; Pevsner, 1968, pp. 86–87; Himmelheber, 1973, p. 387, no. 1076; Reichel, 1974, pp. 113–16; Munich, 1977, pp. 132, 140, no. 11; Alastair Duncan, *Art Nouveau Furniture* (New York, 1982), no. 160.

The design of the chair, which formed part of Heiseler's library suite (see nos. 34–37), is dominated by a series of C-shaped curves. Issuing from the back, which is shaped like a shield, the arms end in clawlike carved knobs that are the chair's only ornamentation and that recall furniture designs by PANKOK (see no. 65). The upholstered back is reminiscent of a stretched animal skin, a feature common to much of the library furniture (see no. 37). The chair is not built up from individual elements; rather, various forms merge to create an overall shape, something to which Endell referred when publishing the Heiseler furniture in 1900: "Each piece of furniture, each house, should have a unified overall character, a unified effect, and a unified movement of individual forms. No part should ever exist in isolation, but each should contribute to the effect of the whole" (Endell, 1900, p. 306).   H.O.

Fritz Erler
1868-1940

Erler was born in the town of Franken-stein near Wroclaw (Breslau), where the paintings of Böcklin, Feuerbach, and Achenbach in the local museum left a last-ing impression on him. He became a pri-vate student of Albrecht Bräuer (1830-1897), a professor at the Wroclaw art school, who advocated a precise study of natural forms and proportions and who awakened in his students a sense of the beauty of everyday things, pointing out to them, for example, the decorative pos-sibilities inherent in the almost math-ematical regularity of plant cross-sec-tions.

In the winter of 1892 Erler went to Paris to attend the Académie Julian, where his teachers were Adolphe Bou-guereau and Gabriel Ferrier. His first large canvases, worked up from sketches made on the Norman and Breton coasts, were accepted for the Paris Salons of 1893 and 1894. Although reminiscent of Böck-lin, these wild, primitive landscapes also pointed to the planar treatment and shal-low space that were to become hallmarks of Erler's graphic style.

Erler returned to Wroclaw in late 1894, and moved to Munich the following year. Works of his shown at the Munich Kunstverein attracted the attention of the critic Fritz von Ostini, who recom-mended the artist to Georg Hirth. When Hirth published the first issue of *Jugend* in 1896 it bore a cover by Erler, who went on to provide over fifty covers and count-less vignettes, borders, and illustrations for the magazine (see no. 39). Until about 1905, the cover illustrations were closely linked with the magazine's title, and their bold, planar designs, skillfully integrating the title lettering in ever new ways, were extremely effective as advertising. In his vignettes and decorative borders, Erler favored more ornamental, floral designs, and frequently included one or more fig-ures in them.

In 1898 the family of Dr. Albert Neis-ser, who had supported Erler for some years, commissioned him to decorate the music room of their new house in Wroc-law. Erler was given complete responsi-bility for the interior and its furnishings, and the music room ranks as one of the earliest Jugendstil interiors in Germany, as the English journal *The Studio* reported

Fritz Erler, 1929

in 1899: "This has been a rare opportunity for the display of the artist's gifts, for he has been left practically untrammelled. In this temple of music everything is from the one artist's brain and hand; the ar-chitectural forms of ceiling and wainscot, of doors and windows; the decorative work of all kinds, in carved wood, in forged and chased metals, in the furniture and stuffs, and in the beautiful paintings of the broad frieze and other colour – lending adornment of the room … hav-ing thought out his theme, [Mr. Erler] has let the riches of his fancy play about the working out of its charming varia-tions, while absolutely conserving the unities" (Burnley Bibb, "Fritz Erler, I: Decorations for a Music-Room," *The Studio*, vol. 17 [1899], pp. 26-28). A year later he and other Munich artists formed the Scholle group with the aims of in-creasing public interest in their art and of gaining better representation at the Glas-palast exhibitions. By this time Erler had become a household name in Munich's artistic circles, and he received numerous commissions for book designs and ex li-bris, posters and portraits.

Erler also undertook a number of com-missions for murals in public and private buildings throughout Germany, and in 1907 he was awarded a professorship in recognition of his achievements in the field of painting. He continued to devote himself to mural painting and to portrai-ture; as an official war artist during World War I, he painted nationalistic celebra-tions of heroism, and he continued to work in this style under the Third Reich during the latter part of his career.

References

H. E. von Berlepsch-Valendas, "Fritz Erler – München," *Deutsche Kunst und Dekoration*, vol. 1 (1897-98), pp. 93-102; Karl Mayr, "Fritz Erler," *Deutsche Kunst und Dekoration*, vol. 7 (1900-1), pp. 273-88; Mayr, "Illustrationsstil," 1901; Fritz Erler, "Meine Entwürfe zu Faust und Hamlet im Münchner Künstlertheater," *Kunstgewerbeblatt*, n. s., vol. 21 (1910), pp. 97-98, 106-10; Ostini, 1921; Fritz Erler, "Aus Schlenderweil: Grillen ei-nes Malers," *Die Kunst*, vol. 65 (1932), pp. 65-73; Munich, Künstlergenossenschaft, *Sammelausstel-lung Fritz Erler* (1932); Munich, 1958, pp. 163-64; Bernd Dürr, "Die Münchner Künstler-gemeinschaft die Scholle," in *Leo Putz 1869-1940* (Merano, 1981), pp. 23-45; Schroeter, 1988.

Chr. S.

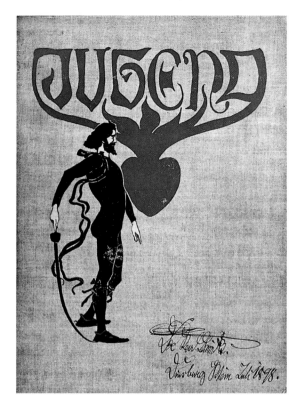

39 *Jugend,* 1898

Printed periodical, 12¹/₄ x 9¹/₄″ (31 x 23.5 cm)
Bayerische Staatsbibliothek, Munich.
4° Per. 80¹ (3

References

Hirth, ed., 1908, p. 72, no. 606 (ill.); Munich,
1969-70, pp. 33, no. 3, 45, no. 82, 77; Berlin,
1970-71, pp. 80-81, no. 168a; Brussels, 1977,
pp. 266-67, no. 635.

In 1921 Fritz von Ostini, for many years
chief editor of *Jugend,* wrote of Erler's
contributions to the magazine: "The rich-
ness and variety of his work...were
enormous; whatever was most personal
to him, most typically Erler, was what
we most liked to include.... One sensed
the romanticism of French knights and
the strength of the Vikings, things that
seemed grotesquely Oriental and others
that reflected the utmost modernity with
the means of expression of a man who
used his eyes" (Ostini, 1921, pp. 27-28).
From the early 1890s Erler had been fascinated by the romantic and fantastic fairy-
tale world of Hans Christian Andersen
and the brothers Grimm. Several trips to
Rügen and the French Atlantic coast left
deep impressions on him, and soon a
dark, somber, romantic mood dominated
his pictures, and characters who seemed
to belong to a long-past age peopled his
scenes. The vignettes, illustrations, and
title pages that Erler designed for *Jugend*
between 1896 and 1900 include knights,
kings, bold seafarers, and commanding,
but at the same time seductive, ladies.
They are all figures from an idealized
world, in which such concepts as honor,
love, courage, and steadfastness are of
great importance.

The man depicted in this design represents a nobleman of the late Middle Ages
who seems to be fixing an opponent with
a firm gaze and to be challenging him to
combat. Georg Hirth, the publisher of
Jugend, had insisted with the first issue in
1896 that the pictures on the title pages be
related to the idea of youth. Erler expressed different aspects of the theme in
his various designs. In this one, which
was used as the cover of the eleventh issue
of *Jugend* in 1898, the combination of a
dueler dressed in black with red lettering
designed by the artist presumably seemed
to Erler a more suitable way of representing the self-confidence and combative
ideals of youth than a realistic depiction of
a man of the nineteenth century. Other
works by Erler similar in style and motif
are to be found in the 1897 and 1898 issues
of *Jugend.* These illustrations won wide
acclaim at the turn of the century, mainly
for their highly individual, rugged
character.   Chr. S.

40 Poster for the Cococello Club, 1902

Printed by Hubert Köhler, Munich
Color lithograph, 34¹/₂ x 15³/₄″ (87 x 40 cm)
Signature: Erler (lower left)
Stadtmuseum, Munich. B 21/2

References

Fritz von Ostini, "Münchener künstlerische Fest-
karten," *Die Kunst,* vol. 14 (1906), p. 196 (ill.);
Westheim, 1907, p. 225; Munich, 1964, p. 35,
no. 143; Suckale-Redlefsen, 1975, pp. 46, no. 7,
47; Munich, 1975-76 (2nd ed., 1978), p. 185,
no. 86, pl. xii; Brussels, 1977, p. 283, no. 677;
Hollmann, et al., 1980, Part 1, p. 77, no. 854,
Part 2, pl. 62, no. 854.

Erler's poster, one of a series commissioned by the Cococello Club, adver-
tised a "satirical carnival party whose
theme was a parody of the founding of art
societies by rich patrons" (quoted in Hollmann, et al., 1980). The motif and its
treatment well express this theme. The
female figure hovering on a yellow cloud
is a subtle caricature of a goddess of art,
holding palette, lyre, and moneybag, her
majestic gaze held not by some vision of
beauty but by a shower of gold. At her
feet crouches a grinning devil, a frequent
and generally ambiguous requisite of
Jugendstil painting.   C.S.v.W.S.

Hermann Gradl

1869-1934

Very little is known about Hermann Gradl, a professional painter and later sculptor and craftsman who in December 1890 moved from Düsseldorf to Munich. Like his younger brother Max Josef (1873-1934), he attended the Munich Kunstgewerbeschule, and was active around 1895 as a landscape painter in the tradition of the Munich School.

Floral motifs stylized to the point of purely geometric ornament characterized a joint project with which the Gradl brothers made their debut in 1898 at the Munich Glaspalast exhibition: clock housings in wood and metal, decorated with symbols of time, and made by the firm of Johann Jagemann, Munich. By this time Max Josef was a successful commercial artist, while Hermann concentrated on the design of objects for series manufacture. At the next Glaspalast show, in 1899, he was represented with pewter pieces made by Ferdinand Hubert Schmitz, a Cologne firm that since 1898 had been producing, under the trade name Orivit, home furnishings in cast and stamped pewter, copper, brass, white metal, bronze, and silver. Hermann Gradl was thus among the first designers known to have worked for Orivit. Even in the catalogue of the 1900 Exposition Universelle in Paris the designers of the firm's extensive presentation were left anonymous. However, Max Osborn recorded that Gradl was responsible for Orivit's pewter wall fountain, with its characteristic decor of water lilies, fish, and stylized waves, which was shown in Paris (now in the Museum für Kunst und Gewerbe, Hamburg).

Presumably, Gradl also contributed to the Orivit line shown at the St. Louis world's fair in 1904, during which a demonstration of the very advanced Huber press used to manufacture objects of precious metals and pewter was planned. The only pieces for which he was credited in the catalogue, however, were pewter objects made by Ludwig Lichtinger, which had also been shown in Paris in 1900, at the 1901 "Internationale Kunst-ausstellung" in Dresden, and in 1906 in a special exhibition at the Württembergischer Kunstgewerbeverein in Stuttgart. His name was also associated with the pewter items manufactured by Walter Scherf & Co., Nuremberg, and displayed at the Turin exhibition of 1902.

In collaboration with Albert Bäuml, head of the Nymphenburg porcelain manufactory, Gradl expanded the traditional lines of the firm to include patterns in the modern style (see nos. 41-42). His employment as a designer by Nymphenburg can be documented as late as 1905, and apparently ended when the manufactory turned toward a more functional style. Apart from a very few, no longer extant sculptures, Gradl's design activity seems to have come to an abrupt close at that time.

Reference

Niggl, 1984 (with bibliog.)   R.N.

41 Pieces from the "Fish" Service, 1899

Made by Königlich-Bayerische Porzellan-Manufaktur, Nymphenburg (established 1747)
Porcelain, with printed and painted overglaze decoration and gilding; a) tureen, height 7^1/$_8$″ (18 cm) (with lid), b) plate, diameter 9^1/$_4$″ (23.5 cm)
Marks: a) 688 XXI 106 (painted), b) factory mark (stamped), XXI. 151 (painted)
Bröhan-Museum, Berlin

References

A. Schmidt, "Weltausstellung in Paris 1900: Das Porzellan," *Sprechsaal,* vol. 33 (1900), p. 1630; *Architektonische Rundschau,* vol. 18 (1902), p. 19 (ill.); Berlin, Sammlung Karl H. Bröhan, *Porzellan-Kunst,* Part 2, *Kunst-Porzellane und Keramik um 1900* (Oct. 8-Dec., 1969), p. 116, nos. 911-14, fig. 139; Michael Archer, "Acquisitions in the Department of Ceramics at the Victoria and Albert Museum (1968-1970)," *Burlington Magazine,* vol. 113 (1971), p. 334; Darmstadt, 1972-73, p. 47, no. 122; Düsseldorf, Hetjens-Museum, *Europäische Keramik des Jugendstils, Modern Style, Art Nouveau* (1974), p. 206, no. 318; Zurich, 1975, p. 230, no. 437; Berlin, *Bröhan,* 1977, pp. 382, no. 538, 383-84; Brussels, 1977, pp. 180, nos. 340a, b, 181; Gerhard P. Woeckel, *Die Tierplastik der Nymphenburger Porzellan-Manufaktur* (Munich, 1978), p. 63; Claus Pese, *Das Nürnberger Kunsthandwerk des Jugendstils* (Nuremberg, 1980), p. 204; Karl H. Bröhan, Rosewith Braig, and Dieter Högermann, *Bröhan-Museum Berlin* (Brunswick, 1984), pp. 28-29; S. Wichmann, *Jugendstil Floral,* 1984, p. 96, no. 196; S. Wichmann, 1984, p. 96, no. 196; Niggl, 1984, pp. VI, figs. 12-13, VII, fig. 14; Bielefeld, 1986, pp. 62, fig. 17, 63, no. 158; Berlin, Bröhan-Museum, *Berliner Porzellan vom Jugendstil zum Funktionalismus 1889-1939* (1987), p. 12.

Documents in the archives of the Nymphenburg porcelain manufactory, among them a letter dated September 18, 1899, from Albert Bäuml, show that Gradl designed the "Fish" service in the fall of 1899. The service (style 688, decoration 624) was made for series production and, as a note on an archive photograph confirms, it was shown in the ceramics section of the Exposition Universelle that opened in Paris in the spring of 1900, together with other products of the factory that were mainly in historical and traditional styles.

With the "Fish" service, his first work for Nymphenburg, Gradl created a modern porcelain design with organic decoration derived from the marine world; his pattern drawings are naturalistic, with a

scientific accuracy and faithfulness to detail that includes even the worm on the fishhook. The colored outlines were transferred to the porcelain from zinc etchings and then painted. As A. Schmidt, reporting on the porcelain section of the Paris exhibition, said:

> The manufactory has also been taking bold steps in the modern direction for some time now. The finest examples of this are a range of decorative dessert plates, twelve different patterns, with severely stylized but rich and opulent plant forms on colored grounds, outstanding for their very fine color compositions. A dinner service, kept to the very simplest forms, but very skillfully and elegantly decorated with red poppy flowers, and another set with finely painted green fish and with violet water plants loosely and sparingly strewn over it in a very elegant manner, are also among the works in the modern style.

Gradl is mentioned as a designer working for the Nymphenburg manufactory in the catalogue of the 1902 international exhibition in Turin. Porcelain services by him were exhibited there in rooms designed by BERLEPSCH-VALENDAS, and the "Fish" service was displayed on a piece of presentation furniture made by the Jakob List carpentry works in Munich.

Gradl's luxury fish service continued to be produced, but after 1914 it was no longer one of the standard sets in the pattern books and catalogues that the Nymphenburg porcelain manufactory published. R.N.

Max Rossbach and Hermann Gradl
42 Pieces from the "Modern" Service, 1899–1902

Made by Königlich-Bayerische Porzellan-Manufaktur, Nymphenburg (established 1747)
Porcelain, with painted overglaze decoration;
a) plate, diameter 7⅝″ (19.5 cm); b) cup, height 3″ (7.5 cm); c) saucer, diameter 5¹¹/₁₆″ (14.5 cm)
Marks: a) factory mark, Nymphenburg (stamped), 1344, 0756, 24 (painted); b) factory mark, Nymphenburg (stamped); c) factory mark, Nymphenburg (stamped), 1344, x (painted)
Bröhan-Museum, Berlin

References

Gmelin, 1901–2, pp. 304, fig. 494 (ill. in interior), 325; W. Fred, "Die Turiner Ausstellung," *Die Kunst,* vol. 6 (1901–2), p. 451 (ill.); Turin, 1902, p. 40, no. 45; Brussels, 1977, p. 181, no. 341; Berlin, *Bröhan,* 1977, pp. 378, no. 536, 379–81, no. 537; Niggl, 1984, pp. IX–XI, figs. 17–18; Reto Niggl, "Hermann Gradl," *Antiquitäten-Zeitung,* no. 1 (1985), p. 8.

Max Rossbach (see p. 148) designed the Nymphenburg "S," or "Modern," serv-ice, as can be verified by a coffeepot in-scribed with his name in the manufac-tory's collection. Gradl's responsibility for this decoration (number 1344, "Ve-nus-Frauenhaar," maidenhair) is proved by an entry in the Nymphenburg list of patterns. A bill for Gradl's fee for the work, dated May 10, 1902, has also sur-vived. The "Modern" set had already been exhibited at the Exposition Uni-verselle in Paris in 1900, decorated with an onion-flower pattern (number 1343), and it may also have been shown there with the red poppy decoration (num-ber 1302) by Gradl or Rossbach men-tioned in a contemporary review of the exhibition (see no. 41). Gradl and Ross-bach provided other floral-pattern de-signs as well for the "Modern" service. Although the table in the "grand" dining room in the 1902 Turin exhibition – de-signed by Berlepsch-Valendas and made by Möbelfabrik M. Ballin, Munich – was laid with the "Modern" service, the maidenhair decoration cannot be iden-tified with certainty from period illustra-tions.

The floral elements and organic model-ing of the design show that it was inspired by nature. The Munich architect and crit-ic Leopold Gmelin affirmed – without mentioning Gradl or Rossbach by name – that the Nymphenburg manufactory had again shown modern, progressive designs in the Turin exhibition: "The great porce-lain manufactories have been rather re-served, and it almost looks as if they are acceding to the pressures of the present cautiously and with some reluctance. The Nymphenburg factory is perhaps most open to the new ideas in decoration."

The different items of the "Modern" service, with their numerous decorative variants, were not included in the pattern books or catalogues published by the manufactory after 1914.   R.N.

Paul Haustein

1880-1944

When Haustein moved to Munich from Dresden in the summer of 1897 at the age of seventeen he took a decisive step in securing his independence and developing his gifts: he now found himself in one of the major German art centers. His acquaintance with PAUL, a school friend six years older than himself who had also attended the Kunstgewerbeschule in Dresden, certainly helped him to gain admittance to the group of avant-garde artists in Munich, and he became Paul's neighbor in Kaulbachstrasse.

Haustein at first continued his training in the applied arts, and attended the Munich Kunstgewerbeschule for two semesters before switching to painting. In the spring of 1898 he passed the entrance examination for the Academy and until 1899 studied under Johann Caspar Herterich (1843-1905), a pupil of the history painter Carl von Piloty, who was sympathetic to the Secessionist movement. Haustein thus took the opposite path to that of many Jugendstil artists, most of whom changed from painting to arts and crafts, and he was one of the few who had received a basic training in the applied arts. After three years Haustein discontinued his formal training. He contributed to *Jugend,* and joined the Vereinigte Werkstätten für Kunst im Handwerk in 1898, the year of its foundation; his designs and experimental work for the SCHARVOGEL ceramics manufactory were also outstanding.

Haustein rapidly became known as a book designer, and by 1901 Otto Grautoff described him in his book *Die Entwicklung der modernen Buchkunst in Deutschland* as "one of the most important figures in Jugendstil...using stylized floral ornamentation." Haustein's designs for Georg Hirth's manifesto *Wege zur Kunst* of 1899 (published in 1901) and his work for the Eugen Diederichs Verlag in Leipzig show that he was one of the progressive group of artists whose designs reflected the recognition of the need for a renaissance in book production and the demand for a unified conception in the design of typography. Haustein was offered two appointments around 1900, the artistic directorship of the Meissen porcelain manufactory and a teaching post in book design at the Kunstgewer-

Paul Haustein, c. 1903-4

beschule in Magdeburg, but he remained in Munich until 1903, when he became a member of the Darmstadt artists' colony.

The artist's gift for metalwork first became evident during his work for the Vereinigte Werkstätten; of particular note is a series of mounted copper enamel vessels (see nos. 43-44) with relief decoration that is very typical of the central Munich Jugendstil group. His highly individual silver and jewelry designs for the Vereinigte Werkstätten were praised in the 1908 book *Das Neue Kunstgewerbe in Deutschland* by Josef August Lux, who noted that they were "inspired by the English Arts and Crafts movement." In 1905 metalwork became his vocation when PANKOK made him head of the metal workshop in the Königliche Lehr- und Versuchswerkstätten (the future Kunstgewerbeschule-Weissenhof) in Stuttgart, where he remained until his death.

Haustein's work spanned half a century and bridged the gap between mass production and art, crafts and industrial design, and craftsman and designer. Haustein did not become a product designer in the strictest sense, but his almost forty years of teaching at the Stuttgart Kunstgewerbeschule meant that he was able to pass on to two generations of pupils his highly developed and many-sided craftsmanship and skill. He produced exemplary work in cooperation with the metal

industry – for example, P. Bruckmann in Heilbronn and the Württembergische Metallwarenfabrik in Geislingen – and many of his pupils, including Paula Strauss, went on to devote themselves to industrial design.

References

Otto Grautoff, "Paul Haustein und seine Arbeiten auf der Ausstellung der Darmstädter Künstlerkolonie 1904," *Die Kunst,* vol. 12 (1905), pp. 57-88; Gustav E. Pazaurek, "Paul Haustein, Stuttgart," *Die Kunst,* vol. 14 (1906), pp. 374-88; Paul Johannes Rée, "Paul Haustein," *Journal der Goldschmiedekunst,* vol. 30, no. 49 (1909), p. 423 ff.; *The Studio Year Book of Decorative Art* (1909), pp. 9, 141; Erich Willrich, "Zu Paul Hausteins Arbeiten," *Dekorative Kunst,* vol. 15 (1912), pp. 393-411; *Jahrbuch der Staatlichen Kunstsammlungen Baden/Württemberg,* vol. 13 (1976), pp. 263-65; Darmstadt, 1976-77, vol. 4, pp. 85-91; Ulrike von Hase, *Schmuck in Deutschland und Österreich 1895-1914* (Munich, 1977), p. 208; Pese, 1980, pp. 54-57; Darmstadt, Hessisches Landesmuseum, *Jugendstil: Kunst um 1900* (1982), pp. 137-38.   H. R.

43 Flask, c. 1901

Made by Vereinigte Werkstätten für Kunst im
Handwerk, Munich (established 1897)
Copper, translucent enamel, and silver;
height 6³/₄″ (17.2 cm)
Marks: Halfmoon, crown, 800, Pegasus
(stamped on mount)
Hessisches Landesmuseum, Darmstadt. 72:48

References

Deutsche Kunst und Dekoration, vol. 8 (1901),
p. 433 (ill.); Bott, 1973, pp. 56, no. 43, 58;
Darmstadt, 1976–77, vol. 2, pp. 85, no. 297, 90;
Darmstadt, Hessisches Landesmuseum, *Jugendstil: Kunst um 1900* (1982), p. 137, no. 158.

44 Flask, c. 1901

Made by Vereinigte Werkstätten für Kunst im
Handwerk, Munich (established 1897)
Copper, translucent enamel, and silver;
height 7¹/₂″ (19 cm)
Marks: Halfmoon, crown, 800, Pegasus
(stamped on mount)
Württembergisches Landesmuseum, Stuttgart.
G6, 423

References

Deutsche Kunst und Dekoration, vol. 9 (1901),
p. 433 (ill.); *Mitteilungen des Württembergischen
Kunstgewerbevereins Stuttgart* (1907), p. 84, no. 6;
Munich, 1958, p. 186, no. 588; Munich, Stadtmuseum, 1972, p. 527, no. 2134.

Enamels such as these were made by
Haustein during a brief period just after
the turn of the century. Within a year of
Haustein's departure from Munich for
Darmstadt in 1903, Otto Grautoff reported that although the young artist had
devoted himself to fine metalwork in the
Vereinigte Werkstätten as a "labor of
love…unfortunately Haustein has at
present no possibilities of activity in this
field" (Otto Grautoff, "Paul Haustein und
seine Arbeiten auf der Ausstellung der
Darmstädter Künstlerkolonie 1904," *Die
Kunst,* vol. 12 [1905], p. 58). This, however, was to change when he became head
of the metal workshop in Stuttgart.
Haustein's brilliantly colored enamels
were comparable to wares being made internationally, such as those by Maurice
Dufrène and others, which were sold in
Paris in Julius Meier-Graefe's shop, La
Maison Moderne, and to which they have
been compared in recent literature.

K.B.H./H.R.

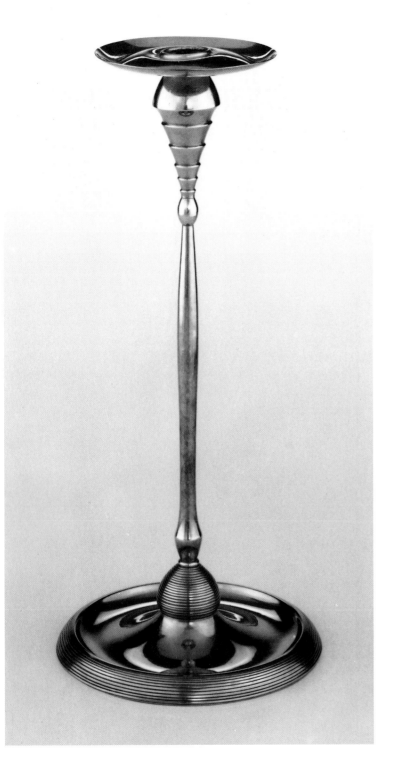

45 Candlestick, 1902

Made by Vereinigte Werkstätten für Kunst im Handwerk, Munich (established 1897)
Brass, height 13³/₄″ (35 cm)
Württembergisches Landesmuseum, Stuttgart.
L 1977-882

References

"Aus Münchens Kunstindustrie," *Dekorative Kunst,* vol. 10 (1902), p. 136 (ill.); *Kunstgewerbeblatt,* n.s., vol. 14 (1903), p. 35 (ill.); Bott, 1973, pp. 44, no. 41, 45; Darmstadt, 1976-77, vol. 2, p. 85, no. 299; Uecker, 1978, p. 178, no. 0254.

In a brief comment on "Munich's art industry," *Dekorative Kunst* reported in 1902 that of the artists of the Vereinigte Werkstätten engaged in metalwork, "only Paul Haustein is a specialist," the other artists doing work equally in all mediums (*Dekorative Kunst,* vol. 10 [1902], p. 140). In fact, the intricate shape and grooved decoration of the neck of this candlestick suggest a smith's training, whereas the comparable candlesticks of PANKOK and PAUL are much simpler in form and sparing of handwork. Haustein designed a series of similar candlesticks for the Dresden metalwork firm of Georg Pöschmann at about the same time.

K.B.H./H.R.

Thomas Theodor Heine
1867-1948

Heine was a prolific painter, whose work was much respected by his colleagues, a sculptor, and a designer of furniture for the Vereinigte Werkstätten, yet his most important contribution to Munich Jugendstil was his enormous oeuvre of graphic art and caricatures. Born in Leipzig, Heine showed a precocious talent for controversy, being expelled from school at the age of seventeen for his caricatures of the local gilded youth that were published in the *Leipziger Pikante Blätter*. He then studied painting in Düsseldorf and Munich (1885-88), where he settled. Over the next five years he associated with a group of young painters – Lovis Corinth, Ludwig Dill, Wilhelm Trübner, and others – who spent their summers in the countryside, mostly in Dachau, a town near Munich that had become the "Bavarian Barbizon and Fontainebleau" to the local adherents of *plein air* painting. There Heine did a series of sensitive landscapes that prompted Corinth to declare, "Whatever he painted, one thing was immediately obvious: his canvases were always distinguished by an artistic skill that could not have been closer to perfection."

According to Meier-Graefe, Heine would probably "have remained just another painter if his father had not cut off his allowance." The crucial year was 1892. Encouraged by a painter-friend, Heine submitted some of his drawings to magazines, and was accepted by the somewhat staidly humorous *Fliegende Blätter,* a family weekly. Its youthful publisher, Albert Langen, was immediately struck by Heine's tense and vibrant line, by a style that incorporated elements from Japanese prints and Toulouse-Lautrec, and in 1895 he hired Heine to provide illustrations and covers for the publications of his fledgling publishing enterprise. Yet Heine still found time to paint, producing a series of remarkable canvases that, influenced by French Symbolism, reflected his own personal situation by probing the relationship between the sexes.

The collaboration between Heine and Langen gave birth to an undertaking that would make both of them famous, *Simplicissimus,* a satirical illustrated weekly, which first appeared on April 1, 1896. Langen had marshaled artists of the first

Thomas Theodor Heine, c. 1905-7

rank – Olaf Gulbransson, PAUL, Ferdinand von Reznicek, Rudolf Wilke – who established the magazine's unique blend of political and social criticism, acerbic caricatures, and lyrically reflective poems and drawings. The "salt and brain" of the paper, as Corinth put it, was certainly Heine, who largely determined its content and thrust, and who over the next thirty-seven years again and again emerged as its sharpest satirist. Indeed, a charge of lese majesty brought Heine a six-months' prison term in 1898. His last caricature for *Simplicissimus* bore the fateful date of April 1, 1933. Persecuted because of his "non-Aryan origins" and his early criticism of National Socialism, Heine was forced to flee Munich. Prague (to 1938), Oslo (to 1942), and Sweden were the stations of an émigré existence lived under continual threat of capture by the Nazis. In his host countries Heine continued his activities as caricaturist and painter, achieving particular popularity in Sweden through his drawings in daily and weekly newspapers. Heine died in Stockholm, a Swedish citizen, in 1948.

References

Esswein, 1904; Julius Meier-Graefe, *Entwicke-lungsgeschichte der modernen Kunst* (Stuttgart, 1904); Lovis Corinth, "Thomas Theodor Heine und Münchens Künstlerleben am Ende des vorigen Jahrhunderts," *Kunst und Künstler,* vol. 4 (1906), p. 143 ff.; Eugen Roth, *Simplicissimus: Ein Rückblick auf die satirische Zeitschrift* (Hanover, 1954); Hamann and Hermand, 1967; Wilfried Wiegand, "Karikatur: Zum Kunstwerk erhoben," *Die Welt,* no. 50 (Feb. 28, 1967), p. 9; Lang, 1970; Munich, 1977-78; Stüwe, 1978.   E.v.D.

46 Poster for *Simplicissimus,* 1896

Printed by Dr. C. Wolf & Sohn, Munich
Color lithograph, 31⁷/₈ x 23¹/₄″ (81 x 59 cm)
Signature: Thomas Theodor Heine (lower left)
Stadtmuseum, Munich. B 5/21

References

Westheim, 1907, p. 225; Joseph Popp, "Bahnbrecher der deutschen Plakatkunst, 2: Thomas
Theodor Heine," *Das Plakat* (1917), pp. 265, 270,
272, fig. 16; Robert Koch, "The Poster Movement and 'Art Nouveau,'" *Gazette des Beaux Arts,*
vol. 50 (1957), pp. 293-94; Munich, 1958, p. 231,
no. 863; Paul Wember, *Die Jugend der Plakate:
1887-1917* (Krefeld, 1961), p. 19, no. 396;
Darmstadt, Hessisches Landesmuseum, *Plakate
um 1900* (Jan. 26-Apr. 1, 1962), no. 53; Hamburg,
1963, p. 66, no. 627; Hellmut Rademacher, *Das
deutsche Plakat von den Anfängen bis zur Gegenwart*
(Dresden, 1965), p. 82; Berkeley, University Art
Gallery, University of California, *Jugendstil &
Expressionism* (Nov. 16-Dec. 8, 1965), pp. 15,
no. 23, 33; Hellmut Rademacher, *Masters of German Poster Art* (New York, 1966), p. 41; Lothar-
Günther Buchheim, *Jugendstilplakate* (Feldafing,
1969), no. 65; Kubly, 1969, pp. 92-94, 178, no. 3;
Munich, Haus der Kunst, *Internationale Plakate
1871-1971* (1971-72), no. 191; Berlin, 1972, p. 163,
no. 415; Munich, Die Neue Sammlung, *Eine Auswahl aus dem Besitz des Museums* (1972), no. 35;
Schindler, 1972, p. 95; Munich, 1975-76 (2nd ed.,
1978), p. 181, no. 27; Darmstadt, 1976-77, vol. 2,
p. 169, no. 320; Brussels, 1977, p. 284, no. 679;
Hollmann, et al., 1980, Part 1, p. 109, no. 1209,
Part 2, pl. 86, no. 1209.

Heine's first poster for *Simplicissimus,* the
magazine he cofounded in 1896, establishes the highly original combination of
satire and illustration that made him the
leading German poster designer of his
time. A young lady with palette and
brushes, personifying Art (also the spirit
of youth, or *Jugend*), is being cheerfully
abducted by a devil, personifying Satire,
who reads an issue of the magazine seem-
ingly unaware of the fact that the girl is
using his tail to write the title *Simplicissimus* on the poster itself. The poster thus
becomes a symbol of the magazine it ad-
vertises, a visual description of the art and
satire within its covers. This poster design was also used as a cover design for
early bound volumes of *Simplicissimus* before it was replaced by the bulldog symbol (no. 47).   K. B. H./C. S. v. W. S.

47 Poster for *Simplicissimus*, 1897

Printed by Dr. C. Wolf & Sohn, Munich
Color lithograph, 30¹/₈ x 18¹¹/₁₆″ (76.5 x 47.5 cm)
Signature: TTH (lower left)
Philadelphia Museum of Art. Purchased: Marie
Josephine Rozet Fund. 1988-17-1

References

Westheim, 1907, pp. 224 (ill.), 225; *Ex Libris: Buchkunst und Angewandte Graphik,* 21st year, n. s., vol. 5 (1911), p. 199; *Das Plakat,* vol. 12, no. 1 (Jan. 1921), p. 11; Munich, 1958, p. 229, no. 851; Hellmut Rademacher, *Das deutsche Plakat von den Anfängen bis zur Gegenwart* (Dresden, 1965), pp. 80, 82; Kubly, 1969, pp. 94, 178, no. 4; Bevis Hillier, *Posters* (London, 1969), p. 193; Schindler, 1972, p. 95, fig. 81; Suckale-Redlefsen, 1975, p. 48, fig. 1; Stanley Applebaum, *Simplicissimus* (New York, 1975), cover, p. xxi; Munich, 1975-76 (2nd ed., 1978), pp. 57, fig. 31, 181, no. 30b; Steve Heller, *Simplicissimus: The Art of Germany's Most Influential Satire Magazine* (New York, 1979), cover; Munich, *Kandinsky,* 1982, p. 196, no. 40; New York, 1982, p. 89, no. 6.

What is probably Heine's best-known poster, made for *Simplicissimus,* shows a bright-red bulldog that has broken its chain and is growling ferociously at the viewer. A more suitable visualization of the magazine's biting satire is hardly imaginable. Its title is the poster's sole text, for by that time *Simplicissimus* was a household name in Germany. Only two colors, red and black, are used to provide accents that heighten the effect of the shimmering white paper.   C. S. v. W. S.

48 Poster for Die Elf Scharfrichter, 1903

Published by Vereinigte Druckereien und Kunst-anstalten, Munich
Printed by Schön & Maison, Munich
Color lithograph, 43³/₄ x 26″ (111 x 66 cm)
Signature: TTH (lower left)
Kunsthalle, Bremen

References

Walter von Zur Western, "Moderne Arbeiten der angewandten graphischen Kunst in Deutschland, IV: Das Plakat," *Zeitschrift für Bücherfreunde,* vol. 7 (1903-4), p. 106; Hamburg, 1963, p. 67, no. 631; Berkeley, University Art Gallery, University of California, *Jugendstil & Expressionism* (Nov. 16-Dec. 9, 1965), pp. 15, no. 22, 32; Hellmut Rademacher, *Das deutsche Plakat von den Anfängen bis zur Gegenwart* (Dresden, 1965), pp. 82, 89; Brussels, Kursaal D'Ostende, *Europa 1900* (June 3-Sept. 30, 1967), p. 84, no. 778; Kubly, 1969, pp. 98-99, 178, no. 12; Lang, 1970, p. 113, colorpl. 90; Bremen, Kunsthalle, *Kunst im Alltag: Plakate und Gebrauchsgraphik um 1900* (Apr. 24-June 26, 1977), pp. 193-94, no. 217, 199; Brussels, 1977, p. 284, no. 681; Munich, *Kandinsky,* 1982, p. 260, no. 210; New York, 1982, p. 146, no. 95.

Apart from his ferocious *Simplicissimus* bulldog (no. 47), Heine's poster for the cabaret Die Elf Scharfrichter (The Eleven Executioners) is probably his most famous. Many other artists, including Serapion Grab and PAUL, designed posters for this Munich troupe, which, founded in 1901, achieved renown through its association with such important playwrights as Frank Wedekind. But it was Heine, with his gift of simplification, who made the most memorable statement. The figure of the leading lady, Marga Delvard, is given monumental presence by the reduction of her gown to a single, flowing plane, ironically counterpointed by a bevy of glaring devils' heads. Bizarre and ornamental creatures of the kind found in Japanese woodcuts were often employed by Heine – for example, in the covers for his *Thorheiten-Album* (1903) and for Knut Hamsun's novel *Hunger* (1896), as well as in many of his paintings.

   As in most of his posters, the graphic impact is heightened by a sparing use of colors, in this case only three. It is the strong dose of parody that makes many of Heine's designs so compelling and unforgettable.   E. v. D.

Fritz von Miller

1840–1921

Fritz von Miller, c. 1910

References

Kunstgewerbeblatt, n. s., vol. 6 (1895), p. 40;
"Unsere Bilder von der Pariser Weltausstellung,"
Kunst und Handwerk, vol. 50 (1899-1900), p. 279;
Kunstgewerbeblatt, n. s., vol. 12 (1901), pp. 46-47,
49; "Neue Arbeiten Fritz von Millers," *Kunst und
Handwerk,* vol. 57 (1906-7), pp. 109-23; *Journal
der Goldschmiedekunst,* vol. 30 (1909), pp. 277-95;
J. von Schmädel, "Professor Fritz von Miller,"
Kunst und Handwerk, vol. 61 (1910-11), pp.
36-83; G. J. Wolf, "Fritz von Miller," *Kunst und
Handwerk,* vol. 72 (1921-22), pp. 1-11; *Das Fach-
blatt* (Reichsinnungsverband des Juwelier-, Gold-
und Silberschmiedehandwerks), vol. 4 (1941),
p. 1 ff.   H.O.

Munich-born Miller, son of the well-known bronze-caster Ferdinand von Miller, received his early training in his father's workshop, experiencing at first hand the casting and chasing of the statue of Bavaria in Munich and of many other large-scale bronze monuments.

After attending the art academies in Munich, Berlin, and Dresden, Miller was apprenticed as a goldsmith to Hunt and Roskell in London, before going to Paris for three years to work as a modelmaker and enameler. From 1868 to 1912 he was professor at the Munich Kunstgewerbe-schule, where he revitalized the goldsmith's work being done there and exerted a lasting influence on a large number of students, including Karl Gross, Wilhelm Heiden, Emil Lettré, Max Olofs, RIEGEL, Karl Rothmüller, Alexander Schönauer, and Wilhelm Wiedemann.

In 1876 Miller set up his own goldsmith's workshop in Munich, where until 1920, in cooperation with his students, he created numerous pieces of gold- and silverwork that attracted considerable attention at exhibitions of applied art through-out Europe. Miller favored historical styles, using Gothic, Renaissance, and Mannerist models, until 1895, after which he developed a vocabulary of stylized natural forms, often placing them in surreal combinations and oppositions.

Miller rejected preparatory drawings and models, choosing to rely exclusively on a free creative process founded in the nature and technical possibilities of his materials and in a spontaneous development of form. As he himself wrote, "it is only the hand of the craftsman, guided by his eye and his sensibility in the course of work, and genuine, natural growth that give life to natural materials" (unpublished MS., Miller family archives). Miller thus insisted on giving free rein to his imagination and artistic processes. Nevertheless, he received a number of commissions for objects to be presented to such notables as members of the Wittelsbach family and the Habsburg branch of the Hohenzollern family and to various dignitaries and prize winners.

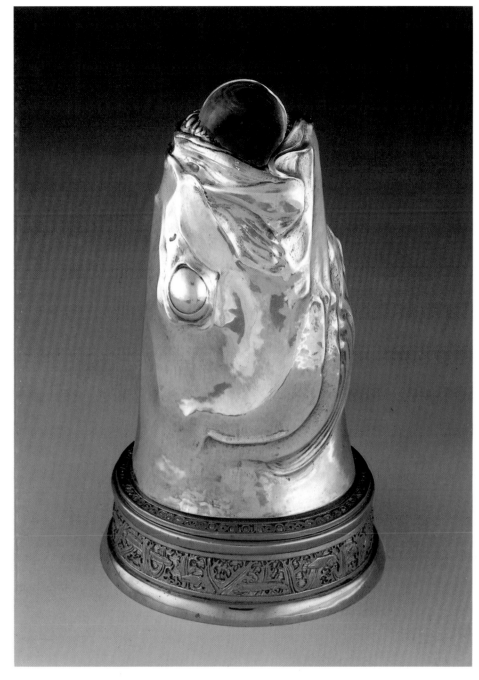

49 Goblet, c. 1905

Silver, gilded silver, rock-crystal, and brass;
height 10⁷/₈″ (27.5 cm)
K. Barlow Ltd., London

References
Kunst und Handwerk, vol. 56 (1905-6), p. 247,
figs. 550-51; Munich, 1976, pp. 211, no. 456,
213, fig. 456; Munich, Villa Stuck, 1979, p. 19,
no. 124.

This kind of footless goblet, known as
Sturzbecher (literally, falling goblet), can
be set down only when its contents have
been drained, and was part of an ancient
drinking custom that had been revived
among Munich's artists in the early
nineteenth century (see Ingo Tornow,
*Das Münchner Vereinswesen in der ersten
Hälfte des 19. Jahrhunderts* [Munich, 1977],
pp. 57, 258, 264, 267, 344).

The goblet in the shape of a fish head
with a rock-crystal sphere in its mouth
is related to Miller's large-scale centerpieces, which usually combined realistic
animal forms with a natural object; the
jewel or trophy thus fuses with the animal
body of precious metal to give rise to
assoiations concerning the symbolic significance and magic properties of natural
forms and materials.

This goblet was illustrated without its
base in a 1906 issue of *Kunst und Handwerk,* where the chasing and engraving
were noted as apprenticeship work by
Max Olofs, and it has frequently been
cited as the work of Olofs. The *Sturzbecher* is included in the detailed lists that
Miller made of his own work and that are
still in the family's possession. These
single out the silver chasing and engraving for special mention, and name the re-
cipient as Miller's eldest son Rupert. Like
his grandfather and father, Rupert von
Miller was a member of the Harbni
Order, a parody of an order of medieval
knights, which existed from 1850 to 1939
and was noted for eccentric drinking ritu-
als. Members presented the order with
cups and goblets for this purpose, and this
goblet seems to have come from the order's effects.   H.O.

Adelbert Niemeyer
1867-1932

Niemeyer, like his colleague RIEMER-SCHMID, was a leading representative of the applied arts movement in Munich during the Jugendstil period. He studied painting at the Düsseldorf Akademie der Schönen Künste from 1883 to 1888, when he moved to Munich, where he continued his studies under Friedrich Fehr, having failed to gain admission to the Academy. He was subsequently a student of the Académie Julian and a pupil of Benjamin Constant in Paris. In 1892 he was one of the founders of the Munich Secession.

Niemeyer began to take an interest in the applied arts around 1899 and, in the aftermath of the 1900 Paris Exposition Universelle, he studied intensively the manufacture of glass, porcelain, furniture, and wrought iron. Though remaining a painter all his life, he had decided by 1902 to devote himself to the applied arts, and in that year he took the practical step of founding the Werkstätten für Wohnungseinrichtungen in Munich, in partnership with the upholsterer Karl Bertsch (1873-1933) and the painter Willy von Beckerath (1868-1938). This interior decoration workshop exhibited a reading room at the 1904 St. Louis world's fair, where it was awarded a gold medal; it also received the same award for furniture and decorative arts exhibited at the "III. Deutsche Kunstgewerbe-Ausstellung" in Dresden in 1906. In the same year the Nymphenburg porcelain manufactory set up a studio for Niemeyer, who had already been a designer for the company for several years. In 1907 the Werkstätten für Wohnungseinrichtung Karl Bertsch (as it was renamed in 1906) merged with the Dresdner Werkstätten für Handwerkskunst to become the Deutsche Werkstätten für Handwerkskunst G.m.b.H. München: Niemeyer remained a prolific designer of furniture for the company until his death.

In 1907 Niemeyer took over the class for ornament and drawing from nature at the Munich Kunstgewerbeschule. He was now in increasing demand, not only as a designer for the ceramic and glass industry, but also as an interior architect for such exhibitions as the Brussels Exposition Universelle, the Munich applied art exhibition in Paris, the Islamic exhibition in Munich, and the international hunting exhibition in Vienna, all of which were held in 1910. Niemeyer was also responsible for a section of the interior architecture at the important "Bayerische Gewerbeschau" held in Munich in 1912, and at the Deutscher Werkbund exhibition in Cologne in 1914. After World War I, Niemeyer assumed responsibility for the ceramic and glass-engraving class at the Munich Kunstgewerbeschule, helped to develop the concept of the easily assembled and modestly priced wooden house for the Deutsche Werkstätten, and continued to design for the ceramic industry, most notably for the Meissen manufactory and the Schwarzburger Werkstätten für Porzellankunst in Unterweissbach, Thuringia.

Adelbert Niemeyer, c. 1926

References

Haenel, 1906, pp. 504-11; Scheffler, "Niemeyer," 1907, pp. 481-504; G. von Pechmann, "Der Gute Ton im Kunstgewerbe: Zu den neueren Arbeiten von Adelbert Niemeyer-München," *Die Kunst,* vol. 24 (1911), pp. 265-87; E. W. Bredt, "Adelbert Niemeyers Haus Krawehl," *Deutsche Kunst und Dekoration,* vol. 31 (1912-13), pp. 42-84; Paul Niemeyer, "Aus dem Leben Adelbert Niemeyers," in Heinz Thiersch, ed., *Wir fingen einfach an: Arbeiten und Aufsätze von Freunden und Schülern um Richard Riemerschmid* (Munich, 1953), pp. 76-81; Nickl, ed., 1984.   B.D.v.Z.

50 Vase, 1905

Made by Königlich-Bayerische Porzellan-
Manufaktur, Nymphenburg (established 1747)
Porcelain with painted overglaze decoration and
gilding, height 10³/₄" (27.5 cm)
Marks: 816, factory mark (stamped), B, 24
(painted)
Staatliche Porzellan-Manufaktur Nymphenburg,
Munich

References
Schumacher, et al., 1906, p. 166 (ill.); Heyck, ed.,
1907, p. 419, pl. 37; Alexander Koch, ed., *Handbuch neuzeitlicher Wohnungskultur: Band Speisezim-
mer* (Darmstadt, 1913), p. 190 (ill.); Effi Horn,
"Nymphenburg's Blüte in neuer Zeit," *Das
Bayerland,* vol. 52, nos. 11-12 (1941-42), p. 384;
Margarete Braun-Ronsdorf, *200 Jahre Nymphenburger Tafelgeschirr* (Darmstadt, 1954), p. 27,
fig. 19; Munich, 1958, p. 197, no. 627.

Niemeyer's cylindrical, purple-glazed
"neoclassical" vase stands solidly on its
four feet and flares outward at its top as if
already yielding to the lateral pressure of
the flowers it was designed to hold. The
neck and feet are ornamented with, and
accentuated by, the type of checkered design that is more commonly associated
with contemporary decorative work by
the Viennese artists Josef Hoffmann and
Koloman Moser. Niemeyer had employed strict geometrical patterns and
motifs based on the square in a silver tea
service and in a Nymphenburg vase and
coffee service (designed in 1904) that were
shown at the 1905 "I. Ausstellung der
Münchener Vereinigung für Angewandte
Kunst" in Munich. Here, in a work designed in 1905, the geometrical ornament
is relieved by falling blossoms, a repeated
motif that decorates the central section
and provides a combination of stylized
natural forms and geometrical ornament
that also characterizes the glass service designed by Niemeyer for Benedikt von
Poschinger in Oberzwieselau (no. 51).

The vase was first exhibited at the
"III. Deutsche Kunstgewerbe-Ausstellung" in Dresden in 1906, where it
formed the centerpiece of a table shown
in an ensemble (Room 69) made by the
Werkstätten für Wohnungseinrichtung
Karl Bertsch, Munich. Although Niemeyer designed at least one other overall
decorative checkered pattern for this vase
(based on stylized natural forms), his use
of the square ornamental motif seems to

have made a greater impression on his
contemporaries. His friend Felix Schlagintweit described the artist in his memoirs
as "one who with restraint and feeling for
form had developed the more refined aspects of the Biedermeier manner into a
true and noble style of interior decoration," and he related how Niemeyer applied small gold squares in meander form
to cups and plates and, as a result, was
immediately dubbed "the inventor of the
square" (Felix Schlagintweit, *Ein verliebtes
Leben: Erinnerungen eines Münchener Arz-
tes* [Munich, 1943], p. 133).

The Nymphenburg manufactory reis-
sued Niemeyer's vase in 1982; it is
marked with the impressed Nymphenburg lozenge-patterned shield, together
with the letter "A," which has been in use
since 1975.   B.D.v.Z.

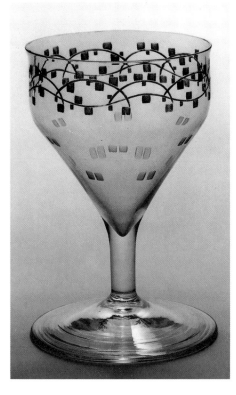

Nymphenburg tea and dinner services exhibited at the "I. Ausstellung der Münchener Vereinigung für Angewandte Kunst" in 1905. When he designed this glass service he certainly had in mind the simple, gold-bordered version of his Nymphenburg dinner service, which becomes less classically severe when softened by the more playful accompanying glassware. At the 1906 Dresden exhibition of applied art this combination of Nymphenburg porcelain and Poschinger glass formed the decoration of a dinner table designed by Niemeyer for the Werkstätten für Wohnungseinrichtung Karl Bertsch in Munich. An additional feature of the glassware's ornamental design is the pairs of cut squares representing falling leaves in the bowl's surface below the gilded ornament; later Niemeyer designs of this kind frequently employ this same motif, but never in such an abstract manner.   B.D.v.Z

52   Vase, c. 1905

Made by Königlich-Bayerische Porzellan-Manufaktur, Nymphenburg (established 1747)
Porcelain with painted overglaze decoration and gilding, height 7$^{1}/_{2}$" (19 cm)
Marks: factory marks (painted), diamond, 874 (stamped)
Stadtmuseum, Munich. K 72-666

References

Margarete Braun-Ronsdorf, *200 Jahre Nymphenburger Tafelgeschirr* (Darmstadt, 1954), p. 27, fig. 19; Munich, 1958, p. 197, no. 628; Woeckel, 1968, no. 43; Düsseldorf, Hetjens-Museum, *Europäische Keramik des Jugendstils, Modern Style, Art Nouveau* (1974), p. 208, no. 322; Brussels, 1977, p. 193, no. 383; Karlsruhe, 1978, p. 265, no. 107.

Niemeyer worked for several German porcelain manufactories, including Berlin, Meissen, and smaller companies in Thuringia. One of his most important achievements was designing utilitarian services for Nymphenburg, "plain sets with tasteful borders" that seemed to one contemporary critic to "recall those good old traditions ... at the time of the Empire" (Heyck, ed., 1907, p. 422). The pattern that decorates this ample, twin-handled vase is close to the border design of those utilitarian wares.

K.B.H./C.S.v.W.S.

51   Glass, c. 1905

Made by Benedikt von Poschinger, Oberzwieselau (active 1880-1919)
Glass with cut decoration and gilding, height 4$^{1}/_{4}$" (11 cm)
Hessisches Landesmuseum, Darmstadt. Kg 64:162

References

Haenel, 1906, p. 508 (ill. in Dresden); Schumacher, et al., 1906, p. 166 (ill.); Heyck, ed., 1907, p. 419, pl. 37; Karl Mayer, "Adelbert Niemeyer," *Dekorative Kunst,* vol. 15 (1907), p. 504 (ill.); Scheffler, "Niemeyer," 1907, p. 504 (ill.); Warlich, 1908, p. 84 (ill.); *The Studio Year Book of Decorative Art* (1910), p. 205 (ill.); Munich, 1958, pp. 197, no. 630, 270; Munich, 1964, p. 120, nos. 985-88; Hans Eckstein, *Die Neue Sammlung* (Munich, 1965), pl. 104; Gerhard Bott, *Jugendstil: Vom Beitrag Darmstadts zur internationalen Kunstbewegung um 1900* (Darmstadt, 1965), pp. 213, no. 266, 238; Bott, 1973, pp. 235, no. 279, 259; Brussels, 1977, p. 245, no. 574; Bott, 1982, p. 226, no. 297.

A cylindrical bowl with a funnel-shape base above the stem characterize all the glasses in the nine-piece service designed by Niemeyer in about 1905. The gilded decoration around the rim incorporates a pattern of intersecting arcs and a wavy line, to which are appended small squares of varying sizes. This design is a highly stylized, almost abstract, version of stem and leaf forms, and combines strictly geometric square shapes with remnants of ornamentally treated plant forms. Checkered patterns and stylized floral borders had formed the decoration of Niemeyer's

Hermann Obrist

1862–1927

Obrist must be considered a central figure of Munich Jugendstil, for he was one of its primary catalysts and spokesmen; without his vigorous presence it is doubtful whether Munich would have become the birthplace and center of Germany's version of Art Nouveau. Born in Kilchberg, Switzerland, the son of a physician, Obrist seemed destined for the life of a scientist. Instead, driven from the strictures of academe by a combination of hearing loss and a predisposition to unexplained "visions," he left the university of Heidelberg in 1887 to undertake extensive travels in England and Scotland, where his experience of the British Arts and Crafts movement undoubtedly influenced his decision to turn his own energies to the applied arts. Following brief studies at the Kunstgewerbeschule in Karlsruhe and an equally brief apprenticeship as a potter, Obrist was awarded gold medals for his ceramics and furniture at the 1889 Paris Exposition Universelle. There ensued a peripatetic existence in Paris (Académie Julian, 1890) and Berlin (1891, as an art critic for the *Börsenkurier*). Having sold his first model for a fountain, he then moved to Florence, where he experimented in marble sculpture and opened an embroidery studio in which his own designs could be carried out. The turning point in his career came in 1894, when he moved his studio to Munich and launched his public career as a rousing advocate of a new vision in the arts.

In April 1896 an exhibition of thirty-five embroideries designed by Obrist and executed by Berthe Ruchet captured the attention of the art world. Opening at Littauer's Salon in Munich and then traveling to Berlin and London, the exhibition was reviewed internationally and critics proclaimed the "birth of a new applied art." Meanwhile, Obrist plunged into activity, helping BERLEPSCH-VALENDAS and others to found Munich's influential Vereinigte Werkstätten für Kunst im Handwerk, lecturing widely on the aesthetic revolution he foresaw, and agitating for a new rapprochement between the artist/craftsman and the public. His monumental embroideries, *Whiplash* (fig. 1) and *Blossoming Tree,* and his inspired drawings (for example, *Fantastic Shell*; no. 54) bore witness to his revolu-

Hermann Obrist, 1902

tionary notion that art must free itself from tired rehashings of worn-out styles and the relentless pursuit of nature as perceived by eyes jaded on centuries of prescribed renderings. With respect to nature, the distinction Obrist drew was to have a crucial impact on both the fine and the applied arts of the twentieth century: not nature, but the dynamic of nature must be the goal of art. He called for an art that would be an "intensification of life." Even more than his embroideries, his models for fountains embodied this principle. Casting aside the nymph-, mermaid-, dolphin-strewn paradigms of his time, he created intense, simplified, functional forms designed to exploit and enhance the sound and sight of water splashing over rock. Unfortunately, these were so far in advance of his time that few were ever commissioned or sold (one such was at the Krupp von Bohlen residence, Essen, 1913) and only a few plaster models remain (Museum Bellerive, Zurich). They were, in effect, too "abstract." Indeed, some of his creations were entirely "abstract," representing

only that "dynamic" he sought – for example, the model for a monument entitled *Movement,* or the famous *Vaulting Pillar* (before 1899). It is not surprising that the budding abstractionist Wassily Kandinsky was soon drawn to his side, that the two formed a close friendship, and that applied arts from the Vereinigte Werkstätten as well as from the Darmstadt artists' colony were included in the January 1902 exhibition of Kandinsky's Phalanx society.

In fact, Obrist's greatest impact was as a teacher. Recognizing that no revolution in the arts could be successful without enlightened public support and artists awakened to "see anew," he lectured incessantly, and in 1901-2, together with DEBSCHITZ, founded the Lehr- und Versuch-Ateliers für Angewandte und Freie Kunst to promulgate his ideals; it is now recognized as an important precursor of the Bauhaus. Indeed, in 1915 Obrist was one of the artists proposed by Henry van de Velde as director for the Weimar Kunstgewerbeschule, which was to become the Bauhaus.

Forced by increasing loss of hearing to withdraw from public life, Obrist left the school in 1904. His essays had been published in 1903, and thereafter his only outlets were infrequent exhibitions of his work and a few commissions for funerary monuments.

References

Wilhelm Bode, "Hermann Obrist," *Pan,* vol. 1, no. 5 (1896), pp. 326-28; Georg Fuchs, "Hermann Obrist," *Pan,* vol. 1, no. 5 (1896), pp. 318-25; Fred, 1901, pp. 17-26; E. W. Bredt, "Verkünden und Handeln," *Dekorative Kunst,* vol. 9 (1902), pp. 218-26; Obrist, 1903; Obrist, 1904; Karl Scheffler, "Kunstschulen," *Kunst und Künstler,* vol. 5 (1907), pp. 206-10; Karl Scheffler, "Hermann Obrist," *Kunst und Künstler,* vol. 8 (1910), pp. 555-59; Munich, *Hermann Obrist,* 1968; Lampe-von Bennigsen, 1970; Schmoll, 1977; Weiss, 1979, pp. 28-34; Ziegert, 1985; Ziegert, 1986, pp. 28-41.   P. W.

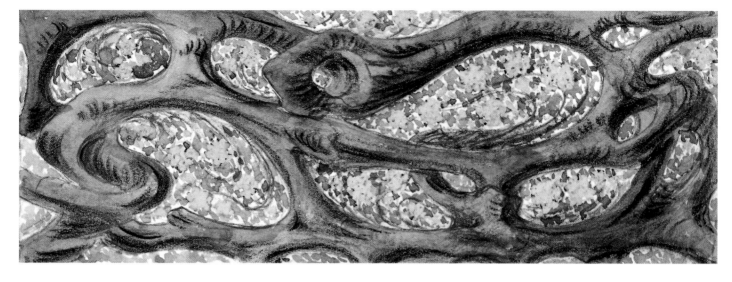

53 Rootlike Ornament, c. 1895

Watercolor, pencil, and chalk on paper,
2⁹/₁₆ x 7³/₁₆″ (6. 5 x 18.2 cm)
Staatliche Graphische Sammlung, Munich. 44 420

References

Munich, 1958, p. 199, no. 640; Paris, 1960-61,
p. 368, no. 1.142; Bern, 1967, no. 5; Zurich,
1967, p. 76, no. 181; Munich, *Hermann Obrist*,
1968, no. 6; S. Wichmann, 1977, pp. 110-11,
fig. 204; S. Wichmann, *Jugendstil Floral*, 1984,
p. 231; S. Wichmann, 1984, pp. 76-77.

In his article of 1904 Obrist wrote that he
wanted his students ultimately to understand that "a flower, a shell, a dry twig, a
root, a skeleton is something other than a
merely associative or intellectual [refer-
ence, but rather] that these are organized
images full of laws, full of structures, full
of expressive forces, full of linear, plastic,
constructive movements of unprecedent-
ed abundance and astonishing variety"
(Obrist, 1904, p. 229). In this ornamental
drawing the latent energy of the root
seems to burst out of bounds, contained
only by the promise of the yellow
blossoms.   P. W.

54 Fantastic Shell, c. 1895

Pencil and charcoal on imitation parchment
paper, 10⁵/₈ x 6³/₈″ (27. 1 x 16.2 cm)
Staatliche Graphische Sammlung, Munich.
44 441

References

Munich, 1958, pp. 199, no. 643, 255; Paris, 1960-
61, p. 368, no. 1.144; Bern, 1967, no. 11; Zurich,
1967, p. 77, no. 187; Munich, *Hermann Obrist*,
1968, no. 34; Weiss, 1979, pp. x, 32, fig. 18;
Weiss, "Kandinsky in Munich," 1982, pp. 34,
123, no. 66; Weiss, "Kandinsky und München,"

1982, pp. 34, 209, no. 70; S. Wichmann, *Jugendstil
Floral*, 1984, pp. 58, no. 99, 59, 233; S. Wichmann, 1984, pp. 58-59; Christoph Kockerbeck,
*Ernst Haeckels "Kunstformen der Natur" und ihr
Einfluss auf die deutsche bildende Kunst der Jahrhundertwende* (Frankfurt, 1986), pp. 188, no. 16, 190,
fig. 16.

A preliminary sketch for this work,
found among the artist's unpublished
notes, is inscribed, "Higher roundness
entirely." On the next page, according to
S. Wichmann (Munich, *Hermann Obrist*,

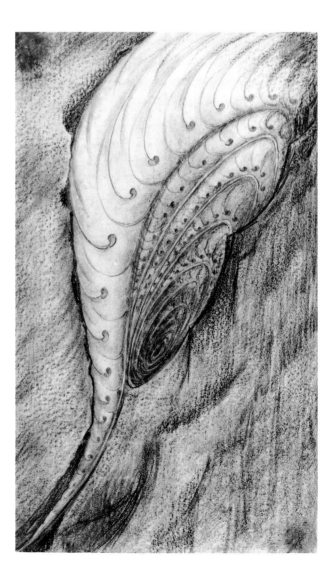

1968), Obrist noted the following cryptic remarks under the title *Ecstatic Vortex*:

> Dynamic: energies, forces
> to make visible through strength
> or weakness of the means. - - -
> Curve intensity/ . . .
> the intensity of convexity,
> through strengthening of the line,
> through/multiplication . . .
> . . . battle, wrestling, encircling
> maestoso: tornado. Whirlwind.
> Cigar glow, cookstove, Andromeda/fog
> Spiral funnel of the rudder in water/
> water vortex in the washbasin,
> bat spiral, crater vortex/
> machineatomic, sculpted
> cigarette smoke, Rococo chapel volute
> torrent, Zermatt, vortex around cliffs
> play of ecstasy around vortex
> seagulls' flight, butterfly vortex, humming-
> birds . . . .

The Wichmann text does not indicate the order in which Obrist wrote these notes, but in any case, the explosion of associative wordplay creates a kind of verbal vortex, a literary parallel to the visual image. The neologism "machineatomic" (*Maschinenatomar*) appears as an astonishing anticipation of Vorticist poetry and underscores why it was that sensitive contemporaries like Karl Scheffler saw Obrist as a man of the future. Obrist's own collection of photographs included such motifs as the iron spiral staircase of the Berlin radio tower, the interior of a gigantic turbo-dynamo, enlargements of primitive microorganisms, an x-ray of a snail shell, a spouting geyser, spiraling fog, fireworks at night, and so forth. Apparently, these served to stoke the imagination of this artist, who thought of art as an "intensification of life."   P. W.

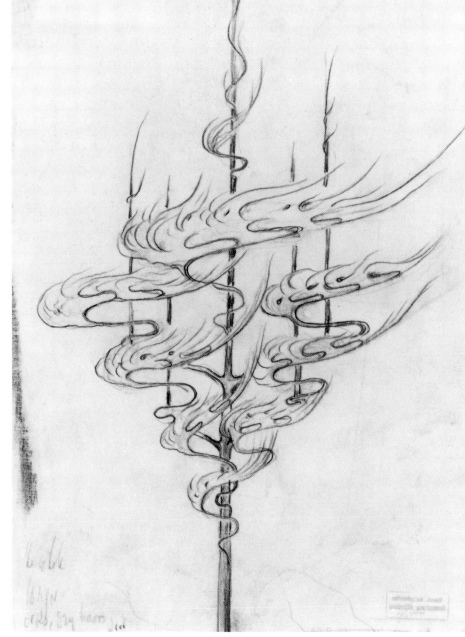

55 Smoldering Plant, c. 1895

Charcoal and pencil on tracing paper, 10⁵/₈ x 7⁷/₈″ (27 x 19.8 cm)
Inscription: the white [indecipherable] (lower left)
Staatliche Graphische Sammlung, Munich. 44426

References

Bern, 1967, no. 25; Zurich, 1967, no. 201; Munich, *Hermann Obrist,* 1968, no. 37; Weiss, "Kandinsky und München," 1982, pp. 34, 208, no. 69; Weiss, "Kandinsky in Munich," 1982, pp. 34, 122, no. 64; S. Wichmann, *Jugendstil Floral,* 1984, pp. 72, no. 130, 233; S. Wichmann, 1984, p. 72, no. 129.

According to S. Wichmann (Munich, *Hermann Obrist,* 1968), the preliminary sketch for this work appears on the same page of Obrist's unpublished notes as that for the drawing of a thorny stem (no. 59) and bears the same inscription, beginning "Spiral ecstasy." The last words of the inscription, "firetree spiral," seem to suit this image of some fantastic plant about to burst into flame. It conveys something of the excitement of the work that has, perhaps, become Obrist's most famous and a paradigm of Jugendstil design – the great *Whiplash* embroidery (fig. 1), so named by Georg Fuchs, who described it in his 1896 article as "this racing movement . . . like the abrupt, powerful convolution of the lash at the crack of a whip" (Georg Fuchs, "Hermann Obrist," *Pan,* vol. 1, no. 5 [1896], p. 324). In this drawing the forms lashing upward about the thorny branches suggest at once the forces of wind and fire. We do not know the plant, but we recognize the energy.

P. W.

56 Chest, 1897

Made by Johann Zugschwerdt (active Munich c. 1900) and Reinhold Kirsch (royal Bavarian court locksmith, active Munich from 1878)
Oak and iron, 18⅛ x 52 x 24″ (46 x 132 x 61 cm)
Stadtmuseum, Munich. 53/363

References

Munich, 1897, p. 211, no. 163; Berlepsch-Valendas, "Umschwung," 1897-98, p. 10 (ill.); "Atelier-Nachrichten: Hermann Obrist," *Deutsche Kunst und Dekoration,* vol. 1 (1897-98), p. 42 (ill.); Gmelin, "Kleinkunst," 1897-98, pp. 19, fig. 13, 20, figs. 14-15, 25-26; "Beschläge und Griffe," *Dekorative Kunst,* vol. 1 (1898), p. 66, figs. 57, 59 (ill.); Rosner, 1898, p. 119; Rosner, 1899, vol. 2, figs. 116, 118; Bode, 1901, pp. 105-6; Fred, 1901, p. 24 (ill.); Munich 1958, p. 198, no. 633; Munich, *Hermann Obrist,* 1968, no. 14; Gerhart Egger, *Beschläge und Schlösser an alten Möbeln* (Munich, 1973), figs. 371, 373; Himmelheber, 1973, pp. 235, 243, 250, fig. 1070, 387, no. 1070; Ottomeyer, 1988, p. 51, no. 1.

The chest, first exhibited together with furniture by BERLEPSCH-VALENDAS, Karl Bertsch, PANKOK, and RIEMERSCHMID at the Munich Glaspalast exhibition of 1897, was among the earliest examples of Jugendstil furniture in Munich. After the exhibition it stood in the study of the artist's villa on Karl-Theodor-Strasse. In type, it recalls Gothic chests with iron fittings, but its structure and ornament are entirely original, related in terms of motif and linear design to Obrist's work in the textile medium. The chest originally rested on two square beams.   H.O.

detail

57 Bedspread, 1897

Made by Berthe Ruchet (Swiss, active Munich 1895–1900)
Silk with silk embroidery, 89³/₄ x 80¹/₄″
(228 x 204 cm)
Signature: HO (intertwined) (corner)
Stadtmuseum, Munich. 49/65

References
Mary Logan, "Hermann Obrist's Embroidered Decorations," *The Studio,* vol. 9, no. 44 (Nov. 1896), pp. 102–3 (ills.); Obrist, "Pourquoi," 1900, pp. 198–99 (ills.); Obrist, "Wozu," 1900, pp. 182–3 (ills.), 197; Fred, 1901, p. 17 (ill.); Munich, 1958, pp. 198, no. 636, 253; Marie Schuette and Sigrid Müller-Christensen, *Das Stickereiwerk* (Tübingen, 1963), p. 58, no. 461; Munich, *Hermann Obrist,* 1968, no. 68; Fanelli and Fanelli, 1976, fig. 23; Munich, 1977, p. 11; Maria Grazia Messina, "Teoria dell'Einfühlung ed Architettura: L'apporto di August Endell," *Ricerche di Storia dell'Arte,* vol. 5 (1977), p. 43, fig. 1; Stuttgart, 1980, pp. 288, no. 298, 299; Bader-Griessmeyer, 1985, pp. 23–25, 30, fig. 5.

This beautiful bedspread never became quite so famous as the somewhat earlier Obrist tapestry *Whiplash* (fig. 1), which took on symbolic significance for the new, Jugendstil movement in art. Yet it, too, gives an idea of the impact that Obrist's designs had on an art scene enervated by eclecticism. Sinuous plants issue like tongues of flame from the two long sides of the spread. The forms also recall crashing, whitecapped waves, like the ones in *Mount Fuji Viewed from the Sea off Kanagawa,* a Hokusai print that was very well known at the time and that Obrist had certainly seen. No less audacious was the embroidery technique of this and other pieces executed by Berthe Ruchet

(see nos. 58, 60). The stitches conform to the organic growth of the stems, leaves, and blossoms, their density and thickness of relief continually changing to produce a vibrant play of light and shade over the shimmering silk threads.   C.S.v.W.S.

58 Tablecloth, c. 1897

Made by Berthe Ruchet (Swiss, active Munich
1895–1900)
Linen with silk embroidery, 124³/₈ x 85⁷/₈″
(316 x 218 cm)
Signature: HO (intertwined) (lower left)
Stadtmuseum, Munich. 49/64

References

Mary Logan, "Hermann Obrist's Embroidered
Decorations," *The Studio,* vol. 9, no. 44 (Nov.
1896), pp. 99 (ill.), 101; Munich, 1897, p. 211,
no. 160; Munich, 1958, pp. 199, no. 637, 252;
Zurich, 1967, p. 78, no. 208; Munich, *Hermann
Obrist,* 1968, no. 69; Fanelli and Fanelli, 1976,
fig. 356; Maria Grazia Messina, "Teoria dell'Einfühlung ed Architettura: L'apporto di August
Endell," *Ricerche di Storia dell'Arte,* vol. 5 (1977),
p. 43, fig. 2; Bader-Griessmeyer, 1985, pp. 25–26,
30, fig. 4.

According to Obrist, his embroideries
were intended "tò evoke the wonderful
charm of ever-changing plant life" (*Dekorative Kunst,* vol. 9 [1902], p. 224), words
that apply to this large tablecloth from the
artist's villa in Munich. All four sides are
adorned with a patterned border consisting of a plant solidly rooted in the earth, a
sinuous stalk rising above narrow, angu-
lar leaves, and delicate pink blossoms re-
sembling those of a plantain.   C. S. v. W. S.

59 Thorny Stem, c. 1898

Pencil on imitation parchment paper, 16¹/₈ x 10″
(41 x 25.3 cm)
Inscription: noch länger unten (lower right)
Staatliche Graphische Sammlung, Munich. 44421

References

Munich, 1958, pp. 199, no. 642, 257; Bern, 1967,
no. 26; Zurich, 1967, p. 78, no. 202; Munich,
Hermann Obrist, 1968, no. 36; Maria Grazia Messina, "Teoria dell'Einfühlung ed Architettura:
L'apporto di August Endell," *Ricerche di Storia
dell'Arte,* vol. 5 (1977), p. 45, fig. 6; Weiss, "Kandinsky in Munich," 1982, pp. 34, 123, no. 67;
Weiss, "Kandinsky und München," 1982, pp. 34,
209, no. 71; S. Wichmann, *Jugendstil Floral,* 1984,
p. 233; Bader-Griessmeyer, 1985, pp. 28, 36,
fig. 19; Christoph Kockerbeck, *Ernst Haeckels
"Kunstformen der Natur" und ihr Einfluss auf die
deutsche bildende Kunst der Jahrhundertwende*
(Frankfurt, 1986), pp. 180, no. 11, 182, fig. 11.

A preliminary sketch in the unpublished
notes of the artist is inscribed: "Spiral ec-
stasy/Spiral of the blossoming tree/Fire-
tree spiral" (transcribed by S. Wichmann
in Munich, *Hermann Obrist,* 1968). The
spiral symbol of dynamic energy became
an obsession with Obrist as it was with
many artists of the time – for example,
Gallé, Gaudi, Guimard, Horta, Redon,
Schmithals, and many others, not to
mention the veil dancing of Loïe Fuller
captured in spiraling sculptured form by
Raoul Larche. In his 1910 essay on Obrist, Karl Scheffler referred to him as "an
ecstatic of form [whose] apparent abstrac-
tions are filled to bursting with sensuos-
ity; in the chaos of his form lies, in
embryonic form, a higher architectonic
order" (*Kunst und Künstler,* vol. 10 [1910],
p. 556).   P. W.

detail

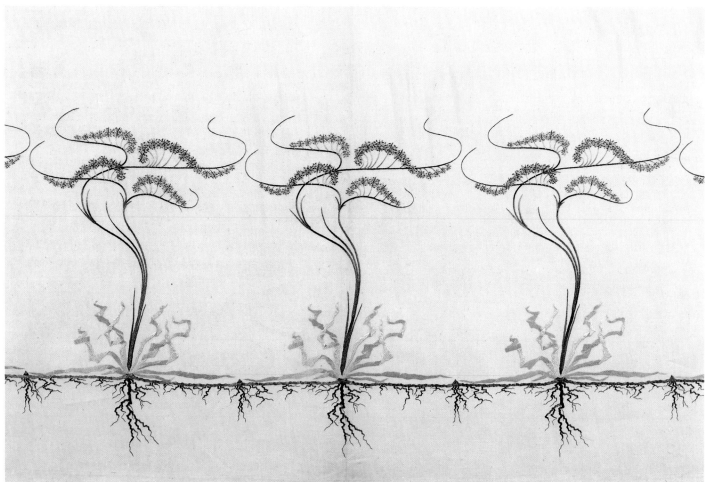

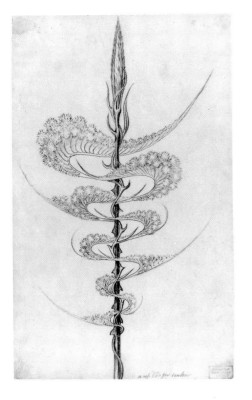

60 Orange Lilies, 1898

Made by Berthe Ruchet (Swiss, active Munich
1895–1900)
Silk and cotton brocade with gold threads and
silk embroidery, 38¹/₂ x 18⁷/₈″ (98 x 48 cm)
Signature: HO (intertwined) (lower left)
Stadtmuseum, Munich. 55/683

References

Henry Nocq, "A Munich," *Revue des Arts Décoratifs,* vol. 17 (1897), pp. 324 (ill.), 326; Obrist,
"Wozu," 1900, pp. 182 (ill.), 191 (ill. in Villa Obrist), 197; Obrist, "Pourquoi," 1900, p. 198 (ill.);
Illustrirte Zeitung, vol. 114b, no. 2962 (Apr. 5,
1900), p. 499, no. 1 (ill.); Brussels, 1977, p. 77,
fig. 112; Munich, *Kandinsky,* 1982, p. 206, no. 60;
New York, 1982, p. 95, no. 20; Bader-Griessmeyer, 1985, pp. 31–32, fig. 17.

This little-known tapestry by Obrist once
adorned his villa in Munich. Its dynamic
effect is produced by means of repetition
– three orange-lily blossoms with sta-
mens descending in a shower, and dan-
gling stems with spear-shaped leaves
blowing obliquely across the plane. The
emblematic force of the design is heightened by brilliant, exotic hues, from sal-
mon pink to green, over a shimmer of
gold. As in the bedspread (no. 57), particular combinations of stitches are used
to achieve varying heights of relief.

C. S. v. W. S.

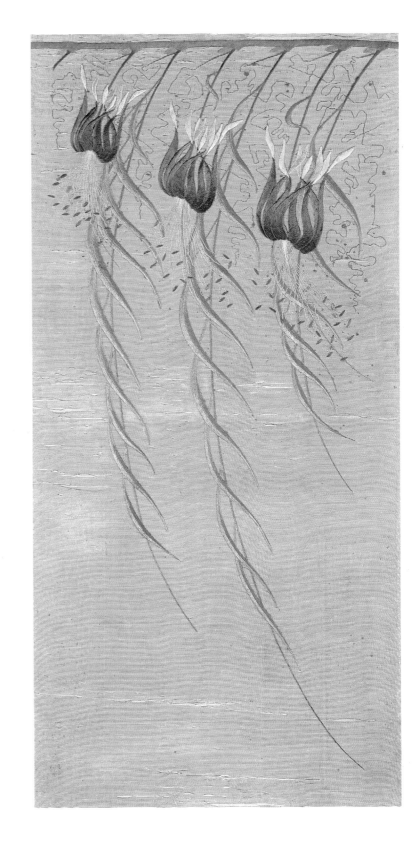

61 Serving Table, c. 1898

Made by Vereinigte Werkstätten für Kunst im
Handwerk, Munich (established 1897)
Oak and wrought iron (top restored), height 29¹/₂″
(75 cm)
Stadtmuseum, Munich. 71/15

References

Obrist, "Wozu," 1900, p. 186 (ill.); Munich,
1958, p. 200, no. 649 (as Pankok); Paris, 1960-61,
p. 368, no. 1.146; Rheims, 1966, p. 232, no. 313,
fig. 313; Irene von Treskow, *Die Jugendstil-Porzellane der KPM: Bestandskatalog der Königlichen
Porzellan-Manufaktur Berlin 1896-1914* (Munich,
1971), pp. 242, no. 269, 243; Munich, Stadtmuseum, 1972, pp. 190, fig. 196, 525, no. 2097;
Himmelheber, 1973, pp. 243, fig. 1078, 387,
no. 1078; Munich, *Kandinsky,* 1982, p. 205,
no. 61; Masini, 1984, p. 173, fig. 462 (as Endell);
Ottomeyer, 1988, p. 52, no. 2.

The table, once owned by the poet Henry
von Heiseler (see no. 34), has a rather unusual construction. The top is supported
by four flaring legs whose ends recall the
detailing of Gothic crockets, and bears
a tray with two wrought-iron handles.
The base forms a receptacle that probably
held a wine cooler. The four diagonally
mounted feet, carved in the semblance
of an animal's hind leg, merge with the
supports. This tense lineature, however,
belies the construction, in which a single,
flowing form has been built up of many
small pieces of wood.

If the design is unique, even eccentric,
Obrist certainly intended it. "Everything
I do," he wrote, "is meant to be comfort-
able, noble, something that can be
achieved only by getting away from
overdecoration and imitation. It is meant
to be adapted to my personal needs. It is
meant to be pretty and charming, and, if
possible, even beautiful and unique. My
aim is to work all this out carefully with
my assistants, and when friends come to
visit me, I want them to admire, even
envy me. I want to enjoy my work in
spite of all the effort involved; I want to
be terribly proud of my home and of every single chair in it, of a home that is not
going to be like that of my neighbor. I do
not want to outdo him by going him one
better, but simply by doing something he
will have a hard time copying" ("Hat das
Publikum ein Interesse daran, selber das
Kunstgewerbe zu heben?" *Kunstgewerbeblatt,* n. s., vol. 11 [1900], p. 92).

The attribution of the serving table to
Obrist is based on an article in the 1900
volume of *Dekorative Kunst*; its resemblance to PANKOK's furniture designs led
earlier commentators to attribute it to
that artist. A variant of the table is preserved in the Bayerisches Nationalmuseum, Munich.   H. O.

62 Sideboard, 1899

Made by Vereinigte Werkstätten für Kunst im
Handwerk, Munich (established 1897)
Oak, oak veneer, and pewter, 60⁵/₈ x 53¹/₈ x 28″
(154 x 135 x 71 cm)
Stadtmuseum, Munich. 71/13

References

Obrist, "Wozu," 1900, p. 186 (ill.); *Illustrirte
Zeitung,* vol. 114b, no. 2962 (Apr. 5, 1900),
p. 499, no. 4 (ill.); Ottomeyer, 1988, p. 52, no.3.

Like the serving table (no. 61), this
sideboard comes from the dining room of
Henry von Heiseler's house. Admirably
suited to its function of storing and displaying tableware, it consists of a two-
door cupboard surmounted by two drawers in the middle and three on each side
and, above them and half as deep, a semi-
circular arched top that culminates in a
small plinth, which was used for display
of a decorative object. The leaf and bud
motifs adorning the engraved pewter
mount on the rear panel of the upper section recur on the knobs of the drawers
below. A companion piece exists in a private collection.   H. O.

Bernhard Pankok

1872-1943

Pankok came to Munich in the fall of 1892, after finishing an apprenticeship as a restorer and decorator in his hometown of Münster and studying painting in Düsseldorf and Berlin. Initially, he worked as a portrait painter and graphic artist, contributing to the journals *Pan* and *Jugend*. In 1897 he designed his first furniture, a chair and a mirror frame for the spectacular "VII. Internationale Kunstausstellung" in the Munich Glaspalast. Both pieces were indicative of Pankok's transition from painter to craftsman, for their construction still left much to be desired in cabinetmaking terms. It was not until 1899, with his furniture designs for OBRIST's villa in the Schwabing district of Munich and for the "Deutsche Kunst-Ausstellung" in Dresden, that Pankok showed himself to be not only an artist of consummate and original gifts, but also a master of woodworking technique and detailing.

The imaginative charm of his style was also evident in the Alcove Room displayed at the 1900 Paris Exposition Universelle and honored with a *grand prix*. It was designed for the Vereinigte Werkstätten für Kunst im Handwerk, evidently in collaboration with such other cofounders of the Werkstätten as BEHRENS, PAUL, and RIEMERSCHMID. With this room, and with his design of the official catalogue of the exhibition's German section (see no. 66), Pankok achieved international recognition.

In 1900 he also received his first commission to design and build a private residence, for the art historian Konrad Lange in Tübingen. The exterior was a successful blend of English country house and traditional Bavarian domestic architecture; the interior, surprisingly departing from Pankok's Jugendstil approach, had a functional simplicity that presaged the straight lines of his next phase, as seen in the drawings for his own country house in Baierbrunn, outside Munich.

In 1901 Pankok became a professor at the recently established Lehr- und Versuchswerkstätte in Stuttgart, a school of applied art that he was to head from 1913 onward, and settled in that city. Pankok's architecture was based on series of closed cubes, illuminated by glazing that was clearly emphasized as a grid pattern. La-

Bernhard Pankok, *Self-Portrait,* 1898.
Westfälisches Landesmuseum, Münster

ter, however, in designing the Rosenfeld house in Stuttgart (1909-23), he developed a quite unexpected sumptuousness, though without having recourse to traditional forms. His architecture, invariably original, lent the German version of Art Deco its unmistakable stamp.

Besides painting and printmaking, architecture and design, Pankok devoted himself to the interior decoration of ships – such as the Lake Constance steamers *Friedrichshafen* and *Überlingen* – and designed the passenger compartments of four Zeppelins. Throughout his career he was an impassioned creator of designs for the theater, producing famous sets and costumes for Mozart's *Don Giovanni* (1909) and *Le Nozze di Figaro* (1912) for Stuttgart, and *Così fan tutte* (1921) for Berlin.

References

Konrad Lange, "Bernhard Pankok," *Dekorative Kunst,* vol. 13 (1905), pp. 129-60 (ills.); Wilhelm Schäfer, "Bernhard Pankok," *Die Rheinlande,* vol. 19 (1910), p. 181 ff.; Hermann Ehrenberg, "Bernhard Pankok als Maler und Radierer," *Die Kunst für Alle,* vol. 32 (1916-17), p. 161 ff.; Emil Gerhäuser, *Stuttgarter Bühnenkunst* (Stuttgart, 1917); Günther, 1971; Stuttgart, 1973; Münster, 1986.   S.G.

63 Armchair, 1897

Made by Vereinigte Werkstätten für Kunst im
Handwerk, Munich (established 1897)
Pearwood with silk upholstery, 34⅝ x 23⅝ x
21⅝″ (88 x 60 x 55 cm)
Marks: 21/219 VW
Label: La Maison Moderne (LMM)
The Danish Museum of Decorative Art,
Copenhagen

References

Gmelin, "Kunsthandwerk," 1897-98, p. 419,
no. 602; Ernst Brües, "Ausstellung zu Krefeld,"
Deutsche Kunst und Dekoration, vol. 2 (1898),
p. 418; *Dekorative Kunst,* vol. 1 (1898), p. 193; *Dekorative Kunst*, vol. 2 (1898), p. 157 (ill.); *Illustrirte Zeitung,* vol. 115, no. 2979 (Aug. 2, 1900), p. 180
(ill.); *Kunstgewerbeblatt*, n.s., vol. 11 (1900), p. 27
(ill.); Walther Gensel, "Das Kunstgewerbe auf
der Pariser Weltausstellung," *Kunstgewerbeblatt*,
n.s., vol. 11 (1900), p. 229 (ill.); "Die Vereinigten
Werkstätten auf der Pariser Weltausstellung,"
Dekorative Kunst, vol. 6 (1900), p. 269 (ill.);
"Deutsche Kunst und Dekoration auf der Pariser
Welt-Ausstellung," *Deutsche Kunst und Dekoration,* vol. 6 (1900), pp. 295, 297 (ills.); Gabriel
Mourey, "Round the Exhibition, III: 'German
Decorative Art,'" *The Studio*, vol. 21 (1901), p. 48
(ill.); Madsen, 1955, pp. 421, 423; Günther, 1971,
pp. 60-61, nos. 2-3, figs. 52-53.

An astonishingly versatile furniture designer, Pankok here created a chair that did not quite suit the dreamy ambience of his Alcove Room, in which it was shown at the Paris Exposition Universelle of 1900. Designed in 1897, it had already been exhibited in Munich and Krefeld in 1898 and at the Munich Secession in 1899. Its design is rather austere and, one senses, not perfectly adapted to the human frame. The squared tops of the legs, like the backrest, bear a pattern of tulips carved in low relief; in a variant of the chair, also exhibited in Paris, these were replaced by figurative motifs. The elegant Jugendstil pattern of the upholstery, fish weaving among water lilies, was the same on both chairs, but appears somewhat overpowered by their stocky, squarish structure.

These early designs do not yet possess the visionary quality of Pankok's work, for example, for the Villa Obrist (see nos. 65, 67-69), in which he proved his ability to unite structure and ornament in a harmonious whole.　　　S.G.

65 Design for Furniture, 1898

Pencil and colored pencil on paper, 13 x 16⁵/₈″
(33 x 42.2 cm)
Signature: B Pankok 98. (lower center)
Württembergisches Landesmuseum, Stuttgart.
1978-89

In 1899 Pankok designed a vestibule and a dining room for the house of his friend OBRIST in the Schwabing district of Munich (see nos. 67-69). It included, in addition to the bench and clock depicted in this drawing, a coat rack of very original construction that stood in one corner of the room. The complete vestibule was displayed at the Munich Secession exhibition of 1899; the bench was also shown at the 1902 exhibition in Turin, in an entrance hall by ADLER. The symmetrical bench (Vereinigte Werkstätten model number 1287; fig. 7) is interesting for the contrast between its smoothly functional seat and back and the armrests surmounted by knobs of the bonelike shape so typical of Pankok. Its extreme length apparently posed difficulties in integrating the decorative forms in the overall structure.

As a whole, Pankok's vestibule made a rather severe and stringent impression, especially in comparison to the overfurnished and overdecorated interiors of late nineteenth-century Germany. The bench originally stood in front of a "triptych" of openings separated by two Neo-Romanesque columns. The rectilinear design of the wall clock is quite untypical for Pankok and may have been dictated by the technical requirements of clockmaking.   S.G.

64 Chair, 1898-99

Made by Vereinigte Werkstätten für Kunst im Handwerk, Munich (established 1897)
Stained oak, 35³/₄ x 17⁷/₈ x 17³/₄″ (91 x 45.5 x 45 cm)
Museum für Kunsthandwerk, Frankfurt. 12979b

References

"Die Vereinigten Werkstätten auf der Pariser Weltausstellung," *Dekorative Kunst,* vol. 6 (1900), p. 269 (ill.); Fuchs, 1902-3, p. 59 (ill.); Hamann and Hermand, 1967, pp. 254, 257; Stuttgart, 1973, p. 77, no. 113; Himmelheber, 1973, fig. 1091, p. 389, no. 1091; Frankfurt, 1974, p. 47, no. 115; Frankfurt, Museum für Kunsthandwerk, *Europäische Möbel von der Gotik bis zum Jugendstil* (1976), pp. 170, no. 225, 171; Heskett, 1986, p. 89.

Pankok's model number 1260 chair has a lightness and grace that may owe something to the style known as the Third Rococo, which was popular in Germany during the 1890s. His sketch for it, in the Vereinigte Werkstätten archives, has a heavier appearance and splayed back legs that are faintly reminiscent of Bavarian folk art and design. A photograph published in *Dekorative Kunst* in 1900 shows the chair in Pankok's Alcove Room at the Exposition Universelle in Paris. The photograph was obviously taken before the room was completely furnished: the covered wall panels had yet to be embroidered, the corner sofa had yet to be installed, and of the furniture that the room later contained, only one of the two armchairs is visible. The corner table seen in the photograph actually belonged to RIEMERSCHMID's Room of an Art Lover (see nos. 99-100).

Pankok's beautiful chair, elegant in contour and delicately carved on the backrest, would certainly have enriched his Alcove Room, with its light, otherworldly mood.   S.G.

66 Endpaper for Exposition Universelle Catalogue, 1899

Color lithograph, 9⁷/₁₆ x 7³/₈″ (24 x 18.8 cm)
Signatures: B Pankok 99. (lower right);
BP [intertwined] LITH. (lower center)
Staatliche Museen Preussischer Kulturbesitz, Kunstbibliothek, Berlin. 01,62/5137

References

Kunst und Handwerk, vol. 50 (1899-1900), pp. 312-13; Munich, 1958, pp. 201, no. 659, 295; Paris, 1960-61, p. 372, no. 1.165; Schmutzler, 1962, colorpl. 1; Hamburg, 1963, p. 69, no. 663; Hofstätter, 1973, pp. 176-77; Berlin, 1970-71, p. 86, no. 178; Berlin, 1972, p. 156, no. 334.

Although Pankok had contributed vignettes to the first issues of *Jugend,* from 1896 on, it was his illustrations for the official catalogue of the German section at the 1900 Paris Exposition Universelle that made him world famous. These graphic compositions were all set in a heavy

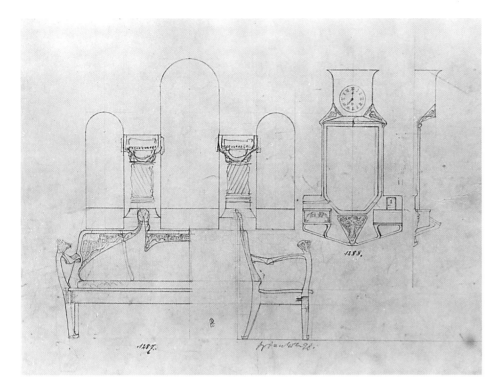

frame or border that resembled preliminary drawings for relief carvings in wood, and indeed, they may well have had some influence on his early furniture designs. The actual illustrations, rendered in fine strokes and dots, were inserted like a picture into this frame.

The endpaper is a composition arranged symmetrically along a vertical axis. It too has a kind of frame, from the bottom of which shapes sprout and grow toward the center, where they branch and merge with a cloud of stippled leaves and blossoms. The motifs are plant-derived: the sinuous vines seem at the same time to flower and scatter their seeds, which fall to the soil, among dark roots, to sprout again.

Pankok's rendering and division of the surface into solid areas alternating with stippled ones take advantage of the coloristic possibilities offered by the lithograph medium.   S.G.

painter producing his first designs for furniture and a demanding patron who was a central figure of Munich Jugendstil in the applied arts: "Obrist...created the basic plan, the structural skeleton, and the distribution [of furniture] in the room, while Pankok was responsible for the artistic design of the furniture, the imaginative style of the decor, etc." The results bore witness to a harmonious combination of "the modern individualism of the designer and the subjective comfort of the client."

The vitrine's most striking feature is the long, slender, sculpturally modeled supports that hold the shelves and glazing. Their grotesquely organic joins, feet, and surmounting forms shaped like crockets recall Gothic buttresses. At the back of the two lower shelves is a structure with no supporting function: a fan vault formed by four arches that rest on a square column – another indication of the Gothic derivation of the piece.

Two designs relating to the vitrine (model number 1498) have survived: a separate study (no. 68) and a signed drawing, dated 1898, showing a similar vitrine in combination with a corner bench, probably representing Pankok's initial conception.   H.O.

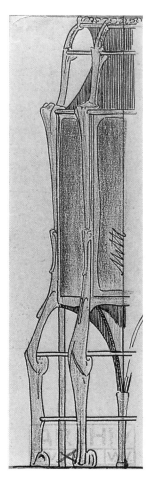

67 Vitrine, 1899

Made by Vereinigte Werkstätten für Kunst im Handwerk, Munich (established 1897)
Stained oak, spruce, and glass, 78³/₄ x 37³/₄ x 24¹/₄″
(200 x 96 x 61.5 cm)
Stadtmuseum, Munich. 49/57

References

Munich, "Secession," 1899, no. 600; Obrist, "Wozu," 1900, p. 195 (ill.); *Dekorative Kunst,* vol. 13 (1905), pp. 362, 364, 367 (ill.); Munich, 1958, p. 200, no. 648; Rheims, 1966, pp. 232–33, 259, fig. 315; Munich, 1970, p. 7, no. 49; Günther, 1971, p. 28; Munich, Stadtmuseum, 1972, p. 525, no. 2096; Stuttgart, 1973, pp. 72, no. 100, 73; Himmelheber, 1973, pp. 230, 244, 388, fig. 1084; Masini, 1984, p. 179, fig. 481; Ottomeyer, 1988, p. 57, no. 4.

This vitrine belonged to the dining room furniture that OBRIST commissioned from Pankok in 1898–99 for his new residence in the Schwabing district of Munich (see nos. 65, 68, 69). An article in the 1905 volume of *Dekorative Kunst* gives an insight into this collaboration between a

68 Design for a Vitrine, 1898–99

Ink and wash on tracing paper, 8¹/₄ x 2¹/₂″
(21 x 6.5 cm)
Vereinigte Werkstätten für Kunst im Handwerk
AG, Munich

References
Munich, 1970, p. 11, no. 80; Günther, 1971,
p. 28, fig. 1; Stuttgart, 1973, p. 73, no. 101.

Along with photographs of the interiors
of the house Pankok designed for OBRIST
(see nos. 65, 67, 69), several pieces of furniture have survived, including the vitrine in stained oak represented in this
sketch (no. 67). Symmetrical in form, it
has a glazed body with open shelves
above and below; the vertical members
flare out into feet, and, at the transition
and end points, thicken into carved,
bonelike shapes.

As a whole, the design has the somewhat bizarre appearance characteristic of
Pankok's early furniture, which was certainly original and imaginative. A similar
vitrine, in mahogany, with an interior
rear panel ornamented with inlays of various woods, is in a private collection.

Pankok, the dreamer and visionary
among his Munich artist-colleagues, lent
German Jugendstil an inimitable accent
with his strange, other-worldly ornament.   S.G.

69 Cupboard, 1899

Made by Vereinigte Werkstätten für Kunst im
Handwerk, Munich (established 1897)
Walnut, spruce, and glass, 65³/₄ x 42 x 16¹/₈″
(167 x 107 x 41 cm)
Stadtmuseum, Munich. 49/58

References
Dekorative Kunst, vol. 5 (1900), pp. 56, 77 (ill.);
Georg Fuchs, "Angewandte Kunst in der Secession zu München 1899," *Deutsche Kunst und Dekoration,* vol. 5 (1899–1900), pp. 2 (ill.), 19; *Die
Kunst,* vol. 12 (1905), p. 367 (ill. in Munich Secession); *Dekorative Kunst,* vol. 13 (1905), p. 367
(ill.); *Die Rheinlande,* vol. 10 (1905), p. 341 (ill.);
Munich, 1958, p. 200, no. 647; Rheims, 1966,
pp. 232, 259, fig. 314 (as Riemerschmid);
Himmelheber, 1973, pp. 244, fig. 1085, 388,
no. 1085; Stuttgart, 1973, p. 73, no. 102;
Ottomeyer, 1988, p. 61, no. 6.

This cupboard, model number 1283 of
the Vereinigte Werkstätten, was made for
the Villa Obrist (see also nos. 65, 67–68).
While the base, with four diagonally
placed, sculpted feet, recalls the three-
dimensional carving of Pankok's early
furniture, the superstructure is largely
constructed of flat panels. The continuous
side panels rest on the protruding feet,
and are decorated with stylized plants and

animals in *à jour* relief. The lowest shelf,
or floor, of the cupboard has ends that
extend through the side panel, creating
a structural joint that at the same time
serves as plastic ornament. The structural
articulation of this piece surpasses anything Pankok had yet achieved.

The cupboard was first shown, as part
of a vestibule, at the 1899 Secession exhibition, where the critic of *Dekorative
Kunst* reviewed it as follows: "The decorative cupboard also reveals an advance

in Pankok's development; the play of his
rich fantasy, which has all too often borne
strange fruit, seems far more lucid and
appealing within this concise overall
silhouette. The feet are the only displeas-
ing feature" (*Dekorative Kunst,* vol. 5
[1900], p. 56).

After the exhibition the cupboard stood
in the study of the Villa Obrist.   H.O.

Bruno Paul

1874–1968

Paul played a major part in the revival of arts and crafts that took place in turn-of-the-century Munich. Born in the Saxon town of Seifhennersdorf, he was sent by his businessman-father, at the age of twelve, to the Kunstgewerbeschule in Dresden. In 1894 he enrolled at the Munich Academy to study painting with Paul Höcker and Wilhelm von Diez; in his spare time he drew vignettes for the journal *Jugend* and contributed to the satirical weekly *Simplicissimus,* producing during his Munich years nearly five hundred caricatures for this magazine (see nos. 70–72).

Paul tried his hand at furniture, initially working in the sinuous Art Nouveau style, but his work gradually evolved into a more rectilinear mode. In 1897, together with BEHRENS, BRAUCHITSCH, HAUSTEIN, Franz August Otto Krüger, OBRIST, PANKOK, RIEMERSCHMID, and others, Paul was a founding member of the Vereinigte Werkstätten für Kunst im Handwerk in Munich. The Hunting Room he designed for this firm, featuring a continuous, inlaid frieze and furniture that was simple and functional by contemporary standards, was awarded a *grand prix* at the Paris Exposition Universelle of 1900.

At the "I. Ausstellung für Kunst im Handwerk," held in Munich in 1901, an interior typical of Paul's early work was on display – a study dominated by graceful arched lines and devoid of applied ornament. It was a prototype for manufacture of the kind later advocated by the Deutscher Werkbund, of which Paul was a co-founder in 1907. With a dining room exhibited in Turin in 1902 he continued his efforts in this direction, then, in his President's Study for the government building at Bayreuth, shown at the St. Louis world's fair of 1904 (see nos. 74–76), Paul proved himself a master of design for mass production. The rectangles and squares of wall and ceiling paneling, and of the built-in cabinets and other furniture, were so skillfully integrated in a serial pattern that the resulting effect was one of highest quality and complete harmony. In 1908 Paul went on to develop a line of *Typenmöbel* (standardized furniture) based on the conception of his St. Louis study. This unit system for small apartments, which could be added

Bruno Paul, c. 1910

to at will, was manufactured serially by the Vereinigte Werkstätten.

In 1907 Paul became director of the school attached to the Berlin Kunstgewerbemuseum, which, at his urging, was combined in 1924 with the Akademische Hochschule für Bildende Künste to become the Vereinigte Staatsschulen für Freie und Angewandte Kunst. Paul served as its director until his resignation in 1933.

Although Paul had designed a few private residences before World War I, it was not until the 1920s that he seriously devoted himself, despite administrative duties, to domestic and commercial architecture. Lucid in design and unerring in proportion, the buildings were generally low and horizontal in emphasis and invariably superb in detail. During the Third Reich, Paul worked as a freelance architect on several small projects, and after World War II was involved in rebuilding activities.

References

Popp, 1916; Ahlers-Hestermann, 1960; Günther, 1971; Lang, 1974; Günther, 1982 (with bibliog.).
S.G.

70 The Munich Fountain of Youth, 1897

Pencil and wash on paper, 15 x 23³/4″ (38.1 x 60.4 cm)
Signature: BR PauL (lower right)
Staatliche Graphische Sammlung, Munich.
Simpl. no. 1250

References

Bremen, Kunsthalle, *Europäischer Jugendstil* (May 16-July 18, 1965), pp. 64, no. 197, 156; Munich, 1969-70, p. 59, no. 181; Gasser, ed., 1977, pp. 82-83; Munich, 1977-78, p. 414, no. 461; Günther, 1982, p. 22; Munich, *Kandinsky,* 1982, p. 204, no. 57; New York, 1982, p. 89, no. 12.

The Munich Fountain of Youth [Jugend], located in the Bohemian Schwabing quarter of the city, takes a good-natured poke at the miraculous passage of the nineteenth-century woman into the modern age. Hatted, high-coiffured, and tightly corseted women dressed in historical-revival clothing approach the rejuvenating waters of Jugendstil to emerge on the other side as sinuous beauties, with their hair down, their feet bare, and their dresses in the style known as Reform – to the consternation of a Neo-Rococo matron eyeing them through her lorgnon. The transformation, however, was only superficial, for Paul appended a couplet that reads, "Why try to cure the world by cutting and cauterizing it,/When you can bring painless relief by stylizing it."

By 1906 Paul had made almost five hundred other drawings for the Munich satirical weekly *Simplicissimus,* toward the end under the pseudonym Ernst Kellermann, so as not to compromise his impending career as an official in the Prussian civil service.   S.G.

Die Zahnbürste

(Zeichnung von Bruno Paul)

„Zum Donnerwetter, Herr, was machen Sie denn da mit meiner Zahnbürste?!"
„Ach, entschuldigen Se gleßigst, ich gloobte, se gehörte zum Schiff."

— 320 —

Erkennungszeichen

(Zeichnung von Bruno Paul)

„Zu dumm, daß man nur im Frack kommen darf, man unterscheidet sich gar nicht von den Kellnern." „Doch, die brechen sich anständig."

71 The Toothbrush, 1897

Color lithograph, 11¼ x 8⅞" (28.7 x 22.5 cm)
Signature: BP (intertwined) (lower right)
Philadelphia Museum of Art. Gift of the Goethe
Institut, Munich, and Goethe House, New York.
1987-61-1

References

Lang, 1974, p. 12; Stanley Applebaum, *Simplicissimus: 180 Satirical Drawings from the Famous German Weekly* (New York, 1975), p. 6.

In turn-of-the-century Munich the weekly *Simplicissimus* was an extremely biting and outspoken critic of German politics and mores. Issue number 32 for 1898-99 was even confiscated by the authorities, and its publisher, Albert Langen, arrested. Paul's caricatures were certainly not the least acerbic part of the magazine.

Paul was a native of Saxony, whose people are known for their creativity and sensibility, leavened with a dose of homegrown cunning that appears naive, and burdened with a dialect that to most German ears sounds slightly ridiculous. The caption to *The Toothbrush,* which appeared in issue number 40 for 1897-98, is written in this broad Saxon. The fat man, caught using his cabinmate's toothbrush,

explains with mock surprise that he thought it came along with the ship.

The figures, in Paul's characteristically bold, broad manner, are composed of large, flat, undecorated shapes, with the addition of very few lines. The poses and facial expressions are strongly exaggerated, but, interestingly, the furnishings of the cabin are not. Paul designed his first luxury cabin for the *Kronprinzessin Cecilie* in 1907 (see also nos. 122-23), leading to a lifelong concern with the furnishings of modern ships. This drawing of 1897 amazingly anticipates the pure forms of tomorrow. The built-in furnishings are devoid of superfluous ornament, and already possess a functionality suited to the technology of the modern liner.   S.G.

72 Mark of Distinction, 1902-3

Color lithograph, 11¾ x 8" (30 x 20.3 cm)
Philadelphia Museum of Art. Gift of the Goethe
Institut, Munich, and Goethe House, New York.
1987-61-2

References

Lang, 1974, p. 70; Stanley Applebaum, *Simplicissimus: 180 Satirical Drawings from the Famous German Weekly* (New York, 1975), p. 9.

In his caricatures for *Simplicissimus* Paul poured derision on the German aristocracy, military, and clergy, not to mention the parvenus who had made their money during the period of expansion following Germany's unification in 1870-71. They now donned the social mark of distinction, the cutaway and white tie, without quite being able to slough off the distinguishing marks of their origins. *Mark of Distinction,* the title of this lithograph, which appeared in issue number 46 for 1902-3, is thus a double entendre. The scene is full of movement, with tightly packed figures, each of which contributes to a statement about this mediocre society that is effective because it immediately creates a gulf between the viewer and the behavior represented.   S.G.

73 Poster for Kunst im Handwerk Exhibition, 1901

Printed by Vereinigte Druckereien und Kunst-
anstalten (formerly Schön & Maison), Munich
Color lithograph, 34⁷/₈ x 23¹/₂″ (88.5 x 59.5 cm)
Signature: BP (intertwined) (center right)
Stadtmuseum, Munich. A 1/90

References

Westheim, 1907, p. 226; Richard Hessberg,
"Bahnbrecher der Deutschen Plakatkunst, 4:
Bruno Paul," *Das Plakat,* vol. 10, no. 1 (1919),
p. 34, fig. 2; Munich, 1958, pp. 233, no. 882, 276;
Paul Wember, *Die Jugend der Plakate: 1887-1917*
(Krefeld, 1961), pp. 32, no. 649, 108; Berlin,
Staatliche Museen Preussischer Kulturbesitz,
Kunstbibliothek, *Frühe Berliner Plakate: 1850-1930*
(July-Oct. 1963), no. 766; Hamburg, 1963, p. 72,
no. 708; Hellmut Rademacher, *Das deutsche Plakat
von den Anfängen bis zur Gegenwart* (Dresden,
1965), pp. 82, 90; Bremen, Kunsthalle,
Europäischer Jugendstil (May 16-July 18, 1965),
pp. 78, no. 305, 178; Hans Eckstein, *Die Neue
Sammlung* (Munich, 1965), fig. 15; Hellmut
Rademacher, *Masters of German Poster Art* (New
York, 1966), p. 43; Bremen, Focke-Museum and
Staatliche Kunstschule, *Frühe Berliner Plakate*
(June 2-July 2, 1967), pp. 2, 8, no. 56; Hagen,
Karl-Ernst-Osthaus-Museum, *Deutsche Plakate
von 1900-1914* (Oct. 26-Dec. 7, 1969), pp. 4-5,
10, no. 4; Berlin, 1970-71, p. 87, no. 183;
Munich, Haus der Kunst, *Internationale Plakate
1871-1971* (Oct. 9, 1971-Jan. 2, 1972), no. 195;
Berlin, 1972, p. 166, no. 443, fig. 166; Munich,
Die Neue Sammlung, *Eine Auswahl aus dem Besitz
des Museums* (1972), fig. 42; Schindler, 1972,
pp. 98, 100, no. 88; Suckale-Redlefsen, 1975,
p. 46, fig. 1; Munich, 1975-76 (2nd ed., 1978),
pp. 23-24, pl. III, 25, 185, no. 81; Darmstadt,
1976-77, vol. 2, p. 174, no. 336; Brussels, 1977,
p. 288, no. 696; Hollmann, et al., 1980, Part 1,
p. 220, no. 2514, colorpl. 10, Part 2, pl. 176,
no. 2514; Prague, 1980, pp. 70, no. 125, 159;
Munich, *Kandinsky,* 1982, p. 197, no. 38; New
York, 1982, p. 87, no. 4; Stuttgart, Graphische
Sammlung, *Ludwig Hohlwein: Plakate der Jahre
1906-1940* (Mar. 2-Apr. 21, 1985), pp. 19, no. 23,
27; Berlin (East), Altes Museum, *Plakatkunst um
1900* (Nov.-Dec. 1985), p. 28, no. 50; H. Wichmann, 1985, p. 324.

Paul's poster for the 1901 exhibition of
the Vereinigte Werkstätten für Kunst im
Handwerk signaled a final break with the
historical revival character of previous
Munich poster design. The motif, two
herons in turquoise and pink on a yellow
ground, was unusual and stood in no direct relation to the theme of the exhibition, unless the birds' grace constituted an
allusion to the artistic aims of its orga-
nizers. Paul's graphic means – flattened
shapes with little interior articulation,
emblematic colors, integration of image
with text – show that Munich artists had
indeed found a new style in poster design.

C. S. v. W. S.

Paul designed the armchair immediately after the Hunting Room that received a *grand prix* at the 1900 Exposition Universelle in Paris. It was part of a study shown at the "I. Ausstellung für Kunst im Handwerk" in Munich in 1901, and later furnished the President's Study exhibited at the 1904 world's fair in St. Louis. The Munich interior represented a considerable improvement over the Paris Hunting Room, which lacked unity and seemed somewhat self-conscious in its exclusion of applied ornament. The study was a harmonious ensemble whose well-conceived construction was ornamental in itself. It also included cabinets with powerfully sweeping lines, a bureau, a floor clock, and a table whose carved legs appeared rather incongruous within the functionality of the overall design. Two examples of this chair (model number 652) supplemented a group consisting of a sofa that seated two and of a second pair of armchairs of pleasing, circular shape. The design of model 652 would seem to lay bare its structure, revealing the forces of thrust and counterthrust with functional elegance.   S.G.

74 Armchair, 1901

Made by Vereinigte Werkstätten für Kunst im Handwerk, Munich (established 1897)
Oak and leather, 34⁷/₁₆ x 25 x 27¹/₂″ (87.5 x 63.5 x 69.9 cm)
K. Barlow Ltd., London

References

Die Kunst, vol. 6 (1902), p. 61 (ill.); *Die Kunst,* vol. 10 (1904), p. 295 (ill.); St. Louis, *Official Catalogue,* 1904, p. 448, no. 2520; St. Louis, *Descriptive Catalogue,* 1904, p. 52 (ill.); *Kunstgewerbeblatt,* n.s., vol. 16 (1905), p. 53 (ill.); *Spemanns goldenes Buch vom eigenen Heim* (Berlin, 1905), fig. 28 (in President's Study); Friedrich Haack, *Die Kunst des XIX. Jahrhunderts und der Gegenwart,* part 2: *Die Moderne Kunstbewegung* (Esslingen, 1925), p. 332; Günther, 1971, pp. 89-90, nos. 75-76, 160, no. 5, figs. 75-76; Günther, 1982, p. 29.

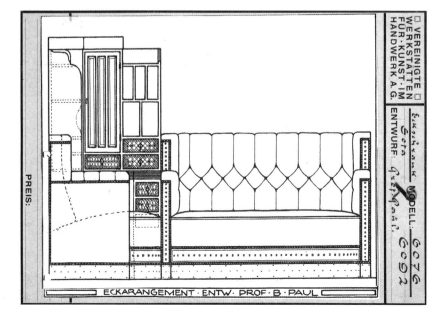

ECKARANGEMENT · ENTW. PROF · B · PAUL

75 Drawing for the President's Study for the Government Building at Bayreuth, 1904

Ink on paper, 5⁷/₈ x 12¹/₈″ (15 x 31 cm)
Vereinigte Werkstätten für Kunst im Handwerk
AG, Munich

References

Karl Friedrich Heitmann, "Das deutsche Kunst-gewerbe auf der Weltausstellung in St. Louis," *Die Rheinlande,* vol. 9 (1905), p. 26; F. Schu-macher, *Strömungen in deutscher Baukunst seit 1800* (Leipzig, 1935), p. 34; Günther, 1971, pp. 92-93, no. 79, fig. 79.

Together with the Hunting Room Paul designed for the Paris Exposition Uni-verselle of 1900, his President's Study for the St. Louis world's fair of 1904 won him the highest awards of the day, and inspired his illustrious contemporary Hermann Muthesius to declare that they "showed to perfection what we want and what we aspire to."

   This drawing is one of a number of de-signs in the Vereinigte Werkstätten ar-chives that depict a corner of the study. The grouping fitted like a piece in a puz-zle into the grid of squares and rectangles that dominated the entire room, creating the impression of a section of paneling extended into the third dimension. The interplay of forms and materials was superb, recalling the designs of Josef Hoffmann and Koloman Moser of Vienna.   S.G.

76 Desk Chair, 1902

Made by Vereinigte Werkstätten für Kunst im
Handwerk, Munich (established 1897)
Ash, 30⁷/₈ x 27³/₈ x 23″ (78.5 x 69.5 x 58.4 cm)
Marks: V. W. 2531, 1770
K. Barlow Ltd., London

References

Kunst und Handwerk, vol. 54 (1903-4), pp. 220, fig. 411, 221, fig. 412; St. Louis, *Official Cata-logue,* 1904, p. 448; St. Louis, *Descriptive Cata-logue,* 1904, p. 52 (ill.); *Die Kunst,* vol. 10 (1904), pp. 294-95 (ills.); *Die Kunst,* vol. 12 (1905), pp. 218-19 (ill.), 225 (ill.); *Spemanns goldenes Buch vom eigenen Heim* (Berlin, 1905), figs. 27-28 (in President's Study); *Kunstgewerbeblatt,* n. s., vol. 16 (1905), pp. 53 (ill. in President's Study), 60; Muthesius, 1905, pp. 78-79; Heyck, ed., 1907, pl. 43; Friedrich Haack, *Die Kunst des XIX. Jahrhunderts und der Gegenwart,* part 2: *Die Moderne Kunstbewegung* (Esslingen, 1925), p. 332; Fritz Schumacher, *Strömungen in deutscher Baukunst seit 1800* (Leipzig, 1935), no. 99, pl. 34; H. T. Bossert, ed., *Geschichte des Kunstgewerbes,* vol. 6 (Berlin, 1935), p. 308; Günther, 1971, pp. 89-90, nos. 75-76, 160, no. 5; Brussels, 1977, pp. 48, no. 50, 55; Günther, 1982, pp. 2, 25, 29; S. Wichmann, *Jugendstil Floral,* 1984, p. 173, no. 354; S. Wich-mann, 1984, p. 173, no. 354.

The chair, with its slanting arms issuing from the back to merge with the front legs, is adapted for work at a desk, ensur-ing the user the necessary freedom of movement. Like the armchair used in the same room (no. 74), its two vertical ties in the backrest distribute the load to the rear feet. This feature was prob-ably inspired by a RIEMERSCHMID chair (no. 93), an unsurpassably elegant model with diagonals extending from backrest to front legs, which caused a sensation at the 1900 Exposition Universelle in Paris.

   Chairs with such sweeping lines and a construction expressive of the play of physical forces characterized Paul's early phase, before his designs began to con-form to more strict, rectilinear principles. Both chairs were designed just after the turn of the century, and formed a beauti-ful contrast to the linear design of the President's Study that they graced in the St. Louis world's fair of 1904.   S.G.

77 Candelabra, 1901

Made by K. M. Seifert & Co., Dresden-Löbtau,
for Vereinigte Werkstätten für Kunst im Handwerk, Munich (established 1897)
Brass, height 15⁷/₈″ (40.3 cm)
Stadtmuseum, Munich. 58/938

References

Munich, 1. Ausstellung für Kunst im Handwerk,
Katalog (1901), p. 61, no. 145; *Die Kunst,* vol. 12
(1905), p. 367 (ill. at Secession); *Die Rheinlande,*
vol. 10 (1905), p. 341 (ill.); Haenel, 1906, p. 504
(ill.); Wilhelm Michel, "Die Münchner Vereinigten Werkstätten auf der kunstgewerblichen Ausstellung in Dresden," *Deutsche Kunst und Dekoration,* vol. 19 (1906-7), p. 101 (ill.); Vereinigte
Werkstätten für Kunst im Handwerk, *Beleuchtungskörper* (Munich, 1912), p. 1; Gemeinnützige
Vertriebstelle Deutscher Qualitätsarbeit GmbH,
Gediegenes Gerät fürs Haus (Dresden-Hellerau,
1912), p. 31; Stuttgart, 1973, p. 130, no. 347;
Brussels, 1977, p. 298, no. 729; Uecker, 1978,
fig. 0284; Graham Dry, "Münchener Jugendstilleuchter um 1900: Aspekte des floralen und
linearen Stils," *Weltkunst,* vol. 57, no. 15 (1987),
pp. 2031, nos. 3-4, 2032-33.

The ceremonial appearance and considerable size of this twelve-armed brass candelabra combine to make it the most
spectacular of all Jugendstil candelabras.
The arms swivel around the middle of the

shaft, forming a three-dimensional structure in the shape of a stylized tree or,
when placed against a wall, creating a
stylized image of a peacock. Designed in
1901, the candelabra was being sold in
several sizes by the Vereinigte Werkstätten until at least 1914, although it appears to have been most popular between
1901 and 1907 and forms a regular decorative feature of rooms by the Vereinigte
Werkstätten that are illustrated in contemporary publications. It was never
published as the work of a specific artist,
and until recently its design was ascribed
to PANKOK, who used similar ribbed ornament to decorate the legs of his furniture for the Lange residence in Tübingen
(1901). Furthermore, the candelabra was
a conspicuous feature of the living room
designed by Pankok for OBRIST's villa and
was exhibited in this context at the tenth
Munich Secession exhibition in 1904. Recent research, however, has shown the
candelabra to be a design by Paul. It was
first exhibited, with a group of similarly
ornamented candlesticks, at the "I. Ausstellung für Kunst im Handwerk" held in
the rooms of the old Bavarian National

Museum in Munich in 1901. Paul's and Pankok's simultaneous use of reticent geometric decoration to underline function – a characteristic also to be found in the work of HAUSTEIN, their colleague at the Vereinigte Werkstätten – represents a corporate endeavor by leading Munich designers to move away from a dependence on the stylized plant forms and sweeping lines that had characterized their early Jugendstil work up to the 1900 Paris Exposition Universelle.   G.D.

78 Candlestick, 1904

Made by Vereinigte Werkstätten für Kunst im Handwerk, Munich (established 1897)
Brass, height 10¹/₄" (26 cm)
K. Barlow Ltd., London

References
Munich, 1. Ausstellung der Münchener Vereinigung für Angewandte Kunst, *Katalog* (Munich, 1905), p. 47, no. 239; "Ausstellung für angewandte Kunst München 1905," *Kunst und Handwerk,* vol. 56 (1905-6), p. 44, fig. 79; Brussels, 1977, p. 298, no. 730; Uecker, 1978, p. 192, no. 0287; Günther, 1982, p. 24.

Paul's designs for small crafted objects are rare by comparison to the extensive and innovative work he did in the fields of furniture and interior design. The Vereinigte Werkstätten employed HAUSTEIN and Franz Ringer to design most of its small metal objects around 1900, though a few very fine pieces by RIEMERSCHMID are also known. Paul's work in this field consisted chiefly of radiator screens with lovely, pierced ornament – for example, for the 1899 "Deutsche Kunst-Ausstellung" in Dresden – and, later, of very elegant door handles made in small numbers for his own residences.

This candlestick is remarkable for its strict symmetry, which has an almost neoclassical flavor. Made by casting, then lathe-turning, its decorative form arose directly from the method of manufacture, thus fulfilling the demands raised around 1900 by Munich artists that the crafts be infused with art. Moreover, this piece marks Paul's transition from a rather modish design in the manner of Henry van de Velde to a more original, forcefully linear style.   S.G.

79 Poster for Angewandte Kunst Exhibition, 1905

Printed by Klein & Volbert, Munich
Color lithograph, 36¹/₂ x 24³/₈" (92.5 x 62 cm)
Stadtmuseum, Munich. B 1/87

References
Archiv für Buchgewerbe, vol. 42, nos. 11-12 (Nov.-Dec. 1905), p. 487, fig. 1; Richard Hessberg,

"Bahnbrecher der Deutschen Plakatkunst, 4: Bruno Paul," *Das Plakat,* vol. 10, no. 1 (1919), p. 36, fig. 4; Suckale-Redlefsen, 1975, p. 50, fig. 1; Munich, 1976, p. 132, no. 260; Brussels, 1977, p. 288, no. 697; Munich, 1975-76 (2nd ed., 1978), pp. 19, fig. 10, 188, no. 121; Hollmann, et al., 1980, Part 1, p. 220, no. 2519, Part 2, pl. 176, no. 2519; Stuttgart, Graphische Sammlung, *Ludwig Hohlwein: Plakate der Jahre 1906-1940* (Mar. 2-Apr. 21, 1985), pp. 19, no. 21, 27.

The poster announced the first exhibition of the Vereinigung für Angewandte Kunst, yet in spite of the modern charac-

ter of the items exhibited, Paul chose to advertise them with an old, heraldic motif, the eagle, radically stylized and perched on a cliff against a starry sky. This national symbol *par excellence* is an indication of a nostalgia that was gaining headway among Munich artists at the time and that could be expected to strike a responsive chord in visitors to the exhibition. The motif was certainly also meant to express the newfound dignity of German craftsmanship.   C.S.v.W.S.

Carl Georg
von Reichenbach

1872-1940

Munich-born Reichenbach, who signed his design work as Irgl Reichenbach, worked in many different mediums, but his main contribution was in the field of interior design. After studying at the Munich Kunstgewerbeschule, he attended OBRIST's and DEBSCHITZ's Lehr- und Versuch-Ateliers für Angewandte und Freie Kunst in Munich from 1905 to 1912. At the same time he spent an extended period in Oberzwieselau in the Bayerischer Wald, learning the craft of glassmaking in Benedikt von Poschinger's works, which specialized in Jugendstil glass. Reichenbach set up his own workshop for the applied arts in Berchtesgaden, and in 1903 in Tegernsee as well, where he mainly produced furnishing items – furniture in the rustic style, and brass lighting fixtures, clocks, textiles, fountains, and glass, which followed the Debschitz School style until well into the 1920s.

But it was the unmistakable designs for glass, both utilitarian and decorative, that Reichenbach produced while at the Debschitz School that made his name as a designer. Presumably he was encouraged to try his hand as a designer of glassware by Karl Schmoll von Eisenwerth, painter and teacher of drawing and graphics at the Debschitz School. Together with Hans Christiansen, DIEZ, and RIEMERSCHMID, Karl Schmoll von Eisenwerth had won a gold medal at the 1900 Paris Exposition Universelle for decorative glass made in Ferdinand von Poschinger's works at Buchenau in the Bayerischer Wald. A portfolio illustrated with original photographs of forty-two glass objects by Reichenbach and Karl Schmoll von Eisenwerth was registered with the Munich patent office on June 9, 1907, showing that the two artists had their decorative glassware jointly protected by a German imperial patent (copy in the Schmoll von Eisenwerth family estate). The decorative glassware that Reichenbach registered at this date included vases, jugs, bowls, tea containers, flasks, wine bottles, and several services of glassware.

Typical Reichenbach glassware displays air bubbles interwoven with colored threads, some of them with prunts. Reichenbach designed the trademark of the Oberzwieselau works and, together

Carl Georg von Reichenbach, c. 1908

with BEHRENS, Albin Müller, NIEMEYER, Riemerschmid, and Curt Stoeving, he probably had the most lasting influence on the Oberzwieselau range, as the large number of surviving pieces testifies.

Reviewing the Debschitz School section of the 1908 Munich exhibition of the Bayerischer Kunstgewerbeverein, the critic of *Kunst und Handwerk* ended on a special note by describing Reichenbach's work:

One may well say that the services, glasses, and vases by Irgl Reichenbach of Tegernsee unite forms that are always successful, or at least never unpleasant, with an excellent use of materials and colors. Looking at these, one automatically thinks of flowing water, the cold beauty of ice crystals, autumnal flowers, or precious stones. The glasses are very pretty in themselves, gracefully and picturesquely encircled with glass threads, all in dark tones, with magnificently colored relief knots aligned with them and acting as points of repose. Everything glows welcomingly, like yellow or red fall berries shining down from the green surface of the glass, which glistens as if running with dew. Other pieces renounce such splendor and simply vary one color. A yellowish green, for instance – but what elegance! Works such as the Reichen-

bach collection contains in its sparkling and glistening display are indeed the reflection of a quite extraordinarily cultured taste. This is the very culmination of the art!

References

Kunst und Handwerk, vol. 58 (1907-8), p. 59; Schack, 1971, p. 50 ff.; Schmoll, 1977, p. 66 ff.

H. S. g. E.

80 Vase, c. 1905

Made by Benedikt von Poschinger, Oberzwieselau (active 1880–1919)
Colored glass, with applied decoration and
prunts; height 2³/₈″ (6 cm)
Private collection

Reference

Berlin, Staatliche Museen, Kunstgewerbemuseum Schloss Köpenick, *Glas: Historismus und
die Historismen um 1900* (Aug. 15–Nov. 20, 1977),
no. 162.

Reichenbach loved to design glasses,
vases, bowls, and boxes decorated with
threading and prunts in strongly contrasting colors. This cylindrical vase has irregular trailed work at the center, held together by large glass prunts; above and
below, on the walls of the vessel, are
scattered smaller decorative pads of glass.
Similar objects by Reichenbach are in
the Badisches Landesmuseum, Karlsruhe
(formerly Woeckel collection), the
Museum für Kunsthandwerk in Schloss
Pillnitz, Dresden, and the Kunstgewerbemuseum, Berlin.

Like many Jugendstil artists who
worked in glass, Reichenbach was inspired by historical models, but unlike
others, he did not turn to Near Eastern
glasswares with enameled and gilded decoration; instead, he looked to Antique
and medieval examples decorated with
threading and prunts, without, however,
imitating them specifically. The technique of decorating glass with such applied ornaments is very old. The thick
consistency of the hot mass of glass ena-
bles long threads to be drawn out and ma-
nipulated around the glass body while it is
still hot, in rings or spirals, or as single
drops or pads of glass (known as prunts)
to be applied to the wall of the vessel.
With his free handling of form and the
interplay of the colors of vessel and decoration, Reichenbach's creations – which
he had made by Benedikt von Poschinger
in Oberzwieselau – constitute a unique
and powerful note in the concert of German and European Art Nouveau glass.

H. S. g. E.

Ernst Riegel

1871-1939

Ernst Riegel (3rd from right) with his students, c. 1912-13

Riegel is without doubt one of the most significant, and least known, of German gold- and silversmiths of the past hundred years. Born in Münnerstadt, he was apprenticed to the silver-chaser Otto Pabst in Kempten, Allgäu, from 1887 to 1890, before becoming an assistant of the Munich goldsmith MILLER in 1895. Miller was the doyen of south German silver- and goldsmiths, and had trained such artists as Karl Gross, Emil Lettré, and Alexander Schönauer. In Miller's studio Riegel was confronted with a rich store of historical examples, and could learn from the sumptuous and elaborate centerpieces in which his mentor excelled.

From 1900 to 1906 Riegel ran his own workshop in Munich, producing finely crafted pieces that rapidly established his reputation. At the age of thirty-five, he was already among the elite of German silversmiths. In 1906 Riegel was represented by a number of works at the "III. Deutsche Kunstgewerbe-Ausstellung" in Dresden, and that year was invited by Grand Duke Ernst Ludwig of Hesse to join the Darmstadt artists' colony, which at that time included such artists as Hans Christiansen, Albin Müller, Joseph Maria Olbrich, and SCHARVOGEL. In these surroundings Riegel's talent matured.

Among the most important works of this period were vessels of cut and polished nephrite, agate, lapis-lazuli, and other semiprecious stones, with finely chased settings. Created for the grand duke, these pieces remain in Schloss Wolfsgarten, near Darmstadt. Riegel also made fine objects and jewelry for members of the grand duke's family and for noble and well-to-do patrons from the Darmstadt and Frankfurt areas.

A further focus was liturgical vessels for churches in Darmstadt and environs. Riegel was especially renowned for the elaborate chains of office, worn on ceremonial occasions by mayors and university presidents, that he made for the cities of Aschersleben, Beuthen, Leipzig, and Worms, among others.

When the creative energy of the artists' colony at Darmstadt began to flag, Riegel sought new challenges, in 1912 becoming professor of goldsmithing at the Kunstgewerbe- und Handwerkerschule in Cologne. One of his first commissions there was to provide new pieces for the city's famous collection of old civic silver. In 1914 Riegel participated in the Cologne Werkbund exhibition, and in 1920 accepted an additional teaching post as head of the goldsmithing class at the Cologne Institut für Religiöse Kunst, an appointment in keeping with his focus on church implements. During the last twenty years of his life Riegel continued to be highly productive, but most of the objects he designed were executed by his students, and they lacked the innovation that had characterized his Munich and Darmstadt work.

For sheer variety Riegel's oeuvre is probably unmatched by that of any other twentieth-century German gold- or silversmith. His work was much in demand, not only among private patrons, but also by museums and city governments. Some of his early objects were acquired by the Gewerbemuseum in Darmstadt, Museum für Kunsthandwerk in Frankfurt, Munich Stadtmuseum, and Kaiser Friedrich Museum in Magdeburg. Many orders for ceremonial pieces reached him from cities like Munich and Cologne. His oeuvre was widely published and illustrated in contemporary art journals, a record sadly not matched by the number of surviving examples.

References

Bott, 1973, pp. 88-89; Darmstadt, 1976-77, pp. 203-10; U. von Hase, *Schmuck in Deutschland und Österreich, 1895-1914* (Munich, 1977), p. 205; Werner Schäfke, *Das Ratssilber der Stadt Köln* (Cologne, 1980), pp. 52-54, 100-101, 106-12; R. Joppien, "Die Kette des Rektors der Universität Köln: Eine Arbeit des Goldschmieds Ernst Riegel," *Museen der Stadt Köln: Bulletin,* vol. 2 (1985), pp. 15-18.   R.J.

81 Goblet, 1903

Silver, gilded silver, and uncut opals; height 9¹/₂″
(24 cm)
Marks: R, 1903
Stadtmuseum, Munich. K 60-507

References

Georg Habich, "Ernst Riegel, München,"
Deutsche Kunst und Dekoration, vol. 15 (1904-5),
pp. 385 (ill.), 386; *Kunst und Handwerk,* vol. 55
(1904-5), p. 245, fig. 456; Munich, Stadtmuseum, 1972, p. 527, no. 2135; Munich, 1976,
p. 211, no. 455; Darmstadt, 1976-77, vol. 4,
p. 204, no. 613; *Antiquitäten-Zeitung,* no. 21
(Oct. 14, 1982), p. 509.

"In the renascence of the goldsmith's art,
which until recently languished in mere
stylistic imitation or was limited to architectural reproduction, Ernst Riegel has
played an outstanding part," wrote the
critic of *Deutsche Kunst und Dekoration* in
1907-8 (p. 57). Nevertheless, Riegel was
influenced in this goblet, as in many of his
works, by earlier Munich traditions, as
evidenced by the combination of various
revived techniques such as the *à jour*-
mounted opals on the base or the twin-
walled cup with its repoussé and pierced
ornament. The form of the vessel recalls
that of Late Gothic "apple goblets," although it has been reinterpreted in the
sense of floral Jugendstil to form a tree
with roots and pruned foliage. Whether
the motif of the crowned bird alludes to
the Grimms' fairy tale *The Seven Ravens*
remains uncertain.   C. S. v. W. S.

82 Goblet, 1903

Silver, height 7⅞″ (20 cm)
Marks: R, stylized hedgehog, 1903
K. Barlow Ltd., London

References

Kunst und Handwerk, vol. 53 (1902-3), p. 249,
figs. 431-32; *Kunstgewerbeblatt,* n.s., vol. 16
(1905), p. 186 (ill.); *The Studio Year Book of
Decorative Art* (1907), p. 207 (ill.); Pforzheim,
Schmuckmuseum im Reuchlinhaus, *Goldschmiede-
kunst des Jugendstils: Schmuck und Gerät um 1900*
(May 10-Sept. 22, 1963), p. 23, no. 1, pl. XXVIII;
Munich, Villa Stuck, 1979, p. 28, no. 159, fig. 46.

Riegel's "seven ravens" goblet, with its
cylindrical cup on a tall, conical shaft, is
remarkably different from that in the
Munich Stadtmuseum (no. 81), which has
the shape of a spherically pruned tree.
Although both have the same subject and
reflect historical influences, the latter is
based on natural forms such as those found
in Late Gothic "apple goblets," while this
piece owes much to Oriental vessels in the
formal austerity of its sharply tapering
shaft. Riegel's early sketchbooks, and his
oeuvre itself, reveal an intensive involvement with historical styles.

Both types of goblet recur frequently in
Riegel's work between 1901 and 1912, yet
the stringency of the shaft design, with its
vertical ribs and pattern of perforations,
seems unusually early for 1903. Such details anticipate the ritual objects that were
commissioned from Riegel in his Darmstadt period in 1908-12 (for example, the
liturgical vessels in the Paulus-Kirche,
Darmstadt, or in the Luther-Kirche,
Worms).

The ornamentation of the cup recalls
those glazed Persian (Kashan) tiles of the
late thirteenth century that display tiny
birds perched or flying among dense
foliage. Riegel employed this motif, in
chased work, on several goblets and
tumblers made between 1901 and 1912,
sometimes adding such exotic species as
parrots and pelicans. The development of
the bird motif found its culmination in
the artist's designs for embroideries of
about 1912, which show facing pairs of
birds between vases, inspired by Near
Eastern and perhaps Sassanid models. In
his pieces of the Munich and Darmstadt
years, Riegel succeeded in merging European with Near Eastern influences in a
way that enriched historicism with new
impulses.   R.J.

Richard Riemerschmid
1868–1957

Riemerschmid, one of the greatest German designers of the twentieth century and the leading representative of the "functionalist" wing of Munich Jugendstil, was a native of the city. An artist as well as an architect of exceptional versatility, he produced designs remarkable for their originality and practicality for furniture, metalwork, glass, ceramics, textiles, and all aspects of interior decoration. His views came to dominate the design establishment in Munich to the extent that OBRIST complained in 1913 that he felt himself a "living outsider" among "you members of the practical art syndicate" and decried "the famous purposefulness" that characterized their designs (letter to Riemerschmid, probably January 26, 1913; Archiv für Bildende Kunst, Germanisches Nationalmuseum, Nuremberg).

Riemerschmid trained initially as a painter, attending the Munich Academy from 1888 to 1890, and did not produce his first furniture designs until 1895 (see no. 83), pieces that were indebted to the Gothic Revival and to the English Arts and Crafts movement, with which he was familiar through the British periodical *The Studio*. In the applied art section of the 1897 Glaspalast exhibition he showed both paintings and furniture (see nos. 84-85), their style already evincing that concern for simple, functional forms, clarity of construction, and truth to materials that was to become a hallmark of his designs and which led Muthesius to observe that "the inherent development of form out of function [was] the prime motive" behind all his work.

In 1897 Riemerschmid cofounded the Vereinigte Werkstätten für Kunst im Handwerk, Munich, but it was not until the following year, when he designed the startlingly original and artistically unified Music Room for the "Deutsche Kunst-Ausstellung" in Dresden (see nos. 91-93), that his stature became fully apparent to his contemporaries. In 1900 he designed another complete interior, the Room of an Art Lover, for the Exposition Universelle in Paris (see nos. 99-100), an ensemble that received a gold medal and consolidated the artist's reputation. He followed it in 1900-1 with the creation of the Munich Schauspielhaus, the theater

Richard Riemerschmid, c. 1927

that is Germany's finest Jugendstil building. Writing in *Die Kunst* in 1901, one contemporary critic observed that Riemerschmid had considered everything in the Schauspielhaus: "The player, the public, the ear, and the eye, the requirements of aesthetics and comfort, all come into their own" (C., "Das Neue Schauspielhaus in München," *Die Kunst,* vol. 4 [1901], p. 367).

It is a measure of Riemerschmid's talent and versatility that he was commissioned in 1903 to produce designs for the Meissen porcelain manufactory, the oldest in Europe (see no. 116). His association with the Dresdner Werkstätten, founded by his brother-in-law Karl Schmidt, began about the same time, when he designed nine rooms for their exhibition in Dresden. The textiles he designed for them with small repeating patterns (see nos. 127-30) broke decisively with the large-scale motifs of earlier work in this medium, yet it was his designing of the Werkstätten's *Maschinenmöbel* that represents possibly his greatest contribution to twentieth-century applied art (see no. 125). First exhibited at the "III. Deutsche Kunstgewerbe-Ausstel-

lung" in Dresden in 1906, this revolutionary program of ready-made suites of machine-made furniture, retailing at reasonable prices, opened up a new era of furniture production and had a decisive influence on German taste in the period before World War I.

A founding member of the Deutscher Werkbund in 1907, Riemerschmid maintained his position as one of Germany's leading designers both before and after World War I, continuing to exert influence through his teaching and organizational activities. Among the major projects he worked on before the war was the planning of Germany's first garden city, at Hellerau near Dresden (1907-13). Riemerschmid's importance as an extraordinarily inventive designer in a restrained, strictly functional mode was reflected in the official appointments he held throughout his career, among them director of the Munich Kunstgewerbeschule (1913-24) and chairman of the Deutscher Werkbund (1921-26).

References

Muthesius, 1904; Rée, 1906; Nerdinger, ed., 1982.   M.F.

83 Secretary, 1895

Stained and painted pine, and wrought iron;
70½ x 35 x 20⅛″ (179 x 89 x 51 cm)
Stadtmuseum, Munich. 68/1413

References
Himmelheber, 1973 (2nd ed., 1983), pp. 206, 234,
244, fig. 916; Nerdinger, ed., 1982, p. 113,
no. 60b; Rammert, 1987, p. 117, no. 60b;
Ottomeyer, 1988, pp. 69-70, no. 12.1.

Following his marriage to the actress Ida
Hofmann in 1895, Riemerschmid began
to design the furnishings of their apart-
ment in Munich's Hildegardstrasse.
These "first experiments," as he called
them, resulted in a suite of Neo-Gothic
furniture, to which this secretary belonged. The use of stone pine, the carved
tendril-and-leaf decoration, the board
construction, and the emphasis on the nature of the material are all indebted to
Late Gothic models. Leopold Gmelin described this approach in 1897: "Hand in
hand with simplicity of construction goes
a preference for modest materials. Just as
no doubt is left as to what a thing is made
of, so its structure is rendered wholly
transparent. Furniture no longer appears
'built up' from separate units or carved in
one piece, but, as in earlier times – most
strikingly, perhaps, in the Gothic and
early Renaissance periods – is clearly
'assembled'" (Gmelin, "Kleinkunst,"
1897-98, p. 19). Further Neo-Gothic elements include the lower section, which
recalls Gothic chests, and the crenelation
at the top, the only architectural feature of
the secretary. However, the main ornamental motif – curved stalks and stylized
blossoms – points to the formal vocabulary of Jugendstil.   H.O.

84 Cloud Ghosts, 1897

Tempera on cardboard, with carved and painted wood frame; 17¹/₂ x 30⁵/₁₆" (45 x 77 cm) (without frame)
Signature: RR (intertwined) 97 (lower left)
Städtische Galerie im Lenbachhaus, Munich.
G 14228

References

Munich, 1897, p. 212, no. 166; Gmelin, "Klein-kunst," 1897-98, pp. 22, 43, fig. 50; Rosner, 1899, p. 107, fig. 99; *Dekorative Kunst,* vol. 5 (1900), p. 8; Munich, 1958, p. 205, no. 685; Munich, Stadtmuseum, 1972, p. 524, no. 2090; Darmstadt, 1976-77, vol. 3, pp. 148, no. 146, 149; Munich, *Kandinsky,* 1982, pp. 214, no. 86, 215; New York, 1982, p. 98, no. 25; Nerdinger, ed., 1982, pp. 90, no. 23c, 91, fig. 1, 99-100; Masini, 1984, pp. 178, fig. 479, 179, no. 479; Munich, 1985-86, p. 31.

Trained as a painter at the Academy in Munich, Riemerschmid painted largely at the beginning and end of his lifelong ar-

tistic career. It was as a "painter" that Riemerschmid was listed in 1897 among the committee members of the decorative arts section (Ausschuss der Abteilung für Kleinkunst) at the international art exhibition at the Munich Glaspalast (see Appendix), where for the first time in the history of such exhibitions, furniture and decorative objects were included as "art," albeit confined there to two small rooms. For the room designed by the architect Theodor Fischer, Riemerschmid contributed a large mural, a landscape with river, and a dresser (see no. 85), as well as this picture. It was listed in the exhibition catalogue simply as "decorative painting," despite the literary-Symbolist associations that seem intended by the subject, a Walpurgisnacht, or witches' sabbath (Munich, 1897, p. 212, no. 166). Several sketches and versions of this work

survive (including two in the Städtische Galerie im Lenbachhaus, Munich, G. 16.359-361, G 15.787), and the image of ghostly figures whirling like clouds in front of a full moon was one that Riemerschmid took up again at the end of his life. The painting was hung in Fischer's room over a door between a frieze and an embroidered *portière* by ENDELL, where the abstract lines of the Endell ornaments could reinforce the illusory nature of Riemerschmid's figures, as they emerge and dissolve in flight (see fig. 4). K.B.H.

GLASPALAST 1897

85 Design for a Dresser, 1897

Pencil and watercolor on paper, 7³/₄ x 8³/₄″
(19.5 x 22 cm)
Architektursammlung der Technischen Universität, Munich. RR 196

References

Munich, 1970, p. 13, no. 124; Nerdinger, ed.,
1982, p. 114, no. 62b; Rammert, 1987, p. 122,
no. 62b.

For the Munich Glaspalast exhibition of
1897 Riemerschmid designed a dresser
that was made by Wenzel Till in yew
(with doors in American maple). The
drawing depicts the dresser in a front
view, the lower section with doors and
the upper with three open shelves, and in
a side view that shows the particular
handling of the open shelving, with little
columns that are an intrinsic part both of
the formal concept and of the construction.
    As a whole, this early piece of furniture
is the first instance in Riemerschmid's
work in which he moved away from a
close adherence to historical models, such
as the Gothic furniture he had studied in
Munich's Bayerisches Nationalmuseum.
Nevertheless, the molding at the top of
the dresser still recalls that in historic German furniture, while the metal fittings are
"Gothic" in detail. The floral element of

Jugendstil is also very much in evidence.
Riemerschmid's endeavor to harmonize
form and function results in a simplicity
that was much acclaimed by his contemporaries.   B.-V. K.

86 Candlesticks, 1897

Made by Vereinigte Werkstätten für Kunst im
Handwerk, Munich (established 1897)
Gilded brass, height 14¹/₈″ (36 cm) (each)
K. Barlow Ltd., London

References

Kunst und Handwerk, vol. 47 (1897-98), p. 324,
no. 492 (ill.); *Dekorative Kunst,* vol. 3 (1899),
pp. 152 (ill.), 209 (ill.); *Deutsche Kunst und Dekoration,* vol. 3 (1898-99), p. 127; Munich, Museum
Villa Stuck, *Jugendstil aus Münchner Privatbesitz*
(Dec. 13, 1972-Feb. 25, 1973), no. 42; Uecker,
1978, p. 194, no. 0290; Darmstadt, Hessisches
Landesmuseum, *Jugendstil: Kunst um 1900* (1982),
p. 260, no. 341; Nerdinger, ed., 1982, p. 273,
no. 278.

One of the first metalwares designed by
Riemerschmid and·one of the first produced by the Vereinigte Werkstätten, the
candlesticks were published in *Kunst und
Handwerk* in 1898, where they were described as among "a first list of works
from the Vereinigte Werkstätten für
Kunst im Handwerk in Munich; they are
mostly lighting devices, but also include
jewelry. The main material of the former
is almost exclusively wrought iron. Of
Riemerschmid's candlesticks, the tall one
is made of bronze." This "tall" candlestick is known in both brass and bronze
versions, and with its tuliplike nozzle displays the same stylized vocabulary of
plant forms as other works of this period
by Riemerschmid (see no. 94) and his
contemporaries (see no. 27).   K. B. H.

87 Candlestick, 1897

Made by Vereinigte Werkstätten für Kunst im Handwerk, Munich (established 1897)
Wrought copper, height 3³/₄″ (9.5 cm)
K. Barlow Ltd., London

References

Kunst und Handwerk, vol. 47 (1897–98), p. 324, fig. 492; *Dekorative Kunst,* vol. 3 (1898), p. 152 (ill.); Munich, 1958, p. 208, no. 702; Günther, 1971, pp. 86–88, fig. 74, 159, no. 4a; Munich, *Kandinsky,* 1982, p. 220, fig. 109; Nerdinger, ed., 1982, p. 273, no. 279.

This candlestick, like the "tall" one (no. 86), was among the first objects produced by the Vereinigte Werkstätten,, and appeared in the 1897–98 volume of *Kunst und Handwerk* as a "small light holder in copper." One of Riemerschmid's most popular designs, it was made, with variations, in several sizes in wrought iron and brass as well as copper, shown in exhibitions from Darmstadt in 1898 to St. Louis in 1904, and offered for sale by the Dresdner Werkstätten, too. In contrast to the intricately wrought candlesticks in a naturalistic floral idiom that Franz Ringer designed for the Vereinigte Werkstätten at this time, Riemerschmid's piece appears simple and functional, with a plain circular tray base and curved side handle.

K.B.H.

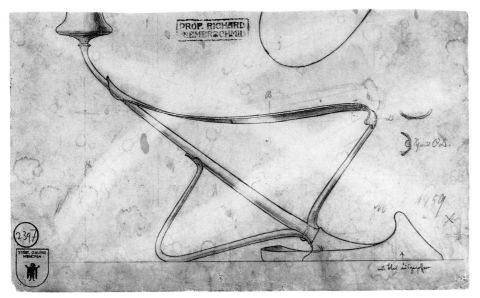

88 Design for a Candlestick, 1898

Ink and pencil on drawing board, 7¹/₄ x 12⁵/₈″
(18.5 x 31.9 cm)
Architektursammlung der Technischen
Universität, Munich. RR 2397

Reference
Nerdinger, ed., 1982, p. 274, no. 281.

The sheet is undated, but written sources
and Riemerschmid's other works enable
it to be ascribed to 1898. At this time
Riemerschmid was also working on designs for electric table lamps and candlesticks for pianos. Common to all these
designs is an extreme economy of form.
The stem of the candlestick (no. 89) rises
obliquely from a solid, heart-shaped foot
and narrows to the top, where it bears a
bud-shaped candleholder. The derivation
of the design from plant forms is evident
particularly in the upper stalk, from
which a narrow leaf grows out to join the
main stem. The lower stalk, which does
not swing out so far, touches the ground
line and supports the main stem.

The attractiveness of the work lies in
both the material used for its execution –
brass – and the purely vegetative concept
of the design, which lacks any additional
decoration.   B.-V.K.

89 Candlestick, 1898

Made by Vereinigte Werkstätten für Kunst im
Handwerk, Munich (established 1897)
Brass, height 6⁷/₈″ (17.5 cm)
K. Barlow Ltd., London

References
Leopold Gmelin, "Das Kunsthandwerk im
Münchner Glaspalast," *Kunst und Handwerk,*
vol 50 (1899-1900), p. 57, fig. 90; Nerdinger, ed.,
1982, p. 274, no. 281.

When on display at the Munich Glaspalast
exhibition in 1899, this candlestick produced by the Vereinigte Werkstätten
(model number 1459) could be compared
to a variety of domestic objects in
wrought iron, copper, and brass made by
such Munich firms as Reinhold Kirsch,
Wilhelm & Lind, and J. Winhart & Co.
These metalwares were richly ornamental, decorated with scrolls, leaves, and
other plant forms, while Riemerschmid's
candlestick – with its simple diagonal
stem set at a 140-degree angle to the base
– is remarkable for its modernist for-
swearing of such embellishments and for
its emphatic assertion of pure line.
Riemerschmid's stringency was not appreciated by Leopold Gmelin, who, reviewing the exhibition for *Kunst und
Handwerk,* remarked that the lamp called
attention to itself "through an almost unnatural restraint in [its] decorative development."   K.B.H.

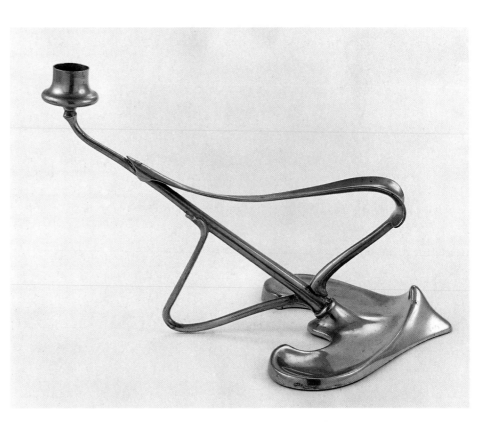

90 Floor Lamp, c. 1898

Made by Vereinigte Werkstätten für Kunst im
Handwerk, Munich (established 1897)
Brass, height 51¹/₂″ (131 cm)
Stadtmuseum, Munich. 64-1225

References

Dekorative Kunst, vol. 2 (1898), pp. 179 (ill.), 241
(ill.), 244 (ill.); "Neues aus den Vereinigten
Werkstätten für Kunst im Handwerk,
München," *Dekorative Kunst,* vol. 3 (1899),
pp. 145, 157 (ill.); Munich, Glaspalast, 1899,
p. 176, no. 2331; *Dekorative Kunst,* vol. 4 (1899),
p. 98 (ill. in Dresden); Schumann, 1899, p. 529
(ill.); *Kunst und Handwerk,* vol. 50 (1899-1900),
p. 62, fig. 100; Paris, 1900, p. 315, no. 3727;
Innendekoration, vol. 11 (1900), pp. 92, 94 (ill. in
Paris); *Illustrirte Zeitung,* vol. 115, no. 2977 (July
19, 1900), p. 108 (ill.); Muthesius, "Neues Ornament," 1901, p. 351 (ill.); Munich, 1. Ausstellung
für Kunst im Handwerk, *Katalog* (1901), pp. 29,
37 (ill.); Günther, 1971, pp. 49-50, nos. 1i,1k,
152, fig. 33; Selle, 1974, p. 109, fig. 8; Nerdinger,
ed., 1982, pp. 17, 135, 153.

As Günther points out, the construction
of the floor lamp, which was shown as
part of the Room of an Art Lover at the
1900 Paris Exposition Universelle, was
based on a "music stand with lamp" exhibited in 1898 at the Munich Glaspalast
and illustrated in *Kunst und Handwerk*
(vol. 47 [1897-98], p. 433). Both lamps
used kerosene, which was held in the
spherical container below the shade. The
tripod, with lateral supports winding
around the center of the shaft, appears
more graceful in this later version, which
was model number 390 in the Vereinigte
Werkstätten line.   C.S.v.W.S.

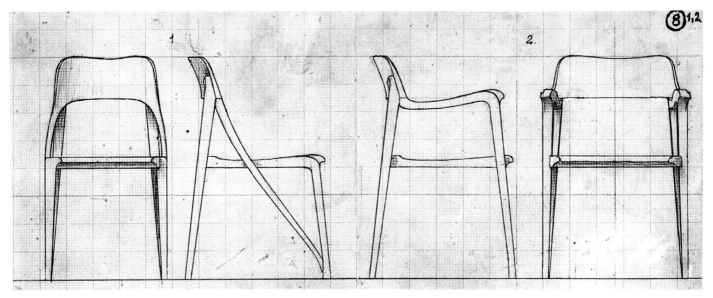

91 Design for Chairs, 1898-99

Ink and pencil on drawing paper, 4¹/₈ x 10¹/₄"
(10.5 x 26 cm)
Architektursammlung der Technischen
Universität, Munich. RR 8.1

References

Günther, 1971, pp. 48, nos. 1d, 1e, 151, fig. 28;
Nerdinger, ed., 1982, pp. 144, nos. 74e, 74f, 469.

The drawing depicts two chairs designed
by Riemerschmid for a Music Room for
the "Deutsche Kunst-Ausstellung" in
Dresden in 1899 and also shown at the
1900 Exposition Universelle in Paris.

The main feature of the music chair
(left; see no. 93) is the diagonal bracing,
which makes visible the distribution of
thrusts as an organic element of the design, as well as constituting an essential
constructional element. Such bracings are
to be found on other chairs of this period,
but never used with such consistency. A
similar simplicity and elegance characterizes the second chair (see no. 92).

B.-V.K.

92 Armchair, 1898-99

Made by Vereinigte Werkstätten für Kunst im
Handwerk, Munich (established 1897)
Oak and leather, 31¹/₂ x 21¹/₈ x 22" (80 x 53.5 x
55.9 cm)
Marks: 1214, 4058
K. Barlow Ltd., London

References

Schumann, 1899, p. 529 (ill.); *Dekorative Kunst,*
vol. 4 (1899), p. 98 (ill. in Dresden); *Innen-Dekoration,* vol. 12 (1901), p. 211 (ill.); New York,
1960, p. 86; Schmutzler, 1962, p. 201, fig. 210;
Rheims, 1966, p. 232, no. 311; Günther, 1971,

pp. 48, no. 1e, 151, fig. 27; Brussels, 1977, pp. 56-57, no. 58; Frank Russell, ed., *A Century of Chair Design* (London, 1980), p. 64, fig. 1; Munich, *Kandinsky,* 1982, p. 216, fig. 89; New York, 1982, p. 166, fig. 130; Nerdinger, ed., 1982, pp. 17, 142-44, no. 74e, 145; Rammert, 1987, p. 151, no. 74e.

This chair (model number 4058) was designed and made at the same time as Riemerschmid's better-known music chair (no. 93) and it, too, was exhibited in the Music Room at Dresden in 1899, although not on the music platform itself, but at the window table opposite. Both chairs share a strikingly modern simplicity of form and the motif of an undulating curve (here, the arms) connecting the front legs to the back rail.

In 1950 the American designer Edward J. Wormley wrote to Riemerschmid on behalf of the Dunbar Furniture Manufacturing Company of Berne, Indiana, asking for his help in reproducing the chair, which he found remarkably well suited to contemporary needs. The chair was produced that year by Dunbar in a slightly altered version, and, in a Dunbar catalogue of about 1951, was described as "an adaptation of the chair by Professor Richard Riemerschmid, first exhibited in Dresden in 1899, [which] testifies to the enduring nature of good design." Riemerschmid later wrote to Wormley that he was proud "to think that the chair designed more than a half century earlier now occupied this place of honor" (correspondence published in Nerdinger, ed., 1982, pp. 532-33). K.B.H.

93 Chair, 1898-99

Made by Vereinigte Werkstätten für Kunst im Handwerk, Munich (established 1897)
Oak and leather, 30⁵/₈ x 18⁷/₈ x 22¹/₂″ (78 x 48 x 57.2 cm)
Marks: 1213, 4059
K. Barlow Ltd., London

References

Kunst und Handwerk, vol. 49 (1898-99), pp. 282, fig. 422, 283, fig. 423 (in Music Room), 286; Schumann, 1899, pp. 509, 527 (ill.); *Dekorative Kunst,* vol. 4 (1899), p. 99 (ill. in Dresden); Max Osborn, "Deutsches Kunstgewerbe auf der Welt-Ausstellung," *Innendekoration,* vol. 11 (June 1900), pp. 96-97 (ills. in Room of an Art Lover); *Kunstgewerbeblatt,* n. s., vol. 2 (1900), pp. 45 (ill.), 49 (ill. in Music Room); *The Cabinet Maker & Art Furniture* (Dec. 1900), p. 150 (ill.); *Deutsche Kunst und Dekoration,* vol. 7 (1900-1), p. 26 (ill.); Munich, 1. Ausstellung für Kunst im Handwerk, *Katalog* (1901), pp. 8, 29 (ill.); Muthesius, 1905,

p. 86 (ill.); Madsen, 1955, pp. 62, fig. 34, 420-21; Frankfurt, 1955, p. 35, no. 352; Ahlers-Hestermann, 1956, ill. facing p. 17; Hans Eckstein, *50 Jahre Deutscher Werkbund* (Frankfurt, 1958), p. 55, no. 47; Munich, 1958, p. 204, no. 678; Seling, ed., 1959, pp. 87, fig. 75, 86; New York, 1960, pp. 114, 179, no. 236; Paris, 1960-61, p. 387, no. 1.187; Schmutzler, 1962, p. 200, fig. 209; Jean Cassou, Emil Langni, and Nikolaus Pevsner, *Durchbruch zum 20. Jahrhundert: Kunst und Kultur der Jahrhundertwende* (Munich, 1962), p. 242, fig. 302; Pevsner, 1968, p. 172; Edgar Kaufmann, Jr., *Introductions to Modern Design* (repr. New York, 1969), p. 12, fig. 9; Günther, 1971, pp. 48, no. 1d, 151, fig. 26; Himmelheber, 1973, pp. 242, fig. 1059, 386, no. 1059; London, Victoria and Albert Museum, *Liberty's 1875-1975* (July-Oct. 1975), p. 44, no. D6; Houston, Rice University, Institute for the Arts, *Art Nouveau: Belgium/France* (Mar. 26-June 27, 1976), p. 145, fig. 172; Frankfurt, Museum für Kunsthandwerk, *Europäische Möbel von der Gotik bis zum Jugendstil* (1976), p. 172, fig. 227; Hans Eckstein, *Der Stuhl:*

Funktion – Konstruktion – Form, von der Antike bis zur Gegenwart (Munich, 1977), p. 129, fig. 172; Brussels, 1977, pp. 48, 57, no. 61; Philippe Garner, ed., *Phaidon Encyclopedia of Decorative Arts* (Oxford, 1978), p. 213; Edith Holm, *Stühle: Von der Antike bis zur Moderne* (Munich, 1978), no. 471; Frank Russell, ed., *A Century of Chair Design* (London, 1980), p. 64, fig. 1; Nerdinger, ed., 1982, pp. 18, fig. 3, 27, 120, fig. 17, 142-44, no. 74f; Munich, *Kandinsky,* 1982, p. 205, fig. 59; New York, 1982, p. 94, fig. 18; Alistair Duncan, *Art Nouveau Furniture* (New York, 1982), no. 164; S. Wichmann, *Jugendstil Floral,* 1984, p. 126, fig. 258; S. Wichmann, 1984, p. 126, fig. 258; H. Wichmann, 1985, p. 194; Rammert, 1987, p. 152, no. 74f.

This chair (model number 4059) remains Riemerschmid's best-known work and was considered remarkable by his contemporaries when first exhibited at the Dresden "Deutsche Kunst-Ausstellung" in 1899 and at the 1900 Exposition Universelle in Paris. Reviewing the Dresden exhibition in the 1899 volume of *Dekorative Kunst*, Paul Schultze-Naumburg praised Riemerschmid's "original ideas of construction which, in his hands, become lines of decoration." Designed as a musician's seat and set on a small platform, the chair was part of a group of music room furniture commissioned from the Vereinigte Werkstätten by the royal Bavarian court piano factory J. Mayer & Co., Munich, who wished to install a music room with their piano "in plain but modern shape" at the Paris and Dresden exhibitions. After 1900 a slightly altered version of the original chair, as well as a version with chamfered decorations, was produced by Liberty & Co., London, and continues in production today. K.B.H.

95 Table, 1899

Made by Vereinigte Werkstätten für Kunst im Handwerk, Munich (established 1897)
Walnut and walnut veneer, 28 x 20¹/₂ x 20¹/₂″ (71 x 52 x 52 cm)
Stadtmuseum, Munich. 49/54

References

Munich, 1958, p. 204, no. 675; Nerdinger, ed., 1982, p. 146, no. 76b; Rammert, 1987, p. 160, no. 76b; Ottomeyer, 1988, pp. 72, 74, no. 13.6.

Riemerschmid was commissioned by Obrist to design furniture for a boudoir and a bedroom in his house in Munich's Schwabing district. Documentation for this furniture is far less complete than for Pankok's work at the Villa Obrist (see nos. 65, 67-69). The bedroom set has not survived (see Nerdinger, ed., 1982, p. 148, no. 77), photographs of the entire room are not extant, and correspondence between the two artists on the subject is limited (September and October 1898, Archiv für Bildende Kunst, Germanisches Nationalmuseum, Nuremberg). Views of the furniture are illustrated in *Dekorative Kunst* (vol. 5 [1900], pp. 190-93), but these give no clear idea of the original context. The pieces were executed by the Vereinigte Werkstätten, whose archives contain all the model numbers and corresponding drawings.

Characteristic of all the furniture in the boudoir set (see also nos. 96-98) is a slab construction that, in the load-bearing members, is a prime determinant of form. The legs or supports taper outward from bottom to top, then bulge out at both sides to form a T at the frame, with which they are set flush – a motif that recalls the Egyptian "papyrus" column. These shafts and capitals work both aesthetically and functionally, serving as a central reinforcement on the chair backs (see no. 97), as a support for the lower shelf in this table (model number 840), and as a support for the shelves of the cabinet.   H.O.

94 Table Lamp, 1899

Made by Vereinigte Werkstätten für Kunst im Handwerk, Munich (established 1897)
Brass and glass, height 17¹/₂″ (44.5 cm)
K. Barlow Ltd., London

References

Muthesius, "Neues Ornament," 1901, p. 358 (ill.); Nerdinger, ed., 1982, pp. 275, no. 286, 286, fig. 58.

Produced by the Vereinigte Werkstätten in 1900 (model number 1251), the lamp is a later version of the 1898 Riemerschmid design preserved in the collection of the Technische Universität, Munich (4029), a model of which was exhibited at the Munich Glaspalast in 1899, at the 1900 Exposition Universelle in Paris, and at the St. Louis world's fair in 1904. In the original design the electrical cord largely supported the weight of the lamp and was strung diagonally, like a bow-string, across the supporting stem between hood and foot. The solution in the version shown here is far more elegant, with the cord concealed entirely in the stem and the bell-shaped foot. Like Riemerschmid's "tall" candlestick (no. 86), the design of foot, stem, and shade is conceived in a delicate floral idiom.   K.B.H.

96 Table, 1899

Made by Vereinigte Werkstätten für Kunst im
Handwerk, Munich (established 1897)
Walnut and walnut veneer, 27⁷/₈ x 23¹/₄ x 23¹/₄″
(71 x 59 x 59 cm)
Stadtmuseum, Munich. 49/53

References

Obrist, "Wozu," 1900, p. 191 (ill. in Villa
Obrist); *Illustrirte Zeitung,* vol. 114b, no. 2962
(Apr. 5, 1900), p. 449 (ill.); Nerdinger, ed., 1982,
p. 146, no. 75b; Rammert, 1987, p. 158, no. 75b;
Ottomeyer, 1988, pp. 72, 74, no. 13.5.

The side table (model number 839), like
the other boudoir furniture for the Villa
Obrist (nos. 95, 97-98), displays the characteristic T shape at the top of the legs.
The four flat legs are set at an angle and
connected at the top by gently arched
sidepieces.   H.O.

97 Chair, 1899

Made by Vereinigte Werkstätten für Kunst im
Handwerk, Munich (established 1897)
Walnut, 35³/₄ x 17⁵/₈ x 16¹/₂″ (91 x 45 x 42 cm)
Marks: 1205, 4256 (stamped)
Stadtmuseum, Munich. 49/55

References

Obrist, "Wozu," 1900, p. 191 (ill. in Villa
Obrist); *Illustrirte Zeitung,* vol. 114b, no. 2962
(Apr. 5, 1900), pp. 499 (ill.), no. 3, 500, no. 6;
H. D. Molesworth and John Kenworthy-
Browne, *Three Centuries of Furniture* (New York,
1972), p. 313, no. 527; Himmelheber, 1973 (2nd
ed., 1983), p. 245, fig. 1060; Nerdinger, ed.,
1982, pp. 120, fig. 16, 146, no. 75c; Rammert,
1987, pp. 158-59; Ottomeyer, 1988, pp. 72, 74,
no. 13.4,1.

The chair (model number 1205), part of
the furnishings for the boudoir of the
Villa Obrist (see also nos. 95-96, 98), was
inspired by a French neoclassical design
called *en gondole,* an armchair in which
armrests and backrest form a semicircle.
The flared back legs of Riemerschmid's
chair extend up beyond the seat to support the open frame of the back, meeting
at the point where a curved crosspiece
provides transverse bracing.   H.O.

98 Desk, 1899

Made by Vereinigte Werkstätten für Kunst im
Handwerk, Munich (established 1897)
Oak, walnut veneer, and silver-plated bronze;
29¹/₂ x 57¹/₈ x 43¹/₄″ (75 x 145 x 110 cm)
Stadtmuseum, Munich. 49/52

References

Obrist, "Wozu," 1900, p. 191 (ill. in Villa
Obrist); *Illustrirte Zeitung,* vol. 114b, no. 2962
(Apr. 5, 1900), p. 500 (ill.); Munich, 1958, p. 204,
no. 674; Herbert Schindler, *Grosse Bayerische
Kunstgeschichte* (Munich, 1963), p. 385; Nerdinger, ed., 1982, p. 146, no. 75a; Rammert,
1987, p. 157; Ottomeyer, 1988, pp. 72, 74,
no. 13.3.

The five-legged, irregularly hexagonal
desk (model number 838) shows the flat
T shape characteristic of Riemerschmid's
furniture for the boudoir of the Villa Obrist (see also nos. 95-97) on the front two
legs, which merge with the case contain-
ing three drawers of equal height. The
unusual design fulfills functional requirements, for the offset top provides a great
deal of working and storage space.   H.O.

manuscript illumination and of the portals of such stave churches as those at Urnes and Hemse in Norway. In contrast to the upward thrust of the junglelike tendrils of the doorframe decoration, the carpet and wallpaper in the actual room bore an extremely delicate pattern of leaves. An interior design of this kind shows how far the new movement had come from the rooms created in previous decades on the basis of Italian and German Renaissance models.   B.-V.K.

99 Design for Room of an Art Lover, 1899–1900

Pencil and colored pencil on paper, 20 x 17⁷/₈″ (50.7 x 44 cm)
Architektursammlung der Technischen Universität, Munich. RR 2430

References

Paris, 1900, p. 315, no. 3727; Munich, 1958, pp. 205, no. 689, 249; Paris, 1960–61, p. 380, no. 1.198; Munich, 1970, p. 14, no. 149; Günther, 1971, pp. 44–45, no. 1a, fig. 21, 149–50; Darmstadt, 1976–77, vol. 2, p. 24, fig. 31; Munich, *Kandinsky*, 1982, p. 214, no. 85; New York, 1982, p. 98, no. 24; Nerdinger, ed., 1982, pp. 152–53, no. 83c, 468.

The drawing belongs to Riemerschmid's designs for the Room of an Art Lover shown at the 1900 Exposition Universelle in Paris. It was a popular theme at the time: M.H. Baillie Scott, for example, produced designs in 1901 for a House of an Art Lover. In this drawing the artist links the frieze-like ornament to broad curving bands that cut into the cavetto between wall and ceiling, thus providing continuous interlaced decoration from the skirting board up to the ceiling. The pattern itself is reminiscent of Carolingian

100 Design for Room of an Art Lover, 1899–1900

Pencil and colored pencil on paper, 21¼ x 30¹¹/₁₆"
(54 x 78 cm)
Architektursammlung der Technischen
Universität, Munich. RR 2436

References

Paris, 1900, p. 315, no. 3727; Munich, 1958,
p. 206, no. 691; Paris, 1960–61, p. 380, no. 1.201;
Munich, 1970, p. 14, no. 147; Günther, 1971,
pp. 44–45, no. 22, 149–50; Darmstadt, 1976–77,
vol. 2, p. 24, no. 31; Nerdinger, ed., 1982,
pp. 116, fig. 10, 152–53, no. 83a.

A number of preliminary sketches for the
door and the stucco frieze in the Room
of an Art Lover show how intensely
Riemerschmid worked on the interlaced
decoration and its arrangement. The view
of the wall contains a section of the
cavetto at the ceiling, a doorframe, and a
continuous interlacing frieze. A striking
feature of the drawing is the self-con-
tained design of the doorframe, with
forms that are not directly related to those
of the frieze interlace. Yet the shape of the
doorframe is closely linked with its decoration, since the arch of the doorway con-
stitutes the arch of a bridge, across which
women and men of various ages are
walking (see no. 101). The idea of movement, proceeding from the sides of the
door and continuing across the arch of the
door lintel, culminates in the intricate
forms of the frieze. The motif of water,
repeatedly hinted at in the decoration of
the doorframe, gives the whole an animated elegance.   B.-V. K.

101 Path of Life, 1899–1900

Oil on panel, 36⅝ x 79½" (93 x 202 cm)
Signature: RR (intertwined) (lower right)
Architektursammlung der Technischen
Universität, Munich. 193

References

Obrist, 1901, p. 351 (ill.); Günther, 1971,
pp. 45–46, no. 1b, 150; Nerdinger, ed., 1982,
pp. 100, no. 29, 153.

The painting was originally positioned
over a door in the Room of an Art Lover
(see no. 100), one of the interiors that
Riemerschmid called "unified, total
works of art" and that represented the applied arts of Germany at the 1900 Paris
Exposition Universelle. The design, with
its eleven hieratic figures, is painted in
muted hues of blue and green which com-
plemented the color scheme of the room
and its furnishings.   C. S. v. W. S.

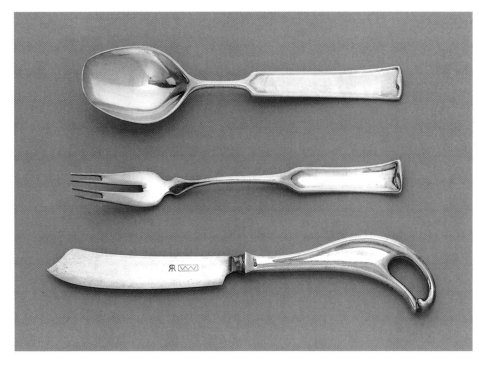

schmid's twelve-piece silver table setting was developed from a design of 1898. It impressed the critic of *Kunst und Handwerk* (vol. 51 [1900-1], p. 356) as "at last reintroducing blades and tines of character." Compared to the tableware then in common use, the knives, with their scimitar blades, seem the most revolutionary feature of the set. Unusual, too, are the design of the fork, which has two paired tines, and the asymmetry of the oyster fork, while the spoon conforms most closely to traditional forms. C. S. v. W. S.

102 Cutlery, 1899-1900

Made by Vereinigte Werkstätten für Kunst im Handwerk, Munich (established 1897)
Silver
a) lengths, knife 9³/₈″ (23.8 cm), fork 7³/₄″ (19.8 cm), spoon 7⁵/₈″ (19.3 cm)
Marks: moon, crown, 800, RR, VW (intertwined)
Stadtmuseum, Munich. Gift of Siegfried Rothkappel, Munich. K 86-3/1-3
b) lengths, oyster fork 6³/₄″ (17.2 cm), butter knife 8¹/₈″ (20.5 cm), cheese knife 8¹/₄″ (21 cm)
Marks: RR, VW (intertwined)
Württembergisches Landesmuseum, Stuttgart. G 4039a, e, f

References

Munich, "Secession," 1899, p. 50, no. 606c-1; "Neues aus den Vereinigten Werkstätten für Kunst im Handwerk, München," *Dekorative Kunst,* vol. 3 (1899), pp. 145, 153 (ill.); *Deutsche Kunst und Dekoration,* vol. 5 (1899-1900), p. 25 (ill.); Paris, 1900, p. 350, no. 4508 (ill.); *Illustrirte Zeitung,* vol. 114b, no. 2971 (June 7, 1900), p. 845 (ill.); *Kunst und Handwerk,* vol. 51 (1900-1), p. 356; Muthesius, "Neues Ornament," 1901, p. 358 (ill.); Turin, 1902, p. 69, no. 176; St. Louis, *Official Catalogue,* 1904, p. 436, no. 2222; Warlich, 1908, pp. 102-3 (ill.); Seling, ed., 1959, p. 347, fig. 301; New York, 1960, pp. 115, 179, no. 237; Pforzheim, Schmuckmuseum im Reuchlinhaus, *Goldschmiedekunst des Jugendstils: Schmuck und Gerät um 1900* (May 10-Sept. 22, 1963), p. 23, nos. 1-2, pl. 26; Munich, Die Neue Sammlung, *Essgerät* (Oct. 14-Nov. 30, 1963), no. 24; Hans Eckstein, *Die Neue Sammlung* (Munich, 1965), fig. 95; Rheims, 1966, p. 350, no. 478; Herwin Schaefer, *Nineteenth Century Modern: The Functional Tradition in Victorian Design* (New York, 1970), p. 167, fig. 246; Nuremberg, Landesgewerbeanstalt, *Gold + Silber: Schmuck + Gerät* (Mar. 19-Aug. 22, 1971), nos. 11, 83; Günther, 1971, pp. 50, no. 1m, 153; Selle, 1974, p. 113, fig. 13; James MacKay, *Kunst*

und Kunsthandwerk der Jahrhundertwende (Munich, 1974), p. 34; Brussels, 1977, p. 132, no. 223; Gasser, ed., 1977, p. 34; Gertrud Benker, *Altes Besteck* (Munich, 1978), p. 171, fig. 340; Solingen, Deutsches Klingenmuseum, *Bestecke des Jugendstils* (Sept. 23-Nov. 25, 1979), pp. 90-91, figs. 103-4; Munich, Villa Stuck, 1979, p. 14, no. 103, fig. 24; Kurt Junghanns, *Der Deutsche Werkbund: Sein Erstes Jahrzehnt* (Berlin, 1982), pp. 68, 69, no. 23; Nerdinger, ed., 1982, p. 294, no. 325; Edward Lucie-Smith, *A History of Industrial Design* (Oxford, 1983), p. 97, fig. 165; Masini, 1984, p. 178, fig. 477; H. Wichmann, 1985, p. 153.

Shown at many international exhibitions at the turn of the century, Riemer-

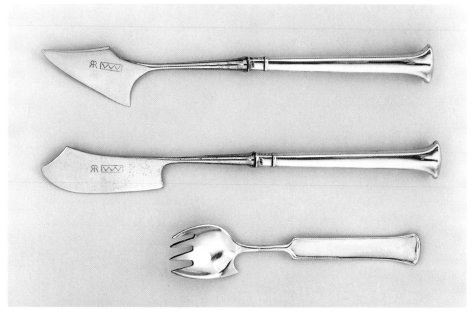

103 Jug, 1900

Made by Reinhold Merkelbach, Grenzhausen
(established 1845)
Stoneware, colored and salt-glazed; height 12⅞″
(32.5 cm)
Mark: 1656
K. Barlow Ltd., London

References

Merkelbach, 1905, pp. 53, no. 1656, 86, fig. 75,
87; Rée, 1906, p. 282 (ill.); Woeckel, 1968, no. 50,
fig. 50; Berlin, Sammlung Karl H. Bröhan, *Porzellan-Kunst* (1969), p. 139, no. 979; Berlin, 1976,
pp. 386, no. 526, 387, no. 526; Brussels, 1977,
p. 218, no. 472, fig. 472; Cologne, 1978, p. 222,
no. 433, fig. 433; Nerdinger, ed., 1982, pp. 281,
fig. 51, 324, no. 395.

One of the earliest models designed by
Riemerschmid for the Merkelbach factory (number 1656), the jug belongs to
a highly regarded series of vessels by Riemerschmid that were mostly produced
between 1900 and 1908. Riemerschmid's
first ceramic designs appear to have been
jugs produced for the Vereinigte Werkstätten by the firm of Villeroy & Boch in
Mettlach and shown at the Paris Exposition Universelle of 1900. However, it was
the Merkelbach series that, through
Riemerschmid's judicious use of traditional forms and techniques as shaped by
his modernist taste, brought the stoneware industry of the Westerwald into the
twentieth century. Riemerschmid's particular approach was appreciated by contemporary critics, even if the results were
not always considered uniformly pleasing, as one commentator in 1907 explained: "Riemerschmid, who ... could
not submit to the constraints of an inher-
ited style, tried to compel the plastic mass
into novel shapes with charming irregularities. He has sufficient appreciation of
the material not to violate the stonelike
mass with lightly constructed shapes. Indeed, he stresses the massiveness a shade
too strongly. In his perception of the
material's characteristics he follows the
old stoneware potters. Although the decorations are strictly modern in origin, and
used in sparse and startlingly capricious
ways, they nestle against the body of the
vessel as the old reliefs did" (quoted in
Berlin, 1976, p. 387). 　　K.B.H.

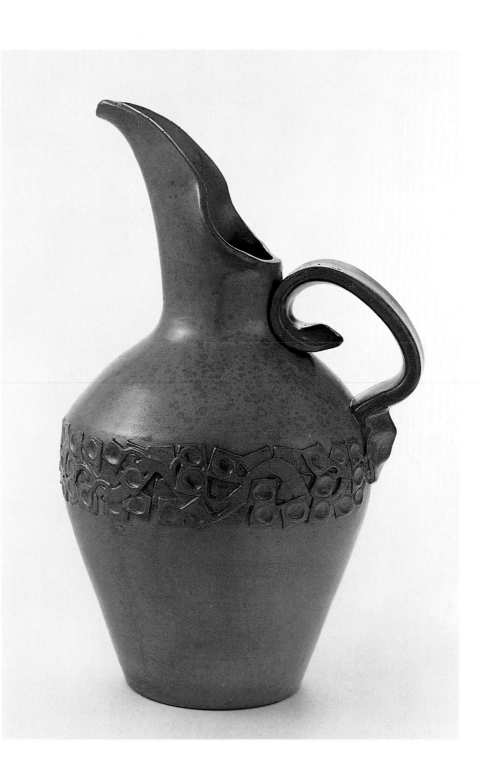

104 Chandelier, 1900

Made by Vereinigte Werkstätten für Kunst im Handwerk, Munich (established 1897)
Brass and glass, height 51¼″ (130 cm)
The Museum of Modern Art, New York. Phyllis B. Lambert Fund. 180.58a-j

References

Deutsche Werkstätten für Handwerkskunst Dresden, *Preisbuch 1908: Beleuchtungskörper* (Dresden, 1908), no. 586; Deutsche Werkstätten für Handwerkskunst GmbH, *Preisbuch 4: Beleuchtungskörper* (Dresden-Hellerau, 1911), p. 54 (ill.); *Baukunst und Werkform,* no. 9 (1952), p. 21; Zurich, 1952, p. 18; *Wissenschaftliche Zeitschrift der Technischen Hochschule Dresden* (1952-53), p. 188, fig. 14; Günther, 1971, fig. 35; H. Wichmann, 1978, p. 192; Nerdinger, ed., 1982, p. 276, no. 289.

Said to have been installed by Riemerschmid in his house in the Pasing district of Munich (see no. 132), the four-armed chandelier was a popular model. It is a variant of a design produced by Konrad König, Munich, and was made by the Vereinigte Werkstätten (model number 586) and, later, by the Deutsche Werkstätten, who offered it for sale in their catalogues of lamps and lighting fixtures. The original design is preserved in the collection of the Technische Universität, Munich (M.166.2). As in almost all of Riemerschmid's pendant fixtures, the weight of the lamps is held by the electrical cords, although here, part of the load is transferred to a skeletal cross frame suspended from the ceiling plate by chains. The ability to reduce the various elements of frame, lamps, cords, and chains to a simple, concisely constructed quadrangular arrangement distinguished Riemerschmid from his contemporaries – even from the English designer W. A. S. Benson, whose pioneering lighting appliances were published in Germany by Hermann Muthesius ("Benson's Electrische Beleuchtungskörper," *Die Kunst,* vol. 6 [1902], pp. 104-10), who in 1904 described the Englishman as the "fruitful instigator" of such pendant electric lights on the Continent (Hermann Muthesius, *The English House,* ed. Dennis Sharp [London, 1979], p. 199).   K.B.H.

105 Garden of Eden, 1900

Oil on canvas, with gessoed and painted wood frame; 63 x 64½″ (160 x 164 cm) (with frame)
Signature: RR 1900 (lower right)
Inscription: "UND GOTT DER HERR / PFLANZTE EINEN / GARTEN IN EDEN" (on frame, bottom)
K. Barlow Ltd., London

References

Die Kunst, vol. 4 (1901), p. 333 (ill.); Nerdinger, ed., 1982, frontispiece, p. 90, no. 22e.

The painting is the second version of a well-known canvas by Riemerschmid that was purchased by the Dresden Gemäldegalerie on May 7, 1897, and destroyed at the end of World War II. Riemerschmid created this version in 1900 for unknown reasons, making a number of changes to the original: he eliminated the figures of Adam and Eve and the animals, moved the Tree of Life off center, reduced the halo that surrounded the tree to a fine line, toned down the colors, and gave the painting a rounded top edge. In doing so, Riemerschmid may have intended to rid the painting of its more overt Symbolist features, but he was also responding to the lively criticism leveled at the first version by conservative members of the Saxon parliament, who railed against its garish colors, ugly figures, and blasphemous halo around the Tree of Life. As in Riemerschmid's designs for the Room of an Art Lover shown at the 1900 Paris exhibition (see nos. 99-100), the painting is framed by gently interlacing tendrils and, at the curved top, by thinly carved rays, which reinforce both the naturalism of the subject and the supernatural aureole surrounding the tree.   K.B.H.

106 Glass from the "Riemerschmid" Service, 1900

Made by Benedikt von Poschinger, Ober-
zwieselau (active 1880-1919)
Clear crystal glass, height 5⁷/₈″ (15 cm)
Stadtmuseum, Munich. K 88/12

References
Muthesius, "Neues Ornament," 1901, p. 359
(ill.); *Velhagen und Klasings Monatshefte* (1903-4),
p. 128 (ill.); Nerdinger, ed., 1982, p. 304, no. 358.

One of the earliest glasses designed by
Riemerschmid, this glass for red wine
comes from the "Riemerschmid" service,
one of a series that the artist created for
the Poschinger firm between 1900 and
World War I. Benedikt von Poschinger
was notably progressive when commis-
sioning outside artists to design his
table glasses, employing, among others,
BEHRENS (no. 11), NIEMEYER (no. 51), and
REICHENBACH from Munich, Curt Stoeving from Berlin, and Albin Müller from
Darmstadt. Highly regarded for their
simple shapes, the Poschinger glasses
were thought to be a considerable improvement on ordinary commercial
glasswares. As the critic of *Die Kunst*
wrote in 1901, "Of the individual objects
reproduced here, the Riemerschmid
glasses are the most noteworthy. They
are not quite as charming as the Behrens
glasses for everyday use, the artist probably being afraid of establishing too close
a relationship to the former. The glasses
should be in more general use, as they are
hardly more expensive than commercial
wares and their elegant, simple shapes are
always pleasing to the eye" (Nerdinger,
ed., 1982, p. 304, no. 358).

The five-piece service consisted of
champagne, red wine, Bordeaux, Madeira, and dessert wineglasses.   K.B.H.

107 Glasses, c. 1901

Made by Benedikt von Poschinger, Oberzwieselau (active 1880-1919)
Clear crystal glass, heights a) champagne 5¹/₂″
(14 cm), b) white wine 5¹⁵/₁₆″ (15 cm),
c) port 3¹⁵/₁₆″ (10 cm)
Private collection

References
Heinz Thiersch, "Richard Riemerschmid 86
Jahre," *Die Innenarchitektur,* vol. 2 (1954-55),
p. 81; Hans Eckstein, *50 Jahre Deutscher Werkbund*
(Frankfurt, 1958), p. 56, no. 57; Munich, 1964,
p. 123, nos. 1024-28; Nerdinger, ed., 1982,
p. 307, no. 364; "Recent Acquisitions of Post-
Medieval Ceramics and Glass in the British
Museum's Department of Medieval and Later
Antiquities (1982-88)," *Burlington Magazine,*
vol. 130 (May 1988), p. 403, fig. 92.

Part of a six-piece service, the glasses are
characteristic of Riemerschmid's more
advanced designs for Poschinger, their
waved outline of convex bulges constituting the only decoration of an otherwise
simple geometric shape. This concentra-
tion on pure form, with its attendant abstract character, appears elsewhere in
Riemerschmid's work and establishes a
point of view that would eventually be
shared by most progressive industrial designers of the twentieth century. One
contemporary critic found Riemerschmid's formal language to be determined by respect for the nature of materials and for an object's practical use: "It is
the shape that serves him, as well as the
function and his own will to create....
You will find that ... the shape was never
invented, but extracted for its own
aesthetic purpose from the nature of
things themselves.... so with Riemerschmid we can speak of a canon of
beauty" (Rée, 1906, pp. 281, 286).

K.B.H.

108 Glasses from the "Menzel" Service, 1903

Made by Benedikt von Poschinger, Oberzwieselau (active 1880–1919)
Blown, optical glass, height 7″ (17.8 cm)
Stadtmuseum, Munich. K 81-5,1

References

Muthesius, 1904, pp. 270 (ill.), 273 (ill.); Dresdner Werkstätten für Handwerkskunst, *Preisliste 1907: Dresdner Kleingerät* (Dresden, 1907), no. 618a-h; Heyck, ed., 1907, p. 422, pl. 71; Deutsche Werkstätten für Handwerkskunst Dresden, *Kleingerät* (Dresden, 1909), nos. 253-60; *Jahrbuch des Deutschen Werkbundes* (1912), p. 63; Hans Eckstein, *Die Neue Sammlung* (Munich, 1965), fig. 102; Schack, 1971, pp. 113, 240, fig. 51; Christel Mosel, *Kunsthandwerk im Umbruch* (Hanover, 1971), p. 34, no. 41; Munich, Die Neue Sammlung, *Eine Auswahl aus dem Besitz des Museums* (1972), fig. 33; Bott, 1973, pp. 235, no. 280, 260; Brussels, 1977, p. 246, no. 580; Darmstadt, Hessisches Landesmuseum, *Jugendstil: Kunst um 1900* (1982), p. 260, no. 342; Nerdinger, ed., 1982, p. 308, no. 366.

The glasses for Rhine wine originally belonged to a seven-piece set marketed under the name "Menzel." Although an early design, it already shows Riemerschmid in full command of the glass medium. Lent stability by a hollow, funnel-like foot and stem, the glasses have a simple and graceful pattern of grooves that underscores its form, produced by an old glassmaking technique revived here to wonderful effect.

C. S. v. W. S.

109 Champagne Bucket, c. 1902

Made by Konrad König, Munich
(active c. 1887-1911)
Brass, height 10″ (25.5 cm)
Stadtmuseum, Munich. K 66-1234

References

Muthesius, 1904, p. 272 (ill.); Warlich, 1908,
p. 75 (ill.); Nerdinger, ed., 1982, p. 296, no. 330.

According to Hermann Muthesius, "the inherent development of form out of function [was] the prime motive" for Riemerschmid's work in all mediums (Muthesius, 1904, p. 276). This is apparent in this vase-shaped champagne bucket, which was made in the little-known family business of the master locksmith Konrad König (Stadtarchiv, Munich, G 157). Apart from the two flattened handles, forked at the bottom and attached with small plates, the only ornaments on the bucket are eight vertical notches on the shoulder and a zigzag border around the neck. The beauty of the metal is enhanced by the matte patina of its surface.   C.S. v. W.S.

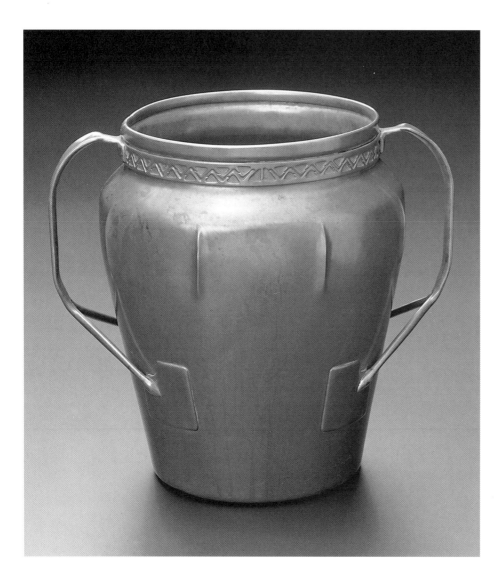

110 Jug, 1903

Made by Reinhold Merkelbach, Grenzhausen
(established 1845)
Stoneware, colored and glazed, with painted
decoration, and pewter; height 7¹/₄″ (18.2 cm)
Mark: 1769 S (impressed)
Stadtmuseum, Munich. K 59-861

References

Kunst und Handwerk, vol. 54 (1903-4), p. 271,
fig. 481; Muthesius, 1904, p. 273 (ill.); Merkelbach, 1905, p. 86, no. 1769, fig. 75; *Deutsche
Kunst und Dekoration,* vol. 17 (1905-6), p. 258
(ills.); *Innen-Dekoration,* vol. 17 (1906), pp. 23
(ill.), 24 (ill.), 141 (ill.); Rudolf Klein, "Die
Deutsche Kunstausstellung in Köln," *Deutsche
Kunst und Dekoration,* vol. 18 (1906), p. 641 (ill.);
Deutsche Kunst und Dekoration, vol. 19 (1906-7),
p. 132 (ill.); *Fachblatt für Holzarbeiter,* vol. 2
(1907), p. 188 (ill.); Warlich, 1908, p. 92 (ill.);
G. E. Lüthgen, *Deutsches Steinzeug, behandelt im
Anschluss an den Wettbewerb für Studentenkunst
Stuttgart 1909* (1909; repr. Munich, 1981), p. 3
(ill.); *Jahrbuch des Deutschen Werkbundes* (1912),
p. 63; Munich, Stadtmuseum, 1972, p. 531,
no. 2185; Gerhard P. Woeckel, "Münchens Kunst
im Jugendstil: Kunsthandwerk um die Jahrhundertwende," *Weltkunst,* vol. 43, no. 15 (Aug. 1,
1973), pp. 1205-6; Brussels, 1977, p. 217,
no. 469; Munich, *Kandinsky, 1982,* p. 219,
no. 105; Nerdinger, ed., 1982, pp. 285, fig. 56,
330-31, no. 408.

In ceramics Riemerschmid's name is associated primarily with stoneware manufactured in the Westerwald, which drew the
highest praise from critics and soon began
to be produced in series. His designs,
which emerged from his own experiments at the potter's wheel, adapted age-
old techniques to modern production
methods; they featured solid forms derived from the properties of the material
and simple patterns in traditional colors.
Representative of the many Riemerschmid designs produced by Merkelbach,
the jug (model number 1769) has a spherical body ornamented in a pattern of offset, rounded lozenges, while the neck is
decorated with a border of stylized leaves
and flowers. The same decoration was
applied by Riemerschmid to another,
closely related Merkelbach jug (model
number 1734) and its accompanying
tankards (model number 1728).

C. S. v. W. S.

112 Armchair, 1903

Made by B. Kohlbecker & Sohn, Munich
(established 1890)
Stained mahogany, wool felt, and brass; 39¹/₄ x
24³/₈ x 20¹/₄″ (99.5 x 62 x 51.5 cm)
Stadtmuseum, Munich. 58/937a

References

Innen-Dekoration, vol. 13 (1902), p. 106 (ill.);
Muthesius, 1904, p. 288 (ill.); Munich, 1958,
pp. 203, no. 670a, 275; Paris, 1960-61, p. 379,
no. 1191; Pevsner, 1968, pp. 83-84, fig. 80;
Munich, 1970, p. 9, no. 59; Himmelheber, 1973,
pp. 243, fig. 1051, 385-86, no. 1051; Prague,
1980, pp. 71, no. 130b, 99; Frank Russell, ed., *A
Century of Chair Design* (London, 1980), p. 65,
fig. 2; Munich, *Kandinsky,* 1982, p. 213, no. 82;
Alistair Duncan, *Art Nouveau Furniture* (New
York, 1982), no. 163; Nerdinger, ed., 1982,
pp. 121, fig. 20, 167-68, no. 97 f; Bouillon, 1985,
pp. 168, 242; Ottomeyer, 1988, pp. 86, 89,
no. 16.5,1.

Riemerschmid designed a pair of armchairs and twenty-two side chairs for the
dining room in the residence of Karl
Thieme and his wife, friends of Riemer-

111 Chair, 1903

Made by B. Kohlbecker & Sohn, Munich
(established 1890)
Stained mahogany, wool felt, and brass; 30¹¹/₁₆ x
18¹/₈ x 21¹/₄″ (78 x 46 x 54 cm)
Stadtmuseum, Munich. 58/936

References

Heyck, ed., 1907, p. 419, pl. 39; Günther, 1971,
p. 86, fig. 73; Munich, Stadtmuseum, 1972,
p. 525, no. 2099; Himmelheber, 1973, p. 387,
no. 1067; Darmstadt, 1976-77, vol. 2, p. 43,
fig. 52; Brussels, 1977, p. 57, fig. 62b; Frank
Russell, ed., *A Century of Chair Design* (London,
1980), p. 65, fig. 3; Munich, *Kandinsky,* 1982,
p. 213, fig. 83; *Antiquitäten-Zeitung,* no. 20,1
(Oct. 14, 1982), p. 530, figs. 2-3; Nerdinger, ed.,
1982, pp. 167, 168, no. 97e; Ottomeyer, 1988,
pp. 86, 91, no. 16.6.

schmid whose drawing room, library, and living room he had designed in 1898. For the large, bay-windowed dining room of the house in Munich's Schwabing district Riemerschmid designed an informal and highly asymmetrical arrangement of furniture, in which each piece was adapted to the floor plan and the sequence of windows. A unifying feature of the overall design, which included lighting fixtures and tiles, was the contrast between the polished red wood of the chairs and the matte blue of their upholstery, a color scheme that was echoed in the other furniture of the room and in the carpet (no. 121).   H.O.

113 Floor Clock, 1903

Made by B. Kohlbecker & Sohn, Munich (established 1890)
Stained mahogany, spruce, and brass; 89³/₈ x 29¹/₂ x 22⁷/₁₆″ (227 x 75 x 57 cm)
Stadtmuseum, Munich. 72/375.

References

Nerdinger, ed., 1982, pp. 167, 168, no. 97c; Ottomeyer, 1988, pp. 86, 91, no. 16.10.

The clock belonged to the dining-room furniture commissioned from Riemerschmid by Karl Thieme and his wife for their Munich residence (see also nos. 111–12). With its bold, simple silhouette, the clock is characteristically clear in construction, while the effect of the spruce inlays combined with the dark red of the wood recalls East Asian lacquerwork, an art that influenced much Jugendstil design.   H.O.

115 Design for a Plate, 1903–4

Ink, pencil, and wash on tracing paper,
13⁹/₁₆ x 11″ (34.5 x 28 cm)
Architektursammlung der Technischen
Universität, Munich. RR 3866

References

Nerdinger, ed., 1982, pp. 316, no. 383k/2, 317;
Johannes Just, *Meissener Jugendstil-Porzellan* (Leipzig, 1983), pp. 151-52; Johannes Just, *Meissen Porcelain of the Art Nouveau Period,* trans. Edward Larkey (London, 1985), pp. 130-31.

The design for a plate, dated 1904 in a later hand, was produced in response to a request by the Königliche Porzellan-Manufaktur Meissen for Riemerschmid to design a more up-to-date range of porcelain to stand beside the "onion pattern" that the manufactory had been making since 1740 (see no. 116). Riemerschmid designed a plate whose cross-section has a much flatter relation between center and rim than the older service. The ornamentation is limited to the rim and consists of stylized branches with rounded leaves. This simple pattern is enlivened by the slight spiraling motion of the stalks, which run toward the edge in several rows. This basic pattern and the scattered leaves occur on all pieces in the service. However, Riemerschmid was concerned not only with the shape and decoration, but with the practical aspect

114 Design for a Textile, 1902

Ink, pencil, and colored pencil on paper,
19¹/₂ x 19¹/₂″ (49.5 x 49.5 cm)
Architektursammlung der Technischen
Universität, Munich. F4

Reference

Nerdinger, ed., 1982, pp. 360, no. 469, 367,
colorpl. 59.

The drawing is one of Riemerschmid's earliest textile designs. A preliminary sketch, executed in ink and pencil on tracing paper and showing the main motif in reduced size, is dated "24.1.02," carries the note "Schwarz auf schwarzem Grund" (black on black ground), and is signed with an encircled "RR." The sheet shown here has the buds in color. The motif consists of interlinked, spiral-shaped vines, the centers of which form the main element of the pattern. Riemerschmid used spirals and bud shapes, or heart-shaped leaves, arranged in different patterns not only in his textile designs but also on wallpapers and linoleum. This design was produced by the Dresdner Werkstätten, and was illustrated among other woven and printed furnishing fabrics designed by Riemerschmid in an article by Rée in *Die Kunst* of 1906 (Rée, 1906, p. 302).   B.-V. K.

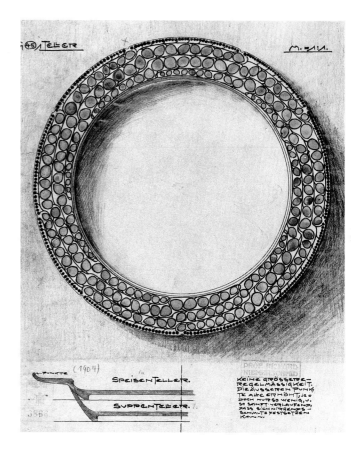

as well: "The outer edges are all raised, but only very slightly, sloping so gently that no dirt can settle anywhere," as his inscription on the sheet states.

With its simple forms and rather traditional pattern, Riemerschmid's porcelain appears light and elegant in comparison with the "onion pattern." B.-V.K.

116 Pieces from a Coffee and Dinner Service, 1903–5

Made by Königlich-Sächsische Porzellan-Manufaktur, Meissen (established 1710)
Hard-paste porcelain with painted underglaze decoration; a) coffeepot, height 8¹/₁₆″ (20.5 cm), b) creamer, height 4¹/₈″ (10.5 cm), c) plate, diameter 14³/₈″ (36.5 cm), d) sugar bowl, height 4¹/₈″ (10.5 cm), e) cups, height 2³/₈″ (6 cm), f) saucers, diameter 5¹/₂″ (13.9 cm)
Marks: crossed swords (underglaze)
K. Barlow Ltd., London

References

Kunstgewerbeblatt, n. s., vol. 17 (1906), p. 237 (ill.); Rée, 1906, p. 283 (ill.); Schumacher, et al., 1906, p. 157 (ill.); Heyck, ed., 1907, p. 422, pl. 72; Warlich, 1908, p. 87 (ill.); K. Berling, *Meissen China: An Illustrated History* (1910; repr. New York, 1972), p. 103, fig. 275; *Jahrbuch des Deutschen Werkbundes* (Munich, 1915), p. 32; Annelore Leistikow-Duchardt, *Die Entwicklung eines neuen Stiles im Porzellan* (Heidelberg, 1957), pp. 55, 104–5, figs. 70–71, pl. 33; Munich, 1958, p. 207, nos. 698–99; *250 Jahre Staatliche Porzellan-Manufaktur Meissen* (Berlin, 1960), fig. 38; Irene von Treskow, *Die Jugendstil-Porzellane der KPM* (Munich, 1971), p. 239, no. 248; Berlin, 1972, p. 173, nos. 504–7; Berlin, *Bröhan,* 1977, pp. 310, 312, no. 450; Brussels, 1977, p. 185, no. 351; Karlsruhe, 1978, p. 266, no. 108; Cologne, Kunstgewerbemuseum, *Europäisches Porzellan und Ostasiatisches Exportporzellan, Geschirr und Ziergerät* (1980), p. 204, no. 147; Otto Walcha, *Meissen Porcelain* (Dresden, 1981), p. 456, no. 204; Hermann Jedding, *Meissner Porzellan des 19. und 20. Jahrhunderts 1800-1933* (Munich, 1981), p. 101, fig. 120; Kurt Junghanns, *Der Deutsche Werkbund: Sein Erstes Jahrzehnt* (Berlin, 1982), p. 70, fig. 32; Nerdinger, ed., 1982, pp. 283, figs. 53–54, 316, 317, no. 383; Vienna, Österreichisches Museum für angewandte Kunst, *Meissner Porzellan von 1710 bis zur Gegenwart* (Nov. 24, 1982 – Apr. 30, 1983), no. 82; Gunther Meier, *Porzellan aus der Meissner Manufaktur* (Stuttgart, 1983), fig. 59; Johannes Just, *Meissener Jugendstil-Porzellan* (Leipzig, 1983), pp. 140–41, nos. 92–93; Johannes Just, *Meissen Porcelain of the Art Nouveau Period,* trans. Edward Larkey (London, 1985), pp. 140–41, figs. 92–93; H. Wichmann, 1985, p. 115; Gillian Naylor, *The Bauhaus Reassessed: Sources and Design Theory* (New York, 1985), p. 29, fig. 9; Bielefeld, 1986, p. 62, no. 156; Heskett, 1986, p. 91.

In February 1903 Riemerschmid was commissioned by the Meissen porcelain factory to design a modern table service "in the same spirit as the best furniture and interior furnishings." The oldest porcelain works in Europe, Meissen had continued, throughout the nineteenth century, to sell vast quantities of porcelain in the "old Meissen style" made from the original molds, an activity for which the firm was criticized at the Paris

117 Jug, 1903

Made by Reinhold Merkelbach, Grenzhausen
(established 1845)
Stoneware, slip coated and salt-glazed, with
colored decoration; height 8¹¹/₁₆″ (22 cm)
Marks: factory mark from 1900, 1773, 2L,
Made in Germany (impressed)
K. Barlow Ltd., London

References

Kunst und Handwerk, vol. 54 (1903-4), p. 271,
fig. 481; Merkelbach, 1905, pp. 54, no. 1773, 86,
fig. 75, 87; Schumacher, et al., 1906, p. 264 (ill.);
Rée, 1906, p. 282 (ill.); Warlich, 1908, p. 44 (ill.);
Munich, Villa Stuck, *Jugendstil aus Münchener
Privatbesitz* (Dec. 13, 1972-Feb. 25, 1973),
no. 129; Düsseldorf, Hetjens-Museum, *Europäische Keramik des Jugendstils* (1974), p. 201,
no. 310; Gabriele Sterner, *Jugendstil: Kunstformen
zwischen Individualismus und Massengesellschaft*
(Cologne, 1975), pp. 126, no. 74, 127, 184;
Berlin, *Bröhan,* 1977, pp. 386, no. 526, 387;
Ekkart Klinge, comp., *Deutsche Keramik des
20. Jahrhunderts* (Düsseldorf, 1978), p. 271,
fig. 753; Tamara Préaud and Serge Gauthier,
Ceramics of the 20th Century (New York, 1982),
p. 40, no. 64; Nerdinger, ed., 1982, pp. 281,
fig. 51, 334, no. 416.

A version of the jug (model number 1773)
was one of several Riemerschmid
ceramics exhibited at the "III. Deutsche
Kunstgewerbe-Ausstellung" in Dresden
in 1906 and that belonged to the *Kleingerät*

Exposition Universelle of 1900. Unlike
the Belgian designer Henry van de Velde,
whose service for Meissen, designed the
previous year, introduced new stream-
lined shapes and abstract linear decoration, Riemerschmid deliberately evoked
such famous traditional Meissen services
as the "onion pattern" of about 1740,
which showed a similar underglaze blue
decoration. Yet unlike the earlier services,
Riemerschmid's is predominantly white,
with a stylized leaf decoration confined
largely to the borders of the individual
pieces. It was this sense of spareness that
appealed to Eduard Heyck in 1907: "Until recently, fine sets of dishes, especially
simple ones, have not been available.
The Riemerschmid service…[although]
rather expensive, [now] exists as [an] example. Hopefully, educated demand will
require that such plain sets with tasteful
borders will be available for purchase by
the less well-off, so that choice is not
confined to miserable kitchenwares or to
naturalistically shaped and painted atroc-
ities."   K.B.H.

(household equipment) sold by the Dresdner Werkstätten. The *Kleingerät* program supplemented the furniture marketed by the workshops (see no. 125) and provided the means to a completely furnished, well-designed interior. According to the *Kleingerät* catalogue and price list of 1907, the objects were required to be "plain things... designed by a strong artistic personality, manufactured in a technically outstanding way, and made of noble materials in order to touch the sense for what is beautiful" (Dresdner Werkstätten für Handwerkskunst, *Preisliste 1907: Dresdner Kleingerät* [Dresden, 1907], n. p.). Like the furniture it accompanied, the jug was produced by a combination of machine and craft techniques, formed in a mold and trimmed on a wheel. Produced in this size only, the model was made in brown salt glaze until about 1911, when it was also manufactured in gray-blue salt glaze.   K.B.H.

118 Tankard, 1902

Made by Reinhold Merkelbach, Grenzhausen (established 1845)
Stoneware, slip coated and salt-glazed, with painted decoration, and pewter; height 4⁵/₁₆″ (11 cm)
Mark: 1729 D (impressed)
K. Barlow Ltd., London

References

Kunst und Handwerk, vol. 54 (1903–4), p. 271, fig. 481; Merkelbach, 1905, pp. 53, 86, no. 1729, 87, fig. 75; Warlich, 1908, p. 92 (ill.); *L'Art Décoratif,* vol. 12 (1910), p. 113 (ill.); Nerdinger, ed., 1982, pp. 281, fig. 51, 327, no. 402b.

This tankard version of Merkelbach's model number 1729 (no. 119), designed in 1902, is decorated not only with the characteristic spiral, but also with curling stems of stylized ivy (*Hedera helix*). Riemerschmid used similar patterns with heart-shaped leaves in textile designs, too, from the earliest, done in 1902 (no. 114), to the furnishing materials he designed for the Dresdner Werkstätten from 1905 (nos. 127-30). Described as a *Bierkrug* (beer mug) in the Merkelbach special price list of 1905, the tankard was designed and produced only in half-liter size and, after about 1909, in this handsome brown (*geflammt*) glaze, which had resulted initially from a mistake in firing.   K.B.H.

119 Jug, 1902

Made by Reinhold Merkelbach, Grenzhausen (established 1845)
Stoneware, slip coated and salt-glazed, and pewter; height 8⁷/₁₆″ (21.5 cm)
Marks: factory mark, 1729, 4.5L, cross (impressed)
Philadelphia Museum of Art. Purchased: The Haney Foundation Fund, The Bloomfield Moore Fund, and The Edgar Viguers Seeler Fund. 1987-10-1

References

Merkelbach, 1905, pp. 53, 118, no. 1729, 119, fig. 91; *Die Kunst,* vol. 22 (1910), p. 461 (ill.); *The Studio Year Book of Decorative Art* (1912), p. 176; *Kunst und Handwerk,* vol. 63 (1912-13), p. 44, fig. 98; *Velhagen und Klasings Monatshefte* (1912-13), p. 319; Heinz Thiersch, "Richard Riemerschmid 86 Jahre," *Innenarchitektur,* vol. 2 (1954-55), p. 80; Munich, 1958, p. 206, no. 696; Hans Eckstein, *Die Neue Sammlung* (Munich, 1965), no. 41; Wolfgang Scheffler, *Werke um 1900* (Berlin, 1966), pp. 112, no. 173, 113; Berlin, 1972, p. 182, no. 607; Munich, Die Neue Sammlung, *Eine Auswahl aus dem Besitz des Museums* (1972), fig. 32; Gabriele Sterner, *Jugendstil: Kunstformen zwischen Individualismus und Massengesellschaft* (Cologne, 1975), pp. 125, fig. 72, 183; Darmstadt, 1976-77, p. 151, no. 272; Brussels, 1977, p. 217, no. 467; Prague, 1980, pp. 72, 108, no. 135; Nerdinger, ed., 1982, p. 326, no. 399; H. Wichmann, 1985, p. 113.

Made in four-and-a-half and three-and-a-half liter sizes and in either gray-blue or brown salt glaze, this jug (model number 1729) was one of several designed by Riemerschmid in 1902. They differed from each other in decoration and sometimes shape, including both a jug and a tankard version (no. 118). Common to all was the elegant spiral motif, which, as a contemporary critic pointed out, was made not by the traditional "scratch" technique, as it would appear, but was molded: "The old scratch technique, that is, the outlining of the ornaments through scratched lines with cobalt applied in between them, was in this way adapted to modern machine production: to avoid scratching the object each time, the lines were pressed broadly into the hollow form so that they appear on the body of the [finished] vessel" (Ernst Zimmermann, "Steinzeugkrüge von Richard Riemerschmid," *Kunst und Handwerk,* vol. 54 [1903-4], p. 270).   K.B.H.

120 Wardrobe, 1903

Made by Wenzel Till, Munich (established before 1897)

Stained maple and mother of pearl, 54⁵/₁₆ x 37³/₈ x 19¹¹/₁₆″ (138 x 95 x 50 cm)

Label: W. Till Möbelfabrik München (inside of door)

Stadtmuseum, Munich. 73/419

References

Deutsche Kunst und Dekoration, vol. 13 (1903-4), p. 231 (ill.); Nerdinger, ed., 1982, pp. 127, fig. 32, 169, no. 98a; Ottomeyer, 1988, p. 94, no. 18.

The wardrobe was originally located in the reception room of the Thieme residence in Munich (see also nos. 111-13, 121). The sides of the piece, formed of a slab and post, taper upward from a base fitted with a curved, applied apron. While the maple wood of the base is stained green, the superstructure is left in a lighter brown. Mother-of-pearl inlays in the shape of irregular trapezoids adorn the front edge of the shelf, the doors, and the posts, where their arrangement gracefully emphasizes the wardrobe's tapered silhouette. The trapezoid motif was repeated throughout the furniture and decoration of the reception room.

The wardrobe was also produced in gray maple for a drawing room by the Dresdner Werkstätten (Nerdinger, ed., 1982, ill. p. 177), and two further variants are also extant.   H. O.

121 Carpet, 1903

Wool, 157¹/₂ x 118¹/₈″ (400 x 300 cm)
Stadtmuseum, Munich. T 86/295

References

Muthesius, 1904, ill. facing p. 272; Nerdinger, ed., 1982, pp. 167, 370, fig. 62, 379, no. 500.

A bill in the possession of the Thieme family suggests that the carpet was made by the Smyrna-Teppichfabrik in Cottbus (Lausitz), not by the Wurzener Teppichfabriken (established 1860), as stated under the illustration of a close variant in the 1904 volume of *Die Kunst* (facing p. 272). As can be seen in early photographs (for example, Nerdinger, ed., 1982, p. 167), the carpet occupied the smaller half of the dining room in the Thieme residence (see nos. 111-13), while a much larger carpet and a runner – both still in the family's possession – were laid out in the other half of the room and in an alcove, respectively. All the pieces have a color scheme of brilliant reds and blues. This carpet, with its large central area and borders of stylized flowering twigs, represents a modern adaptation of classical Persian carpet designs.   C. S. v. W. S.

122 Table, 1904–6

Made by Theodor Reimann, Dresden
Wicker, oak, and spruce, 29^{1}/$_{8}$ x 27^{15}/$_{16}$ x 19^{1}/$_{2}$″
(74 x 71 x 49.5 cm)
Stadtmuseum, Munich. 74/3

References

Nerdinger, ed., 1982, pp. 189, 190, no. 122c;
Ottomeyer, 1988, pp. 109–10, no. 28.2.

This side table, which, together with two
plant stands and a pair of armchairs (see
no. 123), comes from the conservatory of
the Rittinghausen residence at Tutzing
near Munich, originally formed part of
the Kaiser Suite on the ocean liner
Kronprinzessin Cecilie. Apart from PAUL
and J. M. Olbrich, Riemerschmid was the
only artist not residing in Bremen, the
ship's home port, who was invited to par-
ticipate in its interior design. Reports by
Karl Schaefer on these North German
Lloyd commissions appeared in the
1907 volume of *Innen-Dekoration* (vol. 18,
pp. 293–305) and the 1908 volume of
Dekorative Kunst (vol. 16, pp. 76–89), and
these two articles describe and illustrate
the decoration of the rooms in great detail.

While the de luxe staterooms com-
prised a salon, bedroom, and bathroom,
the suite that Riemerschmid decorated
had the advantage of being a series of connected rooms "which as a whole, in terms
of atmosphere and concentrated expression, certainly deserves the highest
praise" (*Dekorative Kunst,* p. 86). H.O.

123 Armchair, 1904–6

Made by Theodor Reimann, Dresden
Wicker and pine, 33^{1}/$_{16}$ x 20^{1}/$_{16}$ x 21^{5}/$_{8}$″
(84 x 51 x 55 cm)
Stadtmuseum, Munich. 74/2, 1

References

Rée, 1906, p. 286 (ill.); *Innen-Dekoration,* vol. 18
(1907), p. 300 (ill.); *Kunstgewerbeblatt,* n. s.,
vol. 18 (1907), p. 236 (ill.); *Kunst und Handwerk,*
vol. 58 (1907–8), fig. 63; *Dekorative Kunst,* vol. 16
(1908), p. 85 (ill.); Deutsche Werkstätten für
Handwerkskunst, *Handgearbeitete Möbel* (Dresden-Hellerau, 1909), p. 229 (ill.); Deutsche
Werkstätten, *Handgearbeitete Möbel* (Dresden-
Hellerau, 1912), p. 225 (ill.); H. Wichmann, 1978,
p. 187; Nerdinger, ed., 1982, p. 189, no. 122a;
Ottomeyer, 1988, pp. 109–10, no. 28.1, 1.

The armchair was one of a pair designed
for the breakfast room of the Kaiser Suite
on the *Kronprinzessin Cecilie* (see no. 122).
The room's color scheme consisted of
natural tones – a smoky brown coffered
ceiling, wooden paneling with friezes of
green leaves, curtains with stylized green
leaf motifs, and a divan upholstered in
green leather. The furnishings were completed by these wicker armchairs, whose
natural color provided a further accent.
The breakfast room was singled out by
Karl Schaefer for special mention: "There
is a very personal romance in the mood of
this small room, which none of the other
designers of the first-class cabins has been
able to match" (*Dekorative Kunst,* vol. 16
[1908], p. 86).

Like the other furniture in the suite, the
chairs have a framework of round wood
covered with wicker weave, whose texture enlivens the characteristically planar
design. Traditionally, wicker had been a
cheap and durable material for use in
veranda and winter-garden furniture.
Jugendstil artists experimented with the
wicker technique with impressive results
that were not necessarily inexpensive –
these chairs, for example, sold for the
considerable sum of 35 marks. H.O.

124 Overdoor, 1909–10

Made by Dresdner Werkstätten für Handwerks-
kunst, Dresden (established 1898)
Painted pine and limewood, 22 x 67³/₄″
(56 x 172 cm)
Staatliche Kunstsammlungen, Museum für
Kunsthandwerk, Dresden. 37 565

References

*Jahrbuch der Staatlichen Kunstsammlungen Dresden
1961-62* (1964), p. 184; Dresden, Museum für
Kunsthandwerk, *Gestaltete Form: Möbel aus
Hellerau* (June 2-Oct. 31, 1973), no. 23, fig. 19;
Dresden, 1976, p. 50, no. 44; Klaus-Peter Arnold,
"Die Geschichte der Deutschen Werkstätten
Hellerau und ihr Beitrag zur deutschen Kunst-
gewerbebewegung" (diss., Halle an der Saale,
1980), vol. 2, p. 277, no. 71; Klaus-Peter Arnold,
*Vom Sofakissen zum Städtebau: Die Geschichte der
Deutschen Werkstätten Hellerau* (forthcoming).

By arranging the richly carved reliefwork
symmetrically and enclosing it in a simple
shape on this overdoor, Riemerschmid
contains the complicated interlacing of
the stalks and leaves that are so characteristic of Jugendstil designs. A drawing
discovered by Klaus-Peter Arnold, Dresden, in Riemerschmid's estate (Städtische
Galerie im Lenbachhaus, Munich, 4491)
suggests that the overdoor was created
shortly before the Brussels Exposition
Universelle of 1910, although the ornamental vocabulary is extremely close to
that designed by Riemerschmid for the
Room of an Art Lover at the Paris Exposition of 1900 (see nos. 99-100). The restraint of Riemerschmid's design here
points forward to the stringent simplicity
practiced by the Bauhaus after World War
I and is evidence of Riemerschmid's contribution to that style.   G. R.

125 Dressing Table and Mirror, c. 1905

Made by Dresdner Werkstätten für Handwerkskunst, Dresden (established 1898)
Pine and wrought iron; a) table 24¹³/₁₆ x 28³/₈ x
14⁹/₁₆″ (63 x 72 x 37 cm), b) mirror 48 x 21¹/₄″
(122 x 54 cm)
K. Barlow Ltd., London

Reference
Deutsche Kunst und Dekoration, vol. 27 (1910-11),
p. 478 (ill.).

The pieces belong to an extensive program of machine-made furniture (*Maschinenmöbel*) designed by Riemerschmid
for the Dresdner Werkstätten and first
exhibited at the "III. Deutsche Kunstgewerbe-Ausstellung" in Dresden in 1906.
The furniture was developed in three
separate programs according to price
range, each program consisting of living
room, bedroom, and kitchen furniture,
with the two upper price categories also
including dining room pieces. With its
extensive use of machinery and its program of complete, ready-made suites, the
Maschinenmöbel has been hailed by critics
as a precursor of modern production furniture. Riemerschmid's contemporaries,
too, considered it revolutionary in its simple, well-proportioned forms, truth to

materials, clarity of structure, absence of
ornament, and modest prices. As Ernst
Zimmermann wrote: "Experience has led
us to associate machine-made products
with all kinds of conceptions other than
that of art.... With its simplicity of style
and purpose, the *Maschinenmöbel* is far
more reasonably priced than those pieces
made with such effort by machines trying
to copy...handwork. Here, a problem
of great significance has been seized with
unusual energy and success and brought to
a resolution that appears to be thoroughly practical" ("Künstlerische Maschinenmöbel," *Deutsche Kunst und Dekoration,*
vol. 17 [1905-6], pp. 253, 257).   K.B.H.

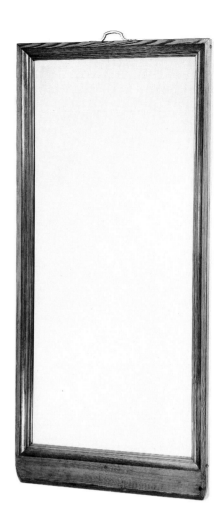

126 Chair, 1904-6

Made by Dresdner Werkstätten für Handwerks-
kunst, Dresden (established 1898)
Oak, 35¹/₄ x 16³/₄ x 17¹⁵/₁₆″ (89.5 x 42.5 x 45.5 cm)
Staatliche Kunstsammlungen, Museum für
Kunsthandwerk, Dresden. 39808b

References

Dresden, 1906, pp. 162-63; Dresdner Werk-
stätten für Handwerkskunst, *Preisbuch 1906*
(Dresden, 1906), pp. 18-21, 28-29; Warlich,
1908, pp. 110, 112; Adolph G. Schneck, *Neue
Möbel vom Jugendstil bis heute* (Munich, 1962),
p. 87; Dresden, Museum für Kunsthandwerk,
Gestaltete Form: Möbel aus Hellerau (June 2-
Oct. 31, 1973), no. 11, fig. 11; Dresden, 1976,
p. 50, no. 43; H. Wichmann, 1978, pp. 66-67, 70;
Gert Selle, *Die Geschichte des Design in Deutschland
von 1879 bis heute* (Cologne, 1978), p. 59, fig. 41;
Klaus-Peter Arnold, "Die Geschichte der Deutschen Werkstätten Hellerau von 1898 bis 1930
und ihr Beitrag zur deutschen Kunstgewerbe-
bewegung" (diss., Halle an der Saale, 1980),
vol. 2, p. 278, no. 77; Munich, Die Neue Sammlung, *Neu: Donationen und Neuerwerbungen 1980/
81* (Mar.-May 1982), pp. 20, 47; H. Wichmann,
1985, p. 197; Klaus-Peter Arnold, *Vom Sofakissen
zum Städtebau: Die Geschichte der Deutschen
Werkstätten Hellerau* (forthcoming).

The elements of the chair are boldly
shaped, their forms adapted to the process
of working the material. It belongs
among the first machine-made furniture
(*Maschinenmöbel*) that Riemerschmid designed for the German middle-class home
before World War I. The individual components were made serially by machine
and assembled by hand. Manufactured in
1906 (model number [79]5), the chair is a
typical example of the *Dresdner Hausgerät*
(Dresden household utensils) produced
by the Dresdner and Deutsche Werkstätten. G.R.

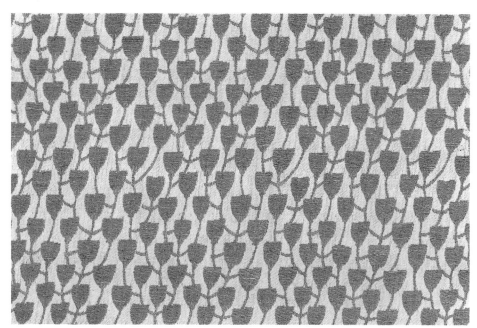

127 Furnishing Fabric, 1905

Made by Dresdner Werkstätten für Handwerks-
kunst, Dresden (established 1898)
Linen, 27⁹/₁₆ x 42¹/₂″ (70 x 108 cm)
Stadtmuseum, Munich

References

Rée, 1906, p. 302 (ill.); Rudolf Klein, "Die
Deutsche Kunstausstellung in Köln 1906,"
Deutsche Kunst und Dekoration, vol. 18 (1906),
p. 643 (ill.); *Innen-Dekoration,* vol. 17 (1906),
p. 142 (ill.); Warlich, 1908, p. 200 (ill.); Munich,
1964, p. 123, nos. 1020-21, fig. 54; Fanelli and
Fanelli, 1976, fig. 386; Gasser, ed., 1977,
pp. 32-33; S. Wichmann, 1977, pp. 82-83,
fig. 164; H. Wichmann, 1978, p. 208; Stuttgart,
1980, pp. 262, no. 209, 263; New York, 1982,
p. 167, no. 132, fig. 132; Nerdinger, ed., 1982,
pp. 362-63, no. 475; S. Wichmann, *Jugendstil
Floral,* 1984, p. 130, fig. 266; S. Wichmann, 1984,
p. 130, fig. 266; H. Wichmann, 1985, p. 179.

This pattern, spreading branches with
bellflowers, was produced in various
color combinations on both woven tapestry cloth and cotton tulle, the different
character of the weave in the latter lending it a less dense, even gauzy, appearance. The small size of the repeating
pattern units is a typical feature of Riemerschmid's fabric designs, and allowed
the fabric to be used for a variety of purposes, from furniture upholsteries to curtain and dress materials.   C. S. v. W. S.

128 Furnishing Fabric, 1905

Made by Dresdner Werkstätten für Handwerks-
kunst, Dresden (established 1898)
Printed linen, 7¹/₂ x 7⁷/₈″ (19 x 20 cm)
Stadtmuseum, Munich

References

Rée, 1906, p. 303 (ill.); *Innen-Dekoration,* vol. 17
(1906), p. 142 (ill.); *Deutsche Kunst und Dekoration,*
vol. 22 (1908), p. 214 (ill.); Warlich, 1908, p. 199
(ill.); Fanelli and Fanelli, 1976, fig. 388; H. Wichmann, 1978, p. 195; Stuttgart, 1980, pp. 262,
nos. 200-2, 263; Nerdinger, ed., 1982, pp. 362,
no. 473, 372, fig. 65.

The textile was produced in various
materials – linen, cotton, silk – and colors, illustrating the great range of which
Riemerschmid's patterns were capable.
This design was also executed in double-
weave (examples in the Württembergisches Landesmuseum, Stuttgart). The
motif here depicts a vine with twining
stems, heart-shaped leaves, and a fruit
cluster, suggesting a rather stylized grape,
but abstracted and simplified beyond
possible identification. Rée, who published this fabric in 1906, spoke of the vi-
tality of Riemerschmid's textile patterns
and how the "life" of the individual motif
contributed to the expression of the
whole design (Rée, 1906, p. 272).

K. B. H. / C. S. v. W. S.

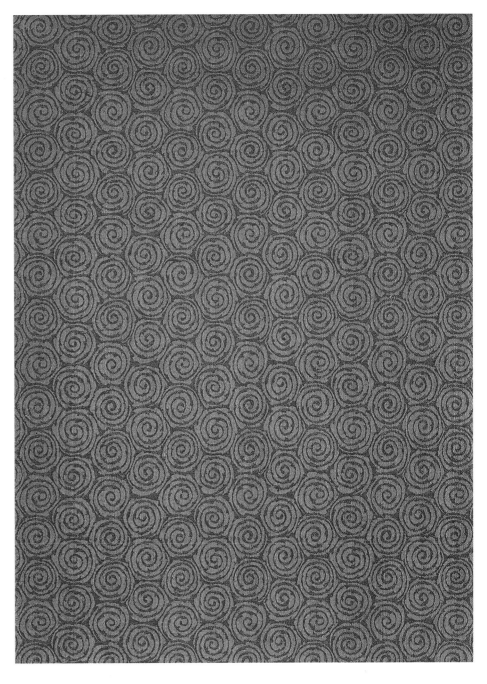

129 Furnishing Fabric, 1905

Made by Dresdner Werkstätten für Handwerks-
kunst, Dresden (established 1898)
Cotton, 39³/₄ x 35⁷/₁₆″ (101 x 90 cm)
Stadtmuseum, Munich

References

Rudolf Klein, "Die Deutsche Kunstausstellung in
Köln 1906," *Deutsche Kunst und Dekoration,*
vol. 18 (1906), p. 642 (ill.); Stuttgart, 1980,
pp. 262, nos. 203-4, 263, fig. 203; Nerdinger,
ed., 1982, p. 363, no. 477.

This jacquard fabric, which was made in
several color variations, is a great deal
more abstract in pattern than the other
Riemerschmid textiles shown here (nos.
127-28, 130), consisting simply of left-
hand and right-hand spirals offset diagonally on a red ground. Riemerschmid also
used a spiral pattern for the decoration of
a stoneware jug series for Merkelbach
(nos. 118-19). While each spiral here is
similarly derived from a geometrically
exact figure, not one is the same as any
other; slight irregularities in size, contour, and disposition, as well as the satu-
rated, vibrating colors, enliven the rows
of closely placed motifs.   C. S. v. W. S.

130 Furnishing Fabric, 1905

Made by Dresdner Werkstätten für Handwerks-
kunst, Dresden (established 1898)
Linen, 37¹³/₁₆ x 42¹⁵/₁₆″ (96 x 109 cm)
Stadtmuseum, Munich. 61/637/3

References

Rée, 1906, pp. 281, 302 (ill.); *Innen-Dekoration*,
vol. 17 (1906), p. 142 (ill.); Georg Lehnert, *Illu-
strierte Geschichte des Kunstgewerbes*, vol. 2 (Berlin,
1908), p. 621, fig. 510; Warlich, 1908, p. 200 (ill.);
Herbert Hofmann, *60 Jahre Deutsche Werkstätten:
1898-1958* (Munich, 1958), n. p.; Fanelli and
Fanelli, 1976, no. 385; Stuttgart, 1980, pp. 260,
no. 197, 261, fig. 197; Munich, *Kandinsky*, 1982,
p. 216, no. 91, fig. 91; Nerdinger, ed., 1982,
p. 363, no. 478.

When publishing this fabric in 1906, Rée
wrote that it was "no accident that Riemerschmid's favorite ornamental motif is
the branch adorned with delicate leaves,
flowers, and buds. In this, an artistic
springtime [*Kunstfrühling*] announces itself" (Rée, 1906, p. 281). Rejecting the
large-scale floral patterns of the period,
Riemerschmid designed delicate small
patterns, and in so doing established new
standards for Jugendstil textiles. A good
example is this design, in muted shades of
gray, blue, and yellow, with undulating
rows of branches and tiny blossoms, reduced to their simplest, most abstract
shapes in the service of a pattern repeat.

K.B.H./C.S.v.W.S.

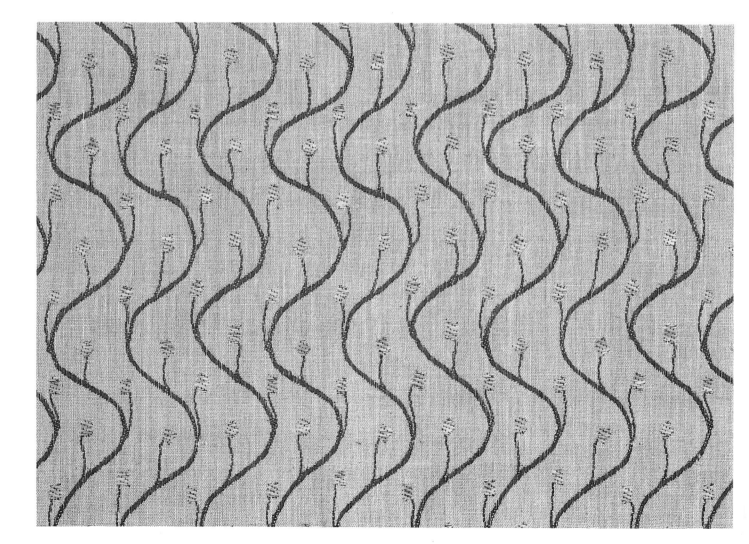

131 Punch Bowl and Cups, 1902-4 and 1906

Made by Reinhold Merkelbach, Grenzhausen (established 1845)
Stoneware, celadon body, colored decoration, glazed; a) bowl, height 14¼″ (36 cm), b) cups, height 2⁷/₁₆″ (6.2 cm) (each)
Marks: a) 1768 S 11 (impressed), b) GG (impressed), 1, 2, 5, 9, or U (inscribed)
Stadtmuseum, Munich. 73-991 (bowl and cup)
Collection of Dr. Beate Dry von Zezschwitz, Munich (five cups)

References

Merkelbach, 1905, pp. 56, no. 1768, 100, fig. 82, 101; Schumacher, et al., 1906, p. 264 (ill.); *Kunstgewerbeblatt*, n. s., vol. 17 (1906), p. 236 (ill.); *Deutsche Kunst und Dekoration*, vol. 19 (1906-7), p. 375 (ill.); *Fachblatt für Holzarbeiter* (1907), pp. 184, 188, 213 (ills.); *Tonindustrie-Zeitung und Fachblatt der Zement-, Beton-, Gips-, Kalk- und Kunststeinindustrie* (1907), p. 997, no. 83; Warlich, 1908, p. 71 (ill.); *Die Kunst*, vol. 20 (1909), p. 319 (ill.); G. E. Lüthgen, *Deutsches Steinzeug, behandelt im Anschluss an den Wettbewerb für Studentenkunst Stuttgart 1909* (1909; repr. Munich, 1981), p. 9 (ill.); *Keramisches Zentralblatt*, 1st year, no. 11 (Feb. 1912), pl. XLIV; *Die Kunst*, vol. 28 (1913), p. 339; *Innen-Dekoration*, vol. 28 (1917), p. 287; "Rheinisches Steinzeug und seine Herstellung," *Die Schaulade*, no. 5 (1929), p. 69; H. T. Bossert,

Geschichte des Kunstgewerbes, vol. 6 (Berlin, 1935), p. 319; Bott, 1973, pp. 349, no. 453, 385; Berlin, 1976, pp. 386, no. 527, 387; Ekkart Klinge, ed., *Deutsche Keramik des 20. Jahrhunderts* (Düsseldorf, 1978), p. 273, no. 761; Darmstadt, Hessisches Landesmuseum, *Jugendstil: Kunst um 1900* (1982), p. 263, no. 343; Nerdinger, ed., 1982, pp. 279, fig. 48, 332-33, no. 412 b.

The earliest, celadon-bodied version of Riemerschmid's eleven-liter punch bowl, designed in 1902, consisted of the stoneware vessel on three legs, with a glass liner and glass lid, both with an undulating surface (see *Deutsche Kunst und Dekoration*, vol. 16 [1905], ill. p. 681). In 1904 Riemerschmid designed a rounded stoneware lid for the bowl, providing a formal completion to the vessel's spherical shape, and repeating the rosette motif which decorates the bowl's rim. The vessel's basic spherical form, balanced on three angled feet, is reminiscent of metalwork designed in the 1880s by Christopher Dresser, with whose work Riemerschmid was surely acquainted (see C. Dresser, *Principles of Decorative Design* [London, n. d. (1873)], figs. 146-47, and London, Camden Arts Center, *Christopher Dresser 1834-1904* [1979], nos. 51, 67-69).

The punch bowl's surface decoration is an essay in abstraction which echoes similarly inspired ornament employed by ENDELL on a radiator screen in his Atelier Elvira in Munich (1898). The wave motif at the base of the bowl and the rising pattern of asymmetric algae-like leaf ornament suggest in abstract terms the vertical movement of bubbles within a beverage, while the spangled pattern of rosettes around the bowl's rim, which continues upward and across the lid, is a stylized representation of bursting and sparkling bubbles. Riemerschmid's punch bowl is an important example of abstract design in Munich applied arts around the turn of the century, eight years before Kandinsky, also in Munich, crossed the border from a representational to an abstract art of painting.

The stoneware cups were designed by Riemerschmid in 1906 to accompany the punch bowl. They replaced plain glass cups of the same shape designed in 1902, which were certainly manufactured – as was the punch bowl's original glass liner and lid – by Benedikt von Poschinger in Oberzwieselau in the Bayerischer Wald.

B. D. v. Z.

132 Design for the Riemerschmid Residence, 1906-7

Pencil on paper, 11¹³/₁₆ x 18¹/₂″ (30 x 47 cm)
Architektursammlung der Technischen
Universität, Munich. RR 858

In 1897 Riemerschmid designed his residence on ground owned by his brother, the manufacturer Anton Riemerschmid, in the Munich suburb of Pasing. The plans were officially approved on February 15, 1898, and the villa was erected on a nearly square ground plan in the park between Rembrandtstrasse and Lützowstrasse. By extending the site to the west and shifting the line of the building seven feet to the north on Lützowstrasse, Riemerschmid was able to start planning an extension to his house in October 1906. The present drawing shows the north front of the villa itself and the utilities tract on the left, together with the corridor connecting them with the studio building on the right.

The additional buildings produced the courtyard arrangement as seen in the drawing, and it was through this extension to the original villa that the whole complex acquired the character of a country house set in a park landscape. The buildings are of differing heights, with hip roofs, while the roof of the villa itself is crowned with a little lookout. The west side of the building, which is particularly exposed to the weather, is entirely covered with clapboard, unlike the other facades. Riemerschmid's arrangement of the buildings was guided by the desire not to have dense building in the "villa suburb" of Pasing. The site has remained virtually unchanged to the present day.

B.-V.K.

133 Hanging Lamp, 1906

Made by Dresdner Werkstätten für Handwerkskunst, Dresden (established 1898)
Brass and glass, height 7¹/₂″ (19 cm)
K. Barlow Ltd., London

References

Dekorative Kunst, vol. 10 (1902), pp. 142 (ill.), 449 (ill. in Turin); Uecker, 1978, p. 194, no. 0291; Nerdinger, ed., 1982, p. 287, no. 291.

A variant of a 1902 design by Riemerschmid that had been made by the Vereinigte Werkstätten, the pendant electric lamp was produced in four different versions and appeared in the catalogues of lamps and lighting fixtures issued by the Dresdner and Deutsche Werkstätten between 1906 and 1934. As in most of Riemerschmid's hanging lamps, and indeed, as was common practice at the time (see no. 104), the lamp is suspended on its two electrical cords. Riemerschmid's designs for lighting fixtures set a high standard for his contemporaries, as the reviewer pointed out when the lamp was first published with other metalwares in 1902: "The metalwork of the Vereinigte Werkstätten is worthy of the company's furniture. Their shared standard of excellence is due to the fact that the same artists work in both techniques. Such strong individuality as ... Riemerschmid's [has] not been without influence. ... [it] has provided a model, not, fortunately, in the form of imitations, but in terms of a common artistic direction" ("Aus Münchens Kunstindustrie," *Dekorative Kunst,* vol. 10 [1902], p. 140).

K.B.H.

134 Table Lamp, c. 1906

Made by Dresdner Werkstätten für Handwerks-
kunst, Dresden (established 1898)
Brass, height 14″ (35.5 cm)
Württembergisches Landesmuseum, Stuttgart.
G 6.204

References

Haenel, 1906, p. 493 (ill. in Dresden);
Schumacher, et al., 1906, p. 159 (ill.); *Deutsche
Kunst und Dekoration,* vol. 19 (1906-7), pp. 133,
135 (ills.); Munich, 1958, p. 208, no. 705;
Munich, Stadtmuseum, 1972, p. 525, no. 2101;
Uecker, 1978, p. 193, no. 0289; S. Wichmann,
Jugendstil Floral, 1984, p. 126, fig. 257;
S. Wichmann, 1984, p. 126, no. 257.

In its total lack of ornament and promi-
nent screw heads, the lamp is almost
without parallel among Riemerschmid's
metalwares. It appears as a rationalized
series of triangular shapes in which even
the three electrical cords emerging
from beneath the shade play a part. However, the lamp seemed less obviously
mechanistic in its original context, the
Gentleman's Room (*Herrenzimmer*) that
Riemerschmid created for the "III. Deutsche Kunstgewerbe-Ausstellung" in
Dresden in 1906, where it stood on an
embroidered cloth-covered table in a
paneled interior. Like Riemerschmid's
Maschinenmöbel (see no. 125), shown at
the same exhibition, this machine-pro-
duced fixture was intended to appeal to
the public through its "simplicity of
style" and "reasonable price" and "not
through its new shape" (Ernst Zimmermann, "Künstlerische Maschinenmöbel,"
Deutsche Kunst und Dekoration, vol. 17
[1905-6], pp. 256-57). The model was
produced with variations by the Dresdner
and Deutsche Werkstätten and as a hanging lamp, designs for these being preserved in the Technische Universität,
Munich (M116.1A, M280, M174).

K.B.H.

Max Rossbach
1871-1947

The painter and designer Max Rossbach was born in Leipzig, the son of Arwed Rossbach (1844-1902), a noted architect and government building surveyor. In 1894 he moved to Munich, where he enrolled in the engraving class at the Academy. After spending a few years in Venice, he returned to Munich and, in about 1897-98, became associated with the Munich Jugendstil artists BERLEPSCH-VALENDAS and Martin Dülfer (1859-1942) and with the Vereinigte Werkstätten für Kunst im Handwerk. When the Vereinigte Werkstätten first exhibited, at the 1898 Glaspalast exhibition, Rossbach showed a painted porcelain cup, jug, and tea caddy. The manufacturer of these first porcelain designs is unknown: services by Rossbach with poppy and dandelion decorations in a Munich private collection bear simply an impressed "VW" (for Vereinigte Werkstätten) enclosed in a rectangle, and it was not until later that Swaine & Co., Hüttensteinach, executed designs (by SCHMUZ-BAUDISS) for the Werkstätten.

In 1899 Rossbach exhibited a tea service made by the Vereinigte Werkstätten in the breakfast room designed by Dülfer for the "Deutsche Kunst-Ausstellung" in Dresden, which anticipated porcelain decorations that Schmuz-Baudiss exhibited at the Paris Exposition Universelle of 1900. Rossbach himself was represented at the 1900 exhibition with porcelain for everyday use.

In about 1900 Rossbach built a house with studio for himself in the Munich district of Solln, which still stands, and designed jewelry for the Vereinigte Werkstätten. Other pieces of jewelry by him were executed at this time by the Munich goldsmith Karl Rothmüller (1860-1930).

Rossbach continued his association with the Vereinigte Werkstätten, showing, for instance, "designs for various mediums, intarsia, embroidery, etc." at a special exhibition titled "Die Pflanze in ihrer dekorativen Verwertung" (The Use of the Plant in Decoration) that was held in 1903 at the Kunstgewerbemuseum in Leipzig.

From 1899, Rossbach, together with GRADL, was instrumental in introducing new styles and decorations at the Nymphenburg porcelain manufactory. The re-

Max Rossbach, with wife Anna, son Adalbert, and nurse, Venice, 1894

form movement at the manufactory was represented at the Paris (1900) and Turin (1902) exhibitions by these artists' "Modern" service (no. 42). Documents preserved at Nymphenburg, among them the decoration lists, provide a fairly precise record of Rossbach's activity as a designer of decorations for the manufactory; shape designs by him are not documented. He worked for the manufactory from 1899 to about 1906 (1908 at the latest), producing designs that were executed in overglaze and underglaze decoration.

In contrast to his animated Jugendstil designs for the Vereinigte Werkstätten, Rossbach's Nymphenburg decorations are dominated by botanical accuracy, ornamental lines, and the "modern stylization" mentioned in the manufactory's pattern lists.

Rossbach soon returned to painting as his main field of activity, and it was as a painter that he exhibited at the St. Louis world's fair in 1904. He occasionally participated in the Munich Glaspalast exhibitions – for example, in 1904 and 1921 – yet despite their indebtedness to the Munich School, only three of Rossbach's

paintings have found a place in Munich's public collections, all of them in the Städtische Galerie im Lenbachhaus.

References

Munich, 1898, nos. 2156-58; *Dekorative Kunst*, vol. 1 (1898), p. 245; *Deutsche Kunst und Dekoration*, vol. 4 (1899), pp. 498, 518-21; *Kunst und Kunsthandwerk*, vol. 2 (1899), pp. 212, 218; *Deutsche Kunst und Dekoration*, vol. 5 (1899-1900), p. 25; *Die Kunst*, vol. 4 (1901), pp. 152-53; *Kunst und Handwerk*, vol. 51 (1900-1), p. 82; *Jahrbuch der Bildenden Kunst*, vol. 1 (1902), col. 192; *Jahrbuch der Bildenden Kunst*, vol. 2 (1903), col. 215; Ulrich Thieme and Felix Becker, *Allgemeines Lexikon der Bildenden Künstler*, vol. 29 (Leipzig, 1935), p. 33; Selle, 1974, p. 113; Ulrike von Hase, *Schmuck in Deutschland und Österreich 1895-1914* (Munich, 1977), pp. 75, 286; Brussels, 1977, p. 184, no. 350; Gerhard P. Woeckel, *Die Tierplastik der Nymphenburger Porzellan-Manufaktur* (Munich, 1978), p. 62; Nerdinger, ed., 1982, p. 320, no. 386a; Reto Niggl, "Hermann Gradl," *Antiquitäten-Zeitung*, no. 1 (1985), p. 8.   R.N.

Jakob Julius Scharvogel
1854-1938

Scharvogel introduced and developed the art of flambé stoneware in Germany, which until the late nineteenth century had been the sole domain of French ceramic artists, such as Carriès, Chaplet, Dalpayrat, Delaherche, and Hoentschel.

Scharvogel's education in Zurich, Darmstadt, and Mainz had destined him for a career in business, but during a long stay in London in 1879 his frequent visits to the ceramics department of the South Kensington (now Victoria and Albert) Museum finally led him to become a potter. After first experiments in pottery and a study of glass manufacture in the Bayerischer Wald in 1880-83, he was engaged as an engineer and deputy director by the ceramics firm of Villeroy & Boch in Mettlach with responsibility for the design department and the ceramic mosaic studio. In 1885 he was sent by the firm to Leipzig, where he was given the task of establishing the Villeroy & Boch depot for central Germany. Scharvogel remained in the firm's employ until 1898; as a supplier of terra-cotta ornament for monumental buildings, he was concerned mostly with the execution of architectural ceramic projects, but also with problems of interior decoration. His personal interest in the production of his own pottery was confined during these years to the painted decoration of tiles.

Scharvogel resigned from Villeroy & Boch in 1898 and moved to Munich, where he set up a small factory in Obersendling for the production of stoneware in the style of antique Japanese models, but with a greater emphasis on new and colorful glazes. He first exhibited his new stoneware (grès-flammé) in 1899 at the Munich Glaspalast exhibition and immediately received recognition for his work, which soon became known as "Scharvogel stoneware." Early pieces, strongly influenced by Japanese models, were of a purely decorative nature, but by 1900 Scharvogel was designing utilitarian objects and had engaged the cooperation of progressive Munich artists, such as BEHRENS, Emmy von Egidy, Ludwig Habich, Walter Magnussen, and SCHMUZ-BAUDISS.

Scharvogel exhibited his flambé glazes at the Paris Exposition Universelle of 1900. He subsequently concentrated on

Jakob Julius Scharvogel. Bronze portrait by Heinrich Jobst, c. 1908. Städtische Kunstsammlung, Darmstadt

the production of utilitarian household pottery, and also developed a new range of tiles using enameled glazes. He exhibited in Turin in 1902 and St. Louis in 1904, and in 1906 took up an appointment in Darmstadt as director of the Grossherzogliche Keramische Manufaktur, where with the assistance of sculptors such as Karl Huber, Heinrich Jobst, and Carl Melville, he devoted his energies to the revival of stoneware and terra-cotta for the purposes of architectural decoration. Important works in this field are the bathing pools in Bad Nauheim (1908), the grand-ducal reception rooms at the Darmstadt railroad station (1912), and the Kaiser-Friedrich bathing pools in Wiesbaden (1912-13). The Darmstadt manufactory exhibited with great success at the Brussels Exposition Universelle in 1910.

Scharvogel resigned his position in 1913, and returned to Munich, where he lectured on architectural ceramics at the Technische Hochschule from 1915 to 1925. Throughout his life, Scharvogel wrote on subjects concerning modern and historical ceramics and the applied arts in general.

References

Deutsche Kunst und Dekoration, vol. 6 (1900), pp. 519, 534-35; Borrmann, 1902, pp. 57-58; Moritz Otto von Lasser, "Aus J. J. Scharvogels Werkstatt," *Deutsche Kunst und Dekoration,* vol. 13 (1903-4), pp. 181-88; Carl Benno Heller, "J. J. Scharvogel und die Gründung der Grossherzoglichen Keramischen Manufaktur Darmstadt," *Kunst in Hessen und am Mittelrhein,* vol. 14 (1975), pp. 101-7; Cologne, Kunstgewerbemuseum, *Meister der deutschen Keramik: 1900 bis 1950* (Feb. 10-Apr. 30, 1978), pp. 268-76. B.D.v.Z.

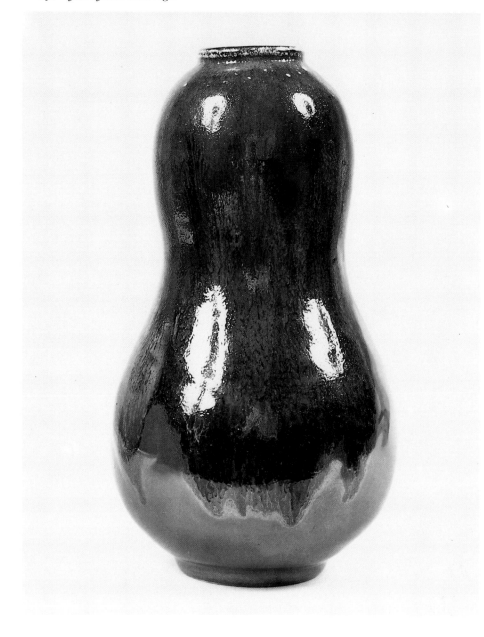

Scharvogel's debt, both technically and formally, to Japanese stoneware. Early examples of Scharvogel's stoneware vases were supplied with circular wooden stands, carved and decorated in the Japanese manner.

E. W. Bredt, with the sins of blatantly commercial late nineteenth-century Westerwald stoneware in mind, praised Scharvogel's contribution to the art of German stoneware in his review of the "I. Ausstellung der Münchener Vereinigung für Angewandte Kunst" in 1905: "Scharvogel has taken up the old challenge with vigor...and he creates objects of stoneware – a material hitherto regarded as plebeian – whose gorgeous colors make them worthy of a place in the palaces of princes" (*Die Kunst,* vol. 14 [1906], p. 38). B.D.v.Z.

136 Plate, C. 1900

Made by Scharvogel Kunsttöpferei München, Munich (established 1898)
Glazed stoneware, diameter 12⅝" (32 cm)
Marks: SKM, stylized crane in circle (impressed)
Staatliche Museen Preussischer Kulturbesitz, Kunstgewerbemuseum, Berlin. WA 75

References

Wolfgang Scheffler, *Werke um 1900* (Berlin, 1966), vol. 2, p. 100, no. 148; Darmstadt, 1976–77, vol. 4, p. 212, no. 638; Cologne, 1978, p. 272, no. 549.

Scharvogel's debt to Japanese ceramics is documented in this stoneware plate not only by the green and yellow, blue and red high-temperature glazes, but also by the raised emblem of two superimposed stylized waves at the plate's center. The spiraling motion of the circular motif, which, like an island, retains the brown glaze of the underlying layer, resists the surrounding mass of solidified colorglazes. The emblem is based on the Japanese symbol for a wave, and, in particular, Scharvogel may have been impressed by a similar circular, stylized, three-wave device that appears on Japanese woodblock prints as the seal of the publisher Eijudo (see Willy Boller, *Meister des Japanischen Holzschnittes,* 2nd, enl. ed. [Olten, 1957], pp. 138–39). Scharvogel's impressed mark on the reverse of the plate is itself a tribute to a Japanese graphic design: it takes the form of a stylized crane in a circle and is closely modeled on the publisher's seal used around 1800 by Tsuruya Kinsuke (see London, Victoria and Albert Museum, *The Toshiba Gallery: Japanese Art and Design* [London, 1986], pp. 134–35, no. 141). B.D.v.Z.

135 Bottle-Gourd Vase, 1899

Made by Scharvogel Kunsttöpferei München, Munich (established 1898)
Glazed stoneware, height 8¼" (21 cm)
Marks: SKM, stylized crane in circle (impressed)
Hessisches Landesmuseum, Darmstadt. 69:9

References

Sprechsaal (Coburg), Dec. 7, 1899, p. 1505; Siegfried Wichmann, "Übernahme floraler Grundformen unter Anregung der ostasiatischen Keramik," in Munich, Haus der Kunst, 1972, pp. 352–59, 1248; Bott, 1973, pp. 90, no. 94, 92; Bott, 1982, p. 264, no. 346, colorpl. 163.

Vases of this double-gourd shape belong to the earliest ceramics made by Scharvogel in his Munich workshops. It is likely that a vase of this kind was among the sixteen that he showed in the Munich Glaspalast exhibition in 1899, the first exhibition to which he contributed. His first customer was Prince Regent Luitpold of Bavaria, who expressed his great satisfaction "that the extensive activity displayed by the capital of Bavaria in the field of the applied arts had been further enriched by this ceramic undertaking."

Vases in double-gourd form were produced by many leading European glass and ceramic manufacturers from 1880 onward (for example, Bernard Moore, Emile Gallé, Alexandre Bigot, and Paul Jeanneney), and Scharvogel may have been particularly impressed by similar vases made by the acknowledged pioneer of the revival of artistic stoneware, Jean Carriès. But the double-gourd shape, and the brown, blue-black, violet, and oxblood colored glazes, also clearly indicate

137 Vase, 1904

Made by Scharvogel Kunsttöpferei München,
Munich (established 1898)
Glazed stoneware, height 7¹/₁₆″ (18 cm)
Marks: SKM, stylized crane in circle (impressed)
Staatliche Museen Preussischer Kulturbesitz,
Kunstgewerbemuseum, Berlin. WA 70

References
Die Kunst, vol. 10 (1904), p. 485 (ill.); Munich,
I. Ausstellung der Münchener Vereinigung für
angewandte Kunst, *Katalog* (1905), p. 49;
"Scharffeuersteinzeug von J. J. Scharvogel –
München," *Die Kunst,* vol. 14 (1906), p. 31 (ill.);
Deutsche Kunst und Dekoration, vol. 28 (1911),
p. 115 (ill.); Munich, 1964, p. 126, no. 1047;
Zurich, Kunstgewerbemuseum, *Keramik* (1965),
p. 161; Wolfgang Scheffler, *Werke um 1900*
(Berlin, 1966), p. 98, no. 144; Munich, *Hermann
Obrist,* 1968, p. 83, pl. 6; Zurich, 1975, p. 125,
no. 221; Brussels, 1977, p. 223, no. 493; Elisabeth
Kessler-Slotta, *Max Laeuger (1864-1952): Sein
graphisches, kunsthandwerkliches und keramisches
Oeuvre* (Saarbrücken, 1985), p. 173, no. 40b.

Scharvogel was president of the Munich
Vereinigung für Angewandte Kunst, and
at its first exhibition, held in 1905, he
showed a large selection of "decorative
and utilitarian objects executed in
enameled flambé stoneware," including
an example of this vase. It had already
been exhibited in 1904 at the Vereinigte
Werkstätten für Kunst im Handwerk in
Munich. The inside of the vase has a
gray-white glaze, while the exterior is
decorated with dark-blue and olive glazes

with beige freckles. The vase with
symmetrical spiral handles was a type of
vessel introduced to Jugendstil pottery in
about 1897 by Max Laeuger in Kandern
in southwest Germany. Siegfried Wichmann interestingly links Scharvogel's
three-handled vase to OBRIST's theories
on the "dynamic energies" that should be
inherent in a work of art, and sees the
vase as an illustration of Obrist's demand
for a "centrifugal tempo" and for a "process of oscillation upward and forward"
that is best expressed by the spiral movement, the predominant characteristic of
the abstract work of SCHMITHALS.

B.D.v.Z.

Hans Schmithals
1878-1964

Schmithals was born in Bad Kreuznach, and studied business in Darmstadt for a short time before leaving for Munich, where in September 1902 he joined the recently opened Lehr- und Versuch-Ateliers für Angewandte und Freie Kunst. He was considerably influenced by the school's founders, OBRIST and DEBSCHITZ, and after graduating, became an instructor there. Nominally, he was to teach the hand-printing of wallpapers, but he adhered to the school's rejection of the division between fine and applied art and was active in diverse fields and mediums.

As a painter, Schmithals took inspiration from Obrist's notion that the spiral is one of the basic forms that visualize dynamic force. In his early pictures, painted between 1902 and 1904, he reduced a glacial landscape, for instance, to a series of vortexes, tubular segments, and rudimentary spheres (see *Composition in Blue,* 1902; Bayerische Staatsgemäldesammlungen, Munich). In color and form, he evoked the centrifugal forces present not only on the glacier's surface, but also in its rifts and caverns – that is, in the third dimension. Schmithals was a daredevil skier and mountain climber, and this elemental experience of nature informed his pastels and paintings in combined mediums and lent them their visionary quality. True to Obrist's teachings, curvilinear shapes and "unraveling forms" acquired increasing prominence in his compositions. Soon they had detached themselves entirely from visual phenomena, from landscape impressions, and came to evoke seething cosmic whirlwinds, as may be seen particularly in *North Star and Draco* (no. 138).

The same radical nonobjectivity is found in the artist's handwoven carpets. In 1908 Schmithals contributed a number of abstract textile designs, together with his first designs for furniture, to an exhibition of the Verband für Raumkunst, Munich.

After a sojourn in Paris from 1909 to 1911, Schmithals returned to Munich, where, together with WERSIN, he founded the Ausstellungsverband für Raumkunst. The group mounted an exhibition in the fall of 1913 that included large woven carpets by Schmithals, who had been able to

Hans Schmithals, c. 1950

gain the support of the Smyrna carpet-making firm in Cottbus. Some of his furniture was on display as well, clean-cut, functional pieces in Caucasian walnut, upholstered in Morocco and with fittings of brass and patinated nickel, manufactured by the Frick company of Pappenheim in Franconia. So impressive was this Munich show that it was included in the 1914 Werkbund exhibition in Cologne.

Little was heard of Schmithals after World War I, and in World War II the greater part of his oeuvre was destroyed. A few surviving paintings were shown at the "Aufbruch zur modernen Kunst" exhibition in Munich in 1958, which led to a rediscovery of Schmithals as one of the early pioneers of abstract art, and the reclusive artist began to repaint some of his lost compositions from memory.

References

Dekorative Kunst, vol. 14 (1906), p. 346; E. K., "Arbeiten von Hans Schmithals," *Die Kunst,* vol. 30 (1914), pp. 264-72; Munich, 1958, p. 213; "Hans Schmithals," in Hans Vollmer, *Allgemeines Lexikon der bildenden Künstler des XX. Jahrhunderts,* vol. 6 (Leipzig, 1962), p. 396; Otto Stelzer, *Die Vorgeschichte der abstrakten Kunst: Denkmodelle und Vorbilder* (Munich, 1964), p. 115; Milan, 1965; Munich, *Hermann Obrist,* 1968, pp. 9-10; Kaiserslautern, Pfalzgalerie, *Katalog der Gemälde und Plastiken des 19. und 20. Jahrhunderts* (1975), p. 139; Schmoll, 1977, pp. 77, 81; Weiss, 1979, pp. 28, 117, 122, 208, n. 84, 210, n. 37, 265, figs. 91, 95.   W. W.

138 North Star and Draco, 1902

Mixed media, pastel, and gold on paper,
18⅞ x 43⁵/₁₆″ (48 x 110 cm)
Stadtmuseum, Munich. 65/62

References

Munich, 1958, p. 213, no. 749; Seling, ed., 1959,
p. 25, fig. 21; Paris, 1960–61, p. 215, no. 648;
Hans Hofstätter, *Geschichte der europäischen
Jugendstilmalerei* (Cologne, 1963), pl. 35; Milan,
1965, ill. inside front cover; Munich, Stadtmuseum, 1972, p. 524, no. 2095; Gabriele
Sterner, *Jugendstil: Kunstformen zwischen Individualismus und Massengesellschaft* (Cologne, 1975),
pp. 119, no. 67, 124, 125, 183; Munich, *Kandinsky,* 1982, p. 220, no. 112, 221; New York,
1982, p. 115, no. 53; S. Wichmann, *Jugendstil
Floral,* 1984, p. 88, fig. 168; S. Wichmann, 1984,
p. 88, fig. 168.

Done while Schmithals was a student at
the Debschitz School, *North Star and
Draco* was inspired by his teacher's ideas
as formulated in *Die Kunst*: the designer
should make visible the "movements and
groupings within natural phenomena" by
understanding the laws of nature, infus-
ing them with imagination, and condens-
ing them into free-form configurations
(Wilhelm von Debschitz, "Eine Methode
des Kunstunterrichts," *Die Kunst*, vol. 10
[1904], p. 235). Here the dragon representing the constellation Draco – his head
is visible at the lower right – coils around
a star in sweeping ornamental curves.
This expanding movement from the
center outward, threatening to explode
the picture plane, is a typical feature of the
artist's style.   C. S. v. W. S.

Theodor Schmuz-Baudiss
1859-1942

Schmuz-Baudiss attended the Kunstgewerbeschule in Munich from 1879 to 1882 and was a pupil of the Academy there from 1882 to 1890. In 1896, while painting at Diessen in the countryside near Munich, he became acquainted with a local potter named Treffler, and, having learned the rudiments of the potter's craft, subsequently abandoned his successful career as a painter in order to become a potter. After much trial and error, he exhibited his vases at the Munich Glaspalast exhibition of 1897, and received immediate recognition for his contribution to the development of contemporary German ceramics.

The first, rough-and-ready ceramics of 1897 retain the rusticity of local Diessen pottery and were executed in a technique designed by Schmuz-Baudiss to increase decorative effect: the leather-hard, yellow-red body of the vessel was covered with a layer of white slip or stannic oxide, and, after drying, the upper white layer was scratched away in ornamental patterns, as in the sgraffito method, to reveal the body. Before firing, the ornament was filled with colored glazes. Schmuz-Baudiss's early work displays a refreshing spontaneity of vision paired with uncertain craftsmanship. In spite of a reliance on the simple technical methods of local pottery, his use and deployment of shapes and stylized floral ornament derived from contemporary Scandinavian porcelain – in particular, that of the Rörstrand factory in Stockholm – reflect the artist's ambition to emulate the leading European porcelain factories of the time.

From 1897 onward, with increasing expertise, Schmuz-Baudiss's pottery became freer; his vases and other vessels, all unique pieces, gradually acquired more flowing forms and relied increasingly on applied sculptural detail, such as plant and animal ornament. Further technical experiments were carried out in collaboration with SCHARVOGEL, whom he supplied with various designs for brown-glazed stoneware. In 1898 Schmuz-Baudiss became a member of the Vereinigte Werkstätten für Kunst im Handwerk, Munich, and began a prolonged study of porcelain manufacture at the Swaine & Co. factory in Hüttensteinach in Thuringia. Porcelain made there for

Theodor Schmuz-Baudiss. Portrait painting, c. 1915-20

the Vereinigte Werkstätten to his designs, partly with oxides brought from Munich, reflects, in its use of underglaze colors and of low-relief plant and natural ornament, a continuing desire to achieve standards set by contemporary porcelain in Scandinavia. While his work in porcelain was more symmetrical and precise, and more attention was paid to detail, his early technique of slip decoration survived in his work for Swaine & Co.: the factory's "Pensée" dinner service, exhibited by the Vereinigte Werkstätten at the 1900 Paris Exposition Universelle, was decorated by a green slip design cut away to reveal the white porcelain surface.

Between 1899 and 1902 Schmuz-Baudiss exhibited with great success in Munich, Berlin, Leipzig, Dresden, Brussels, Paris, and Turin, and his contribution to Jugendstil ceramic art found recognition in the large number of awards he received. By 1902, the year in which he entered the service of the Königliche Porzellan-Manufaktur in Berlin following an offer by the Prussian ministry of trade, he was already being hailed by Richard Borrmann as "the best ornamental designer of ceramics in Germany" and as "Germany's most creative ceramic artist." In Berlin, Schmuz-Baudiss was first responsible for the establishment of an

underglaze department; after he became director of the manufactory in 1908 – a post he held until his retirement in 1926 – he consolidated the manufactory's leading position in Germany alongside Meissen.

References

"Korrespondenzen: München," *Dekorative Kunst,* vol. 1 (1897), pp. 45-46; Singer, 1898, pp. 205-14; G.[L. Gmelin], "Töpfereien von Schmuz-Baudiss in München," *Kunst und Handwerk,* vol. 47 (1898), pp. 313-19; "Unsere Bilder von der Pariser Weltausstellung," *Kunst und Handwerk,* vol. 50 (1899-1900), pp. 280-81, 378; Gmelin, 1901-2, pp. 325-27; Borrmann, 1902, pp. 57-59, 65-71, 101-7; Irene von Treskow, *Die Jugendstil-Porzellane der KPM: Bestandskatalog der Königlichen Porzellan-Manufaktur Berlin 1896-1914* (Munich, 1971), pp. 57-116, 266-68.   B.D.v.Z.

139 Vase, 1897

Earthenware, slip coated and glazed; height 8¹/₈″ (20.5 cm)
Marks: TS-B (incised), 8, lozenge-patterned shield with star above (impressed)
Gewerbemuseum der LGA im GNM, Nuremberg. 8341

References

Singer, 1898, pp. 206, 212 (ill.); *Dekorative Kunst,* vol. 2 (1898), p. 36; *Kunst und Handwerk,* vol. 47 (1898), p. 317.

Schmuz-Baudiss's earliest pottery of this kind reflects the experimental nature of his work. In his zeal to introduce to Munich a pottery of contemporary validity, Schmuz-Baudiss allowed imperfections in his work to reveal the artist's creative hand.

The vase, and the jug (no. 140), bear an impressed mark of the Nymphenburg porcelain manufactory on the base. This does not signify that the designs were carried out by the manufactory, as is generally believed, nor does the mark mean, as one contemporary author stated, that the finished works could be purchased only through Nymphenburg. In about September 1897 Albert Bäuml, leaseholder of the manufactory since 1888, had a Nymphenburg kiln made available to

Schmuz-Baudiss after the artist's return from ceramic studies in Dinkelsbühl, Franconia, in the summer of that year. The kiln was normally used for the production of firebricks. Schmuz-Baudiss employed the obsolete Nymphenburg mark of an impressed lozenge-patterned shield with star above – used on the manufactory's porcelain from 1850 to 1862 – in order that his work would not be mistaken for contemporary Nymphenburg production. The agreement between Schmuz-Baudiss and Bäuml, whose interests at the time were solely of a retrospective nature, was short-lived and appears not to have been a happy one. It came to an end about March 1898: the April issue of *Dekorative Kunst* relates that "Theodor Schmuz-Baudiss had been tolerated in Nymphenburg as an experimental artist until recently," but that "he has set up in his own right and can now work completely independently."

Schmuz-Baudiss's pottery vases are unique pieces and this one bears the im-

pressed number 8, which allows it to be dated to the fall or early winter of 1897. It was bought from the artist in 1898 for 30 gold marks. G.D.

140 Jug, 1897

Earthenware, slip coated and glazed; height 8³/₄″ (22.2 cm)
Marks: TS-B (incised), 19, lozenge-patterned shield with star above (impressed)
Gewerbemuseum der LGA im GNM, Nuremberg. 8343

References

Singer, 1898, p. 209 (ill.); Irene von Treskow, *Die Jugendstil-Porzellane der KPM: Bestandskatalog der Königlichen Porzellan-Manufaktur Berlin 1896-1914* (Munich, 1971), p. 240, no. 257; Nuremberg, 1980, p. 82, no. 91a.

The orange-red body of the jug was first covered with a layer of green slip, which was then cut away to create a raised surface decoration of stylized plant forms.

The handle consists of a pair of applied snakes, whose heads rest within the flared neck of the jug. The surface and applied ornament are based on the artist's study of local natural forms. The impressed Nymphenburg mark and the number 19 indicate that the jug was one of the earliest pieces to have been fired in Schmuz-Baudiss's kiln at Nymphenburg (see no. 139), and it can therefore be dated to late fall or early winter 1897. The jug was among a group of pottery by Schmuz-Baudiss reviewed by Hans Singer in the 1898 volume of *Deutsche Kunst und Dekoration*. "Schmuz-Baudiss's vases give one the immediate feeling," he wrote, "that they have been developed out of an intensive study of the art and technique of pottery, even though one can argue with him here and there. He has not overpowered the material in a mania to create something new and original.... His originality has come from within himself."

The jug was purchased from the artist in 1898 for 30 gold marks. G.D.

Gertraud
von Schnellenbühel
1878-1959

Born in Jena, Schnellenbühel was one of the first students of OBRIST's and DEBSCHITZ's Lehr- und Versuch-Ateliers für Angewandte und Freie Kunst in Munich. Active particularly in the school's metalworking shop, she developed a biomorphic, ornamental version of Jugendstil inspired by the work of Obrist and similar to that of ADLER and Fritz Schmoll von Eisenwerth.

The Badisches Landesmuseum, Karlsruhe, owns an embroidery attributed to Schnellenbühel that may be dated to about 1902 (formerly Wichmann collection). However, she did not really make her debut at the Debschitz School until 1904, and then with characteristic metalwork pieces. These included a silver champagne cup (about sixteen inches high) that was illustrated in the 1904 volume of *Die Kunst* (location unknown). The cup was singled out for mention in the 1905-6 volume of *Kunst und Handwerk,* in a review of work by students of the Debschitz School included in the Nuremberg "Kunstgewerbe-Ausstellung" of 1906.

Schnellenbühel's most mature work in the spirit of the Debschitz School is undoubtedly the famous twenty-four-light candelabra (no. 141). This elegant masterpiece, first published in *Die Kunst* in 1914, immediately made a name for its designer. So highly regarded was the piece that Obrist himself purchased it for his home.

Schnellenbühel's skill and originality are also evident in jewelry designs, which she herself executed at the Lehr- und Versuch-Ateliers. These include a silver necklace set with moonstones (illustrated in the 1905-6 volume of *Kunst und Handwerk*) that, with a silver bracelet, is now in the estate of the painter SCHMITHALS; a necklace in gold, set with rubies and pearls (illustrated in the 1907-8 volume of *Kunst und Handwerk*); and a silver chain (illustrated in the June 1906 issue of *Die Kunst*).

Basing her work closely on that of Fritz Schmoll von Eisenwerth, Schnellenbühel also created a coffee service in silver with ebony and mother-of-pearl inlays, which was praised in the 1906 volume of *Die Kunst* when it was shown in the section devoted to members of the Debschitz

Gertraud von Schnellenbühel, 1914

School at the 1906 "Bayerische Jubiläums-Landes-Ausstellung" in Nuremberg. After 1914, as far as can be ascertained, there was no further mention of her in the relevant publications, and no later work by her is known.

References

Die Kunst, vol. 10 (1904), pp. 223 (ill.), 225 (ill.); *Kunst und Handwerk,* vol. 56 (1905-6), pp. 351, 362, fig. 787; *Die Kunst,* vol. 14 (1906), pp. 361-62; *Kunst und Handwerk,* vol. 58 (1907-8), p. 32, fig. 52; *Die Kunst,* vol. 30 (1914), p. 329; Munich, 1958, no. 757; Paris, 1960-61, no. 1246; Munich, 1964, no. 1048; Rheims, 1966, no. 438; Munich, Stadtmuseum, 1972, no. 2219.　　　H.S.g.E

141 Candelabra, c. 1910

Made by Steinicken & Lohr, Munich (established 1897)
Silver-plated brass, height 19$^{1}/_{16}$″ (48.5 cm)
Stadtmuseum, Munich. 49-62

References

G.J.W., "Zu den Arbeiten aus der Ausstellung 'Raumkunst,'" *Die Kunst,* vol. 30 (1914), pp. 329-31 (ill.); Munich, 1958, p. 215, no. 757; Paris, 1960-61, p. 389, no. 246; Munich, 1964, p. 126, no. 1048; Rheims, 1966, pp. 323, no. 438, 332; Graham Hughes, *Modern Silver throughout the World 1880-1967* (New York, 1967), p. 245; Munich, Stadtmuseum, 1972, p. 527, no. 2129; Munich, 1976, p. 217, no. 485; Darmstadt, 1976-77, vol. 2, p. 152, no. 275; Munich, Villa Stuck, 1979, p. 20, no. 125, fig. 41; Munich, *Kandinsky,* 1982, p. 220, no. 110; New York, 1982, p. 97, no. 22; S. Wichmann, *Jugendstil Floral,* 1984, p. 68, fig. 119; S. Wichmann, 1984, p. 68, fig. 119; Cologne, 1984, pp. 244, fig. 1, 249.

Published in *Die Kunst* when it was exhibited at the Cologne Werkbund exhibition of 1914, this unique twenty-four-light candelabra was described there as "at first glance capricious with its singularly branching lines.... but when seriously considered, the shapes appear full of measure and rhythm, drawn from the artist's inner treasury of forms." One of a number of "beautifully shaped" objects by Schnellenbühel that "combined construction and ornament" in "exemplary" fashion described in the same article, the candelabra resembled none of the others illustrated there. Its intricate and abstract profusion of curving lines is more characteristic of the early products of the Debschitz School, where Schnellenbühel had studied with OBRIST and DEBSCHITZ from about 1902. In fact, the candelabra later belonged to Obrist, and formed part of the furnishings of his villa in Munich's Schwabing district, which included so many other masterworks of the Munich Jugendstil (see nos. 56, 58, 67, 69, 95-98).　　　K.B.H.

Carl Strathmann
1866-1939

Strathmann was admired both as a painter and an ornamentalist and his paintings were rarely illusionistic in the traditional sense. Rather, they were decorative, often studded with colored glass and stones, a technique foreshadowing that of the Viennese Secessionist Gustav Klimt. In the pamphlet *Um die Schönheit* (no. 33), ENDELL wrote that Strathmann's "ornamental talent is nearly inexhaustible. He brings new forms unceasingly.... One laughs at him; one would do better to study him intensively" (quoted in Weiss, 1979, p. 69).

Born in Düsseldorf, Strathmann was the son of a prosperous German businessman, which freed him of financial worries throughout his career. While attending the Düsseldorf Kunstakademie from 1882 to 1886, he became friends with HEINE. Expelled from the academy for "lack of talent," Strathmann continued his studies at the Kunstschule in Weimar, with Leopold von Klackreuth, an exponent of Impressionist *Heimatkunst* (regional art).

Moving to Munich, Strathmann established himself in a well-appointed atelier on Landwehrstrasse and mingled with the Bohemian circle of the painter Lovis Corinth, who described Strathmann's debut canvas, *Le Billet Doux*, as a combination of outdoor painting with psychological realism. Strathmann's graphic works of the early 1890s were strongly influenced by the Symbolists Adolph Knopff and Jan Toorop, whose art caused a furor at the inaugural exhibition of the Munich Secession in 1892. In his watercolors, however, Strathmann's own expressive needs came to the fore, producing images of bizarre eeriness. Although he occasionally approached the somber romanticism of Heine or the grotesque linear stylization of Paul Klee's early drawings, Strathmann created synthetic structures that display a modern sense of formal ambiguity. The artist also created ironic and self-spoofing drawings, which he published in such Jugendstil periodicals as *Jugend, Fliegende Blätter,* and *Pan,* as well as in a portfolio of caricatures titled *Fin de siècle.*

Strathmann's best work was done around 1895, the year after he became a member of the Munich Freie Vereinigung, a progressive faction that had split

Carl Strathmann, before 1900

off from the Secession and included BEHRENS, Corinth, ECKMANN, Julius Exter, Heine, Hans Ode, Hermann Schlittgen, Max Slevogt, and Wilhelm Trübner. Among the major canvases of this period was *Salammbô* (Weimar museum), which, inspired by Flaubert's novel, combined precious stones with painting, leading the Kunstverein jury to reject it as "craftlike." This painting is an example of the ornamental side of Munich Jugendstil, which assimilated the most diverse influences, from Symbolism to Japonism, from Byzantinism to Academicism.

In the course of the next decade – and particularly when he shared a studio with NIEMEYER – Strathmann turned increasingly to the applied arts. He designed patterns for textiles, menus, calendars, wallpaper, book covers, theater curtains, and rugs that reflected his unusual capacity for formal invention and combined heterogeneous stylistic elements into a compelling visual whole of magical charm.

References

Lovis Corinth, "Carl Strathmann," *Kunst und Künstler,* vol. 1 (1903), pp. 255-63; Fritz Schmalenbach, *Jugendstil: Ein Beitrag zur Theorie und Geschichte der Flächenkunst* (Würzburg, 1935), p. 96; Hans H. Hofstätter, in Seling, ed., 1959, p. 142; Bonn, 1976; S. Wichmann, 1977, pp. 108-9.   J.H.v.W.

142 Design for a Plate, c. 1897

Ink, watercolor, and enamel on cardboard, 28¹¹/₁₆ x 28¹¹/₁₆" (72.8 x 72.8 cm)
Stadtmuseum, Munich. 57/801 (Ü)

References

Munich, 1897, p. 214, no. 184a; Bonn, 1976, pp. 34, fig. 58, 35, 48; Weiss, 1979, p. XXI, fig. 63; Munich, *Kandinsky,* 1982, pp. 228-29, no. 124; New York, 1982, p. 204, no. 201.

The design for a ceramic plate, which was probably never executed, was shown in the applied art section of the 1897 Munich Glaspalast exhibition. Known variously as *Satan* and *The Snake in Eden,* it depicts the serpent twined around a tree trunk in the midst of wildly proliferating, imaginary flowers and in a field of white blossoms that reappear in modified form on the octagonal border, among tangled golden foliage and thornbushes. This image with its border provides an example of the convoluted decorative linearism that was a hallmark of the artist's painting. The suggestive and enigmatic treatment of the serpent reveals the influence of the Symbolists, especially of Strathmann's fellow painter STUCK.   C.S.v.W.S.

Franz von Stuck
1863–1928

Stuck was one of the leading artists of Munich Jugendstil and of German art at the turn of the century. The strength of his artistic contribution lay in the multiplicity of his talents, which encompassed drawing, painting, sculpture, applied art, and architecture – a universality typical of Art Nouveau.

Born in Tettenweis, Lower Bavaria, Stuck – who was raised to the nobility in 1906 – studied in Munich at the Kunstgewerbeschule from 1878 to 1881 and at the Academy between 1881 and 1885. During the early years of his career he made drawings and illustrations for popular magazines, such as *Fliegende Blätter,* and later for *Pan* and *Jugend.* His painting *The Guardian of Paradise* was shown at the 1889 Glaspalast exhibition in Munich, where it won a gold medal.

Stuck's paintings adapted the neoclassical vocabulary of Arnold Böcklin and Max Klinger and stood in complete contrast to the then revolutionary movements of Realism and Naturalism. In 1892, with Bruno Piglheim, Fritz von Uhde, and Heinrich von Zügel, Stuck cofounded the Munich Secession. In 1895 he was appointed professor at the Munich Academy and soon became one of the most prestigious art teachers in Germany, including among his pupils Josef Albers, Wassily Kandinsky, Paul Klee, and Hans Purrmann. Stuck's most famous paintings – for example, *Sin* (1893), *War* (1894), *Paradise Lost* (1897), and *Salome* (1906) – were often executed in variations, with frames designed by the artist.

In 1897-98 Stuck designed his own house, the Villa Stuck in Munich's Prinzregentenstrasse, which was built in collaboration with the architects Jakob Heilmann and Max Littmann. Architecture, interior design, furniture, painting, and sculpture here became a comprehensive unity, a *Gesamtkunstwerk* (total work of art), which was also achieved in the work of other Jugendstil artists, such as ERLER and RIEMERSCHMID. The Grecian-style furniture that Stuck designed for the villa was shown at the Paris Exposition Universelle of 1900 and awarded a gold medal there. Stuck's interests also extended to such areas as theater, music, dance, and literature.

Franz von Stuck, c. 1918

For Stuck, the borderlines between fine and applied art were invalid. Similar basic concepts informed the work of the Vereinigte Werkstätten für Kunst im Handwerk and the Lehr- und Versuch-Ateliers für Angewandte und Freie Kunst, as they did the foundation of the Bauhaus by Walter Gropius in Weimar in 1919. Stuck's further aspirations toward a new type of folk art remained an exclusive aesthetic revolution and have been aptly described as "folk art for rich people."

References

Otto Julius Bierbaum, *Franz Stuck* (Bielefeld, 1899); Franz Hermann Meissner, *Franz Stuck* (Berlin, 1899); Georg Habich, "Villa Stuck," *Kunst und Handwerk,* vol. 49 (1898-99), pp. 185-207; Hans Vollmer, *Franz Stuck* (Berlin, 1902); Fritz von Ostini, "Villa Stuck," *Innen-Dekoration,* vol. 20 (1909), pp. 397-428; Herbert Schindler, "Franz von Stuck," *Epoca,* no. 6 (June 1967), pp. 41-49; Munich, *Franz von Stuck,* 1968; Werner Hager, "Zur Villa Stuck," in Renate von Heydebrand and Klaus Günther Just, eds., *Wissenschaft als Dialog: Studien zur Kunst und Literatur seit der Jahrhundertwende* (Stuttgart, 1969), pp. 1-8; Schmoll, ed., 1972; Voss, 1973; Gregor von Rezzori, "A Temple to His Art," *House and Garden,* vol. 158, no. 3 (Mar. 1986), pp. 84-94, 97. U.K.

143 Poster for "VII. Internationale
Kunstausstellung," 1897

Printed by Meisenbach Riffarth & Co., Munich
Photolithograph, 23⁵/₈ x 34³/₈" (60 x 87.5 cm)
Signature: Franz Stuck (center right)
Stadtmuseum, Munich. B 1/29

References

Jugend, no. 22 (May 29, 1897), p. 361 (ill.); *Wester-
mann's Monatshefte,* vol. 83 (1897-98), p. 493 (ill.);
Poster and Art Collector (Nov. 1898), p. 214 (ill.);
Archiv für Buchgewerbe, vol. 52, nos. 7-8 (July-
Aug. 1915), p. 241, fig. 15; *Das Plakat,* vol. 10
(1919), p. 40, fig. 4; Munich, 1958, p. 247,
no. 981; Hamburg, 1963, p. 59, no. 475; Italo
Cremona, *Il Tempo dell'Art Nouveau: Modern
Style, Sezession, Jugendstil, Arts and Crafts,
Floreale, Liberty* (Florence, 1964), no. 241;
Munich, *Franz von Stuck,* 1968, p. 83, no. 77;
Reichel, 1974, pp. 69-70; Munich, 1975-76 (2nd
ed., 1978), p. 181, no. 34; Brussels, 1977,
pp. 290-91, no. 706; Hollmann, et al., 1980,
Part 1, p. 282, no. 3217, Part 2, pl. 225, no. 3217;
Munich, *Kandinsky,* 1982, p. 195, no. 35; New
York, 1982, p. 84, no. 1; Bouillon, 1985, p. 119;
Peter-Klaus Schuster, "Münchner Bilderstürme
der Moderne," *Kritische Berichte,* vol. 14, no. 4
(1986), pp. 60-62.

At the "VII. Internationale Kunstausstellung," held at the Munich Glaspalast in
1897, the Secession showed with the
Künstlergenossenschaft (Society of Artists) for the first time since it had split off
from that official group in 1893. The controversial poster for the Secession's first
exhibition in 1892, also designed by
Stuck, had been emblazoned with a hel-
meted Athena, and in Stuck's poster for
the 1897 exhibition the combative patron-
ess of art and symbol of the Secession
again holds center stage, brilliant in gold
and ivory. She also appears at the upper
right, in profile, confronting a personifi-
cation of painting, the Künstlergenossenschaft's emblem, as if ready to defend the
renegades' ideals. This striking symbolism is made even more effective by a
simplified contour style, a sparing use
of color, and relatively concise text –
features that were to have a lasting influence on poster design.   C.S.v.W.S.

Ignatius Taschner
1871-1913

Although he spent key phases of his career as a sculptor, illustrator, and teacher in Wroclaw (Breslau) and Berlin, Taschner's unbroken ties with his home region made him a quintessential Bavarian artist. He was born in Bad Kissingen, son of a master stonemason, and grew up in intimate contact with his father's craft. In 1885 he was apprenticed to learn the trades of house-painting and stonemasonry, but four years later, in a decision highly unusual for someone of his social background, he entered the Munich Academy to study sculpture with Syrius Eberle.

After winning a silver medal at the Academy, he was awarded first prize in a war memorial competition in Schweinfurt. His sculpture was unveiled in 1895, but this initial success did not continue, and Taschner faced years of poverty. Gradually he was able to obtain private sculpture commissions, and lived by designing stained-glass windows and selling illustrations.

In 1903 increasing success as a sculptor led to the offer of a teaching post at the Kunstgewerbeschule in Wroclaw, and this soon proved an artistic stepping-stone to Berlin. In 1904 the architect Alfred Messel commissioned him to produce the sculptural ornament of the new Wertheim department store there, and Ludwig Hoffmann, Berlin city architect, arranged for Taschner to contribute to the design of an elaborate centerpiece for presentation to the crown prince (Stadt-museum, Munich). In 1905 Taschner opened his own studio in Berlin. He continued to contribute to important building projects in that city, receiving commissions for the city hall, Virchow hospital, and the Märkisches Museum, among others. For the city of Wroclaw he created a fountain dedicated to the novelist Gustav Freytag, and for St. Paul, Minnesota, a monument to the poet Friedrich von Schiller.

His newfound prosperity enabled Taschner to build a house of his own design in Mitterndorf, on the edge of the Dachau moors near Munich, where he pursued his ideal of developing art out of the spirit and practice of craftsmanship. This included a respect for folk art and the life of the people. From the beginning

Ignatius Taschner, c. 1903

Taschner had employed popular motifs and religious themes, and particularly in his illustrations for fairy tales and novels he returned again and again to depictions of rural life past and present. His illustrations for Ludwig Thoma's *Der heilige Hies* (published 1904) and *Der Wittiber* (1912) are among his finest achievements in this field, effortlessly merging Bavarian Baroque and Rococo forms with the stylized, ornamental approach of Jugendstil in woodcuts of great force. The year 1913 saw the unveiling, in Berlin, of Taschner's *Fairy Tale Fountain*, in which figures from his illustrations to Grimms' fairy tales were transformed into sculpture.

References

Joseph Popp, "Ignatius Taschner," *Deutsche Gesellschaft für Christliche Kunst: Jahresmappe* (1900), pp. 17-18; Habich, 1903-4, pp. 1-18; Tim Klein, "Der Märchenbrunnen in Friedrichshain zu Berlin," *Plastik*, vol. 3 (1913), pp. 73-79; Wilhelm Hausenstein, "Ignatius Taschner gestorben," *Zeitschrift für Bildende Kunst,* supp. to n.s., vol. 25, (1913-14), pp. 179-81; "Friede den Menschen auf Erden," *Zeitschrift für Alte und Neue Glasmalerei,* vol. 3 (1914), p. 155; Alexander Heilmeyer, "Ignatius Taschners Hauskunst," *Kunstgewerbeblatt,* n.s., vol. 28 (1917), pp. 145-52; Thoma and Heilmeyer, eds., 1921; Richard

Lemp, ed., *Ludwig Thoma, Ignatius Taschner: Eine bayerische Freundschaft in Briefen* (Munich, 1971); Helga D. Hofmann, *Kleinplastik und figürliches Kunsthandwerk aus den Beständen des Münchner Stadtmuseums 1880-1930* (Munich, 1974), pp. 81-89; Berlin, Georg-Kolbe-Museum, *Die Figuren des Kronprinzensilbers* (1982), esp. pp. 10-14, 26-36.   N.G.

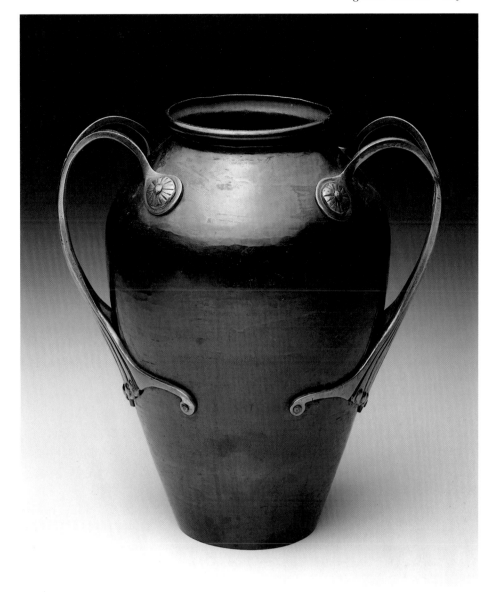

144 Flower Bucket, c. 1903

Made by Steinicken & Lohr, Munich (established 1897)
Colored and lacquered copper, and brass; height 11″ (28 cm)
Stadtmuseum, Munich. 64-261

Reference
Habich, 1903-4, pp. 13-14, 30 (ill.).

The bucket is one of a wide range of small objects – various vessels, candelabras, clocks, and ashtrays – that Taschner designed for industrial production by the Munich firm of Steinicken & Lohr. The designs differ considerably from one another, and include fantastic human and animal forms, elements derived from the folk art of earlier times, and such clear, simple shapes as that of the bucket shown here. Contemporary critics emphasized its suitability for industrial production, commenting on "the austere elegance that is a part of the modern Machine Age." Yet Taschner based the design of the bucket on the age-old form of the amphora. The object's charm derives from the contrast between its dark, solidly three-dimensional body and the linearity of its light brass handles, which are splayed at the bottom. The bucket successfully adapts an artistic design to production in large numbers.   N.G.

Ludwig Vierthaler
1875-1967

Munich-born Vierthaler first came to prominence around 1906 as a designer for metalwork companies in the city. From 1889 to 1892 he was trained as a silversmith and bronze-founder in the works of J. Winhart & Co., and after spending a year at the Kainzinger & Löblein foundry in Nuremberg, he traveled to New York, where he found employment in the metalwork department of Tiffany & Co. On his return to Munich in 1895, he spent a year at the Rupp iron foundry and enrolled at the Kunstgewerbeschule, where he studied under Ferdinand von Miller and Heinrich Waderé. Shortly before 1900 he rejoined Winhart & Co., and by 1906 had taken a leading position in the company, probably as director of design. His designs for the company were included in the "Bayerische Jubiläums-Landes-Ausstellung" held in Nuremberg in that year.

The surface of his copper vases, jugs, jardinières, urns, and other household objects were treated in such a way that subtle color effects were obtained, including bronze-green and purple-red, and the vessels and plates were frequently set with semiprecious stones and mother-of-pearl. Winhart's "artistically superior patinations" were sold under the registered trademark EOSIN. Their design is generally in restrained Munich Jugendstil, but sometimes involves the use of geometric ornament, and, most importantly, a dynamic abstract surface decoration based on underwater plant and animal forms.

Vierthaler's association with Winhart & Co. had come to an end before the Nuremberg exhibition of 1906. In that year he joined Eugen Ehrenböck, a rival Munich metalwork studio founded in 1905, whose copper, iron, and brass products employed multicolored enamel patterns. At the 1906 "III. Deutsche Kunstgewerbe-Ausstellung" in Dresden Ehrenböck was awarded a silver medal. Vierthaler's designs for Ehrenböck were also on display at the Nuremberg exhibition of the same year, and here Ehrenböck was awarded a gold medal. After the exhibition Ehrenböck and Vierthaler went into partnership: the new firm was called Kunst-Metall-Werkstätten, München, E. Ehrenböck & L. Vierthaler.

Ludwig Vierthaler, c. 1910

Their products included household and decorative objects, lighting fixtures, large-scale figures, architectural details, and furniture fittings, and the firm even supplied whole house facades. The partnership was dissolved in 1909. From 1908 to 1910 Vierthaler was working in association with PAUL for the Berlin branch of the Vereinigte Werkstätten für Kunst im Handwerk, Munich. From 1910 onward, Vierthaler continued to design metalwork – for the Homann-Werke in Vohwinkel and for the lighting manufacturer G. Krüger in Berlin – as well as jewelry for A. von Mayrhofer in Munich, while at the same time turning his attention to architectural ceramics. His most important commission in this field was for the figural and ornamental decoration of the Hermann Bahlsen building, designed by Karl Siebrecht for the Deutscher Werkbund exhibition in Cologne in 1914. The ceramics were executed by the Meissen firm of Ernst Teichert. Vierthaler had become a member of the Deutscher Werkbund by 1912, and in 1915 he became a teacher at the Staatliche Handwerker-und Kunstgewerbeschule in Hanover. In 1921 he was appointed professor at the

Hanover Technische Hochschule, with responsibility for the modeling and architectural sculpture classes, but continued to work as a sculptor in bronze during the following years. He later became professor at the Kunstgewerbeschule in Hanover.

References

Kunst und Handwerk, vol. 56 (1905-6), pp. 339-43, 345-49; Nuremberg, Bayerische Jubiläums-Landes-, Industrie-, Gewerbe- und Kunstausstellung, *Offizieller Katalog* (Nuremberg, 1906), p. 132; *Kunst und Handwerk,* vol. 57 (1906-7), inside front wrapper; Hermann Post, "Das Wiedererwachen des Ornaments und die Anlehnung an frühere Stilformen," *Die Kunst,* vol. 26 (1912), pp. 321-28; "Deutsche Form im Kriegsjahr: Die Ausstellung Köln 1914," *Jahrbuch des Deutschen Werkbundes 1915* (Munich, 1915), pp. 143-45; Helga D. Hofmann, ed., *Kleinplastik und figürliches Kunsthandwerk aus den Beständen des Münchner Stadtmuseums 1880-1930* (Munich, 1974), p. 91; Hanover, Kestner-Museum, *Rosenthal: Hundert Jahre Porzellan* (1982), pp. 50, 200-1.

G.D.

145 Dish, 1906

Made by Eugen Ehrenböck, Munich (established 1905)
Patinated copper with enamel decoration, diameter 6 3/16" (15.7 cm)
Württembergisches Landesmuseum, Stuttgart.
G 6,336

Reference

Kunst und Handwerk, vol. 56 (1905-6), pp. 345-46, 349, fig. 751.

Eugen Ehrenböck had designed and made his own metalwork before enlisting the services of Vierthaler in 1906. Ehrenböck had already initiated a revival of the use of enamel decoration on copper and iron household objects, a technique that set him apart from such leading Munich metalwork shops as J. Winhart & Co., Steinicken & Lohr, Gottlieb Wilhelm, Josef Zimmermann & Co., and Theodor Holländer & Co., all of whom participated in the 1906 Nuremberg exhibition. Among the hand-beaten copper dishes designed by Vierthaler that Ehrenböck exhibited in Nuremberg was a group displaying an enameled relief ornament at the center in the form of a beetle, crab, or salamander. The example with a salamander exhibited in 1906 differed from the one shown here in that the surface area of the dish was divided into equal compartments by five radial ridges. The use of the lizard motif in relief, common in English and French ceramics and metalware in the later nineteenth century, is an example of the lasting influence of Japonism in Europe.

Critics at the Nuremberg exhibition were unanimous in their recognition of Ehrenböck's and Vierthaler's technical and artistic achievement. Paul Rée, librarian and secretary of the Bayerisches Gewerbemuseum in Nuremberg, found fault with J. Winhart & Co.'s extensive display, but had nothing but praise for Ehrenböck: "Among the hand-beaten copperware Eugen Ehrenböck's creations aroused the most interest. They owe their charm to a natural choice of form, exquisite patina, and enamel decoration carried out with consummate taste. No wonder that the applied art collections fought with each other to secure such exhibits" (Paul Johannes Rée, "Die Kunstgewerbeausstellung," in *Ausstellungszeitung: Amtliches Organ der ... III. Bayerischen Jubiläums-Landes-, Industrie-, Gewerbe- und Kunstausstellung, Nürnberg 1906,* ed. P.J. Rée [Nuremberg, 1905-6], p. 1072).

G.D.

146 Bowl, 1906

Made by J. Winhart & Co., Munich (established 1883)
Patinated copper with enamel decoration, turquoise, and mother-of-pearl; diameter 7¹/₈″ (19.8 cm)
Württembergisches Landesmuseum, Stuttgart.
G 6,515

References

Schumacher, et al., 1906, p. 248; Munich, 1958, p. 222, no. 802.

Vierthaler's asymmetrical repoussé design for J. Winhart & Co. shows bubble motifs and a squidlike creature whose body is placed toward one edge of the bowl. The creature's arms, curling around the wall of the bowl, conveniently leave the central area free. The choice of this unusual surface decoration was inspired by Ernst Haeckel's *Kunstformen der Natur (Art Forms in Nature),* the first installments of which had appeared in 1899. Haeckel, a leading and highly influential scientist, hoped that his publication would open the eyes of readers to the lesser-known felicities of the plant and animal worlds. When the first section, consisting of fifty plates and an explanatory commentary, was completed in early 1901, Leopold Gmelin, editor of *Kunst und Handwerk,* recommended it in his magazine as an invaluable source for those designers who were as yet unacquainted with Haeckel's work: "There is not a shadow of a doubt that all decorative artists...will profit enormously from this publication, especially as the last parts to appear have paid full attention to the forms and colors of the strange sea creatures that they introduce to us" (*Kunst und Handwerk,* vol. 51 [1900-1], p. 210).

A variant of Vierthaler's exercise in submarine ornament, with less inlaid decoration, was exhibited with other designs for J. Winhart & Co. at the Dresden exhibition of 1906. G.D.

Wolfgang von Wersin

1882-1976

Born in Prague of German and Austrian parents, Wersin began courses in painting there in 1900, while also studying architecture at the city's Technische Hochschule. In 1901 he moved to Munich to continue his training in both fields, but was soon disappointed with the historicist orientation of the Technische Hochschule's school of architecture under Friedrich Thiersch. Excited by the modern Jugendstil of ENDELL and RIEMERSCHMID, and strongly drawn to the crafts, Wersin decided to enter the Lehr- und Versuch-Ateliers für Angewandte und Freie Kunst, Munich, in 1902, the year of its founding by OBRIST and DEBSCHITZ. Although he took his preliminary diploma in architecture at the Technische Hochschule in 1903-4, he discontinued this training because, as he said, Obrist and Debschitz "taught in a much more vital, intellectual, and artistically serious way than any other school."

Obrist's ideas, which Wersin always considered to be those of a man of genius, provide the key to his own approach. Wersin later wrote that he was grateful to the school for "several years of continuous and valuable, if sometimes problematical, impulses and impressions. I devoted myself there to architectural sculpture and applied art, and quite soon, partly in school exhibitions, partly outside the school, I had a good deal of success with fountain sculptures, architectural renderings, and furniture designs that were reviewed and illustrated in art magazines."

After a year of military service in Prague in 1906, Wersin returned to Munich to teach life studies and modeling at the "Obrist School" (as he called it, after its spiritual mentor and not after its director, Debschitz).

In 1908 he left the school, while continuing to maintain his contacts there, enrolled for a time in another school of architecture, and made extensive study trips that took him as far afield as the United States. In 1910 Wersin married Herthe Schöpp (1889-1971), a designer who had also attended the Obrist-Debschitz school and who subsequently collaborated with her husband on many projects. In the years prior to World War I, Wersin pared down his style, freeing it of ornamenta-

Wolfgang von Wersin, 1908. Photograph by Wanda Debschitz

tion to achieve a very personal, stringent, and functional design approach that remained characteristic of him to the end of his career.

Wersin and his wife traveled a great deal in the prewar years, returning more than once to Murano, where they had glassware designs executed on commission by the Deutsche Werkstätten. Successful work in many design fields – including glass, metal, majolica, wickerware, straw mosaics, textiles, carpets, wallpapers, clocks, furniture, and fountains – was interrupted by the outbreak of war, in which Wersin served. In 1918 he resumed his work for the Deutsche Werkstätten, also functioning as art director for a number of important Munich exhibitions. In 1926 he was awarded the title of Professor of Fine Arts. The years 1925 to 1929 were devoted to the Neue Sammlung at the Bayerisches Nationalmuseum, a modern design collection he helped establish and which he headed from 1929 until his dismissal by the Nazis in 1934.

Ever since the prewar period he had pursued a simple, straightforward design in what he termed "eternal forms," and during the 1920s and 1930s he brought it to new heights of perfection – parallel to,

but independent of, the Bauhaus. He provided designs for a great number of firms, principally for the Deutsche Werkstätten, Munich-Hellerau, and various porcelain and glass factories, including Meissen, Nymphenburg, and Rosenthal, as well as Lobmeyr in Vienna.

References

Wersin, 1962; Helga Schmoll gen. Eisenwerth, "Kunsthandwerk und Design," in Munich, Stadtmuseum, *Die Zwanziger Jahre in München* (1979), p. 154 ff.; Linz, 1983, p. 5 ff.   H. S. g. E.

147 Abstract Study, 1903–4

Watercolor and lithography on paper,
4¹/₄ x 7¹/₂″ (10.8 x 18.9 cm)
Inscription: 1903/4 (lower right)
Stadtmuseum, Munich. Wersin Estate

References

Munich, *Kandinsky*, 1982, p. 217, no. 92;
New York, 1982, p. 186, no. 166; Linz, 1983,
pp. 14–16, 66, no. 1.

The abstract study in blue, green, and
white comes from a portfolio done during Wersin's studies at the Debschitz
School. Among the aims of this school
was to help students move from a mere
observation of nature to an understanding
of its underlying principles. Instead of
copying organic configurations, they
were encouraged to detect and trace their
inherent structures, even to the point of
abstraction. A number of designs produced at the school relied on pure
geometrical forms, foreshadowing experiments in Europe during the next decades, particularly at the Bauhaus. Here,
the dominating motif is a sequence of
diminishing squares, emerging from
pentagonal cutouts at the lower edge to
describe graceful arcs. As Helga Schmoll
gen. Eisenwerth suggests in the catalogue
of the Wersin exhibition held in Linz in
1983, this was probably a design for fabric or wallpaper.   C.S. v. W.S.

148 Abstract Study, c. 1903–4

Watercolor and lithography on paper, 4¹/₂ x 7″
(11.5 x 17.8 cm)
Stadtmuseum, Munich. Wersin Estate

References

Munich, *Kandinsky*, 1982, p. 217, no. 93; New
York, 1982, p. 186, no. 167; Linz, 1983, p. 66,
no. 2.

Like Wersin's other *Abstract Study* included here (no. 147), this image in shades
of blue, gray, and white shows variations
on geometric forms, with the sequence
consisting of squares describing a pyra-
mid whose base is superimposed on circular shapes. This study, too, was probably a design for a textile pattern.

C. S. v. W. S.

Appendix

Documents

Program of the Committee of the Section for Decorative Arts of the 7th International Art Exhibition in the Königlicher Glaspalast, Munich, February 24, 1897

1. This exhibition of *objects of the new applied art* aims at selecting, according to strict principles, the best that *modern* applied art has accomplished.
2. It therefore places the main emphasis on *originality of invention* and on *the perfect artistic and technical execution* of such artistic objects as fulfill the *requirements of our modern life.*
3. On the one hand, it excludes everything that appears as a thoughtless and false copy or imitation of past and foreign styles, that is not abreast of the latest developments in modern technology, and that is aimed at the bad taste of the artistically unschooled mass of the people. On the other hand, it also excludes such objects of *modern* applied art as appear to overstep the limits of artistic decorum or appear as exaggerated and misguided through a disregard for materials or through a striving for originality.
4. *In addition, this section is subject to the general program as well as the statutes and other provisions of the 7th International Art Exhibition in Munich.*

v. Berlepsch. Dülfer. Fischer. Obrist. Riemerschmid. Rolfs.

Statutes of the Board for Art in Handicraft, 1897-98

I

The Board for Art in Handicraft aims at furthering the new German arts and crafts. It attempts to accomplish this by:

1. organizing exhibitions of the new arts and crafts (at present, especially by ensuring that the new German arts and crafts are well represented at the Paris World Exposition in 1900);
2. promoting artistic design;
3. founding a G.m.b.H. [limited liability company] with the name United Workshops for Art in Handicraft, whose aims are:
   a) the purchase and exemplary execution of artistic designs,
   b) their direct commercial distribution under the most favorable possible conditions for the participating artists and with an ongoing guarantee of artistic value for the purchasers, and
   c) the education of artistic workers in handicraft techniques; and
4. establishing an information center in Munich, whose functions are:
   a) the provision of information at a modest fee on all aspects of the new arts and crafts to all participating parties, especially with a view to
   b) the furtherance of closer ties between artists, craftsmen, and customers, and
   c) the control of unfair exploitation of artistic creations included in the board's program through appropriate contracts and the prevention of such exploitation through suitable publication.

II

The Board for Art in Handicraft consists of a chairman, a manager, and four members; the latter must be artists by profession. In addition, a legal adviser assists it in the settling of its legal business. If a member resigns, the board makes up its number by a majority vote election and elects its chairman in the same manner. The board forms the jury of exhibitions organized by it and also inspects the designs submitted. If these include works by board members, these members abstain from voting in these cases. The jury must consist of at least three members and, if at all possible, replacements are drawn from the company's artists. The board holds a special meeting every January, at which the chairman is elected, the accounts closed, and the report on the board's activities during the past year discussed.

III

If the board is dissolved, its capital passes to the United Workshops for Art in Handicraft G.m.b.H.

Dr. Rolfs, Chairman. Martin Dülfer. Theodor Fischer. F. A. O. Krüger, Manager. Hermann Obrist. Richard Riemerschmid.

Statement of Purpose and Appeal for Members of the Board for Art in Handicraft, January 1, 1898

Experience over the last few years here in Germany and abroad has shown that ever larger sections of the purchasing public would gladly espouse the new, individual direction in the arts and crafts if they had more and better opportunities to see such new objects of interior decoration and if prices were not higher than those of generally available merchandise in the well-known styles. Those familiar with the situation also know that a considerable number of artists have created individual, beautiful, and functional designs in all areas of the applied arts, but are not in a position to have them carried out or to find customers for them. Furthermore, we know that enough craftsmen and manufacturers exist in Germany who possess both the technical ability to satisfy every artistic demand and the desire to carry out new designs, but who are unable to take the commercial risk of manufacturing pieces in large numbers without knowing how to market them. And the merchants, who are naturally interested in continually offering new and good wares, are in the difficult position of not knowing where the new is manufactured and in what quantities. Because the artists cannot find craftsmen to execute their designs, and because the craftsmen and manufacturers have no opportunity of exhibiting, and prospective purchasers and connoisseurs, none of seeing, buying, or ordering, the new is created sporadically and sold individually and expensively, whereas supply and demand in the new arts and crafts have long since been regulated satisfactorily in our neighboring countries. That is why the German market is flooded with foreign products of this kind of applied art.

The *Board for Art in Handicraft* in Munich, which arranged a showing of choice products, especially of the new German arts and crafts, at the Königlicher Glaspalast in 1897 (under the heading "Kleinkunst" [*objets d'art*]), is now extending its activities to include the task of remedying the state of affairs described above. To this purpose it includes among the aims described in the enclosed statutes the founding of a *Gesellschaft mit beschränkter Haftung* [limited liability company] that is to be set up *in Munich* under the name *United Workshops for Art in Handicraft.* The function of this company is:

1. either to pay artists in cash for their designs and enable them to be carried out under its [the company's] direction or to guarantee

their execution with a share in the profits for, and at no commercial risk to, the artists. Inspection of the designs as to artistic value is always carried out by the board;

2) to order, and pay craftsmen for, a large number of pieces and distribute them throughout the Empire at no commercial risk to the craftsmen;

3) to deliver the pieces ordered by the merchants and to ensure as active a commercial distribution as possible;

4) to offer the buyer products of the new arts and crafts continually, in as many places as possible, and at reasonable prices, and at the same time to provide him with a guarantee of artistic and technical excellence in the form of the board's inspection of all work;

5) to give artists the opportunity of acquiring technical knowledge in the workshops;

6) to promote as effectively as possible contacts between artists, manufacturers, and prospective purchasers on all matters pertaining to the new arts and crafts by means of the *information center* set up by the board; and

7) to prevent, by legal action or publication in the press, unlawful exploitation in the form of unfair imitation or use of artistic designs.

The company is founded with a capital of 100.000 marks, which will presumably increase accordingly as membership expands, and seeks members who are prepared to subscribe at least 500 marks with a deposit of 250 marks. According to law, the sum may not be less than 500 marks, but is subject to no restrictions above that amount. *Payment of this sum is and remains the only obligation that the individual has toward the company. Anyone can become a partner if he pays the above-mentioned sum or more* (rounded off to the nearest 100 marks), *whether he be artist, craftsman, manufacturer, merchant, or private person,* and the dividends he realizes are absolutely separate from payments for designs or articles ordered. Further information may be obtained at all times from the manager of the Board for Art in Handicraft, at present also the provisional manager of the company: the painter F. A. O. Krüger (information center of the K. f. K. i. H. [Board for Art in Handicraft]), Munich XIX (Gern), Kratzerstrasse 1.

Enclosing the statutes of the board and the draft contract of the United Workshops for Art in Handicraft, we therefore appeal for a capital contribution of at least 500 marks with a deposit of 250 marks and would request that capital contributions of 500 marks or more be transferred to the Bayerische Vereinsbank, Munich, by February 15, 1898.

Munich, January 1, 1898.

Hofrat Dr. Rolfs, Chairman.
Architect Martin Dülfer.
Architect Theodor Fischer.
Painter F. A. O. Krüger, Manager.
Sculptor Hermann Obrist.
Painter Richard Riemerschmid.

Major Exhibitions, 1897–1906

1897   Internationale Kunst-Ausstellung, Dresden

VII. Internationale Kunstausstellung, Munich

1898   Internationale Kunst-Ausstellung des Vereins Bildender Künstler Münchens (A.V.) "Secession," Munich

Münchener Jahres-Ausstellung, Munich

1899   Deutsche Kunst-Ausstellung, Dresden

Münchener Jahres-Ausstellung, Munich

Internationale Kunst-Ausstellung des Vereins Bildender Künstler Münchens (A.V.) "Secession," Munich

1900   Exposition Universelle, Paris

1901   Internationale Kunstausstellung, Dresden

VIII. Internationale Kunstausstellung, Munich

I. Ausstellung für Kunst im Handwerk, Munich

1902   Deutsch-Nationale Kunstausstellung, Düsseldorf

Esposizione Internazionale, Turin

1904   Grosse Kunstausstellung, Dresden

X. Ausstellung der Münchener Sezession: Der Deutsche Künstlerbund, Munich

Louisiana Purchase Exhibition, St. Louis

1905   I. Ausstellung der Münchener Vereinigung für Angewandte Kunst, Munich

1906   III. Deutsche Kunstgewerbe-Ausstellung, Dresden

Ausstellung für Angewandte Kunst, Munich

Bayerische Jubiläums-Landes-Ausstellung, Nuremberg

Selected Bibliography

Ahlers-Hestermann, 1956
Ahlers-Hestermann, Friedrich. *Stilwende: Aufbruch der Jugend um 1900.* 2nd. ed. Berlin, 1956.

Ahlers-Hestermann, 1960
Ahlers-Hestermann, Friedrich. *Bruno Paul: oder die Wucht des Komischen.* Berlin, 1960.

Bader-Griessmeyer, 1985
Bader-Griessmeyer, Gabriele. *Münchner Jugendstil-Textilien: Stickereien und Wirkereien von und nach Hermann Obrist, August Endell, Wassily Kandinsky und Margarete von Brauchitsch.* Schriften aus dem Institut für Kunstgeschichte der Universität München, vol. 4. Munich, 1985.

Berlepsch-Valendas, "Umschwung," 1897-98
Berlepsch-Valendas, Hans Eduard von. "Endlich ein Umschwung." *Deutsche Kunst und Dekoration,* vol. 1 (1897-98), pp. 1-12.

Berlepsch-Valendas, 1902
Berlepsch-Valendas, Hans Eduard von. "Ansichten." *Kunstgewerbeblatt,* n. s., vol. 13 (1902), pp. 125-43.

Berlin, 1970-71
Berlin, Staatliche Museen Preussischer Kulturbesitz. *Art Nouveau und Jugendstil: Kunstwerke aus dem Besitz der Staatlichen Museen Preussischer Kulturbesitz.* 1970-71.

Berlin, 1972
Berlin (East), Staatliche Museen, Kunstgewerbemuseum and Nationalgalerie. *Stilkunst um 1900 in Deutschland.* 1972.

Berlin, 1976
Berlin, Sammlung Karl H. Bröhan. *Kunsthandwerk, 1: Jugendstil, Werkbund, Art Déco; Glas, Holz, Keramik.* Berlin, 1976.

Berlin, *Bröhan,* 1977
Berlin, Sammlung Karl H. Bröhan. *Kunsthandwerk, 2: Jugendstil, Werkbund, Art Déco; Metall, Porzellan.* Berlin, 1977.

Bern, 1967
Bern, Berner Kunstmuseum. *Hermann Obrist, Louis Soutter, Jean Bloé Niestlé, Kurt Seligmann.* May 24-June 25, 1967.

Bielefeld, 1986
Bielefeld, Kulturhistorisches Museum. *Jugendstil: Gegenstände aus Bielefelder Privatbesitz.* Sept. 14-Oct. 26, 1986.

Bode, 1901
Bode, Wilhelm. *Kunst und Kunstgewerbe am Ende des neunzehnten Jahrhunderts.* Berlin, 1901.

Bonn, 1976
Bonn, Rheinisches Landesmuseum. *Grotesker Jugendstil: Carl Strathmann 1866-1939.* Mar. 25-May 2, 1976.

Borrmann, 1902
Borrmann, Richard. *Moderne Keramik.* Monographien des Kunstgewerbes, ed. Jean Louis Sponsel, no. 5. Leipzig, 1902.

Bott, Gerhard. *Kunsthandwerk um 1900: Jugendstil, art nouveau, modern style, nieuwe Kunst.* Kataloge des Hessischen Landesmuseums, no. 1. Darmstadt, 1965.

Bott, 1973
Bott, Gerhard. *Kunsthandwerk um 1900: art nouveau, modern style, nieuwe Kunst.* 2nd. ed., rev. and enl. Carl Bruno Heller. Darmstadt, 1973. 3rd. ed., rev. and enl. Carl Bruno Heller. Darmstadt, 1982.

Bott, 1977
Bott, Gerhard, ed. *Von Morris zum Bauhaus: Eine Kunst gegründet auf Einfachheit.* Hanau, 1977.

Bouillon, 1985
Bouillon, Jean-Paul. *Journal de L'Art Nouveau 1870-1914.* Geneva, 1985.

Braungart, 1921
Braungart, Richard von. *Julius Diez.* Munich, 1921.

Brussels, 1977
Brussels, Palais des Beaux-Arts. *Jugendstil.* Oct. 1-Nov. 27, 1977.

Buddensieg, 1984
Buddensieg, Tilmann. *Industriekultur: Peter Behrens and the AEG, 1907-1914.* Trans. Iain Boyd Whyte. Cambridge, Mass., 1984.

Carstanjen, 1898
Carstanjen, Friedrich. "Peter Behrens." *Pan,* vol. 4, no. 2 (Sept. 1898), pp. 117-20.

Cologne, 1978
Cologne, Kunstgewerbemuseum. *Meister der deutschen Keramik: 1900 bis 1950.* Feb. 10-Apr. 30, 1978.

Cologne, 1984
Cologne, Kölnischer Kunstverein. *Der westdeutsche Impuls 1900-1914: Kunst und Umweltgestaltung im Industriegebiet; Die Deutsche Werkbund-Ausstellung Cöln 1914.* Mar. 24-May 13, 1984.

Cremers, 1928
Cremers, Paul Joseph. *Peter Behrens: Sein Werk von 1900 bis zur Gegenwart.* Essen, 1928.

Damann, Walter H. *Deutsche Schriftkünstler der Gegenwart, III: Otto Eckmann.* Hamburg, 1921.

Darmstadt, 1972-73
Darmstadt, Hessisches Landesmuseum. *Jugendstil: Aus der Sammlung Prinz Ludwig von Hessen und bei Rhein und aus dem Viktoria & Albert Museum, London.* Dec. 8, 1972-Jan. 28, 1973.

Darmstadt, 1976-77
Darmstadt, Hessisches Landesmuseum. *Ein Dokument deutscher Kunst: Darmstadt 1901-1976.* 5 vols. Oct. 22, 1976-Jan. 30, 1977.

Dresden, 1899
Dresden, Deutsche Kunst-Ausstellung. *Offizieller Katalog.* 1899.

Dresden, Internationale Kunstausstellung. *Offizieller Katalog.* 1901.

Dresden, 1906
Dresden, III. Deutsche Kunstgewerbe-Ausstellung. *Offizieller Katalog.* 1906.

Dresden, 1976
Dresden, Staatliche Kunstsammlungen, Schloss Pillnitz, Bergpalais. *Kunsthandwerk und Industrieform des 19. und 20. Jahrhunderts.* 1976.

Eckmann, Otto. *Neue Formen: Dekorative Entwürfe für die Praxis.* Berlin, 1897.

Endell, August. *Um die Schönheit: Eine Paraphrase über die Münchener Kunstausstellungen 1896.* Munich, 1896.

Endell, "Formenschönheit," 1898
Endell, August. "Formenschönheit und dekorative Kunst." *Dekorative Kunst,* vol. 2 (1898), pp. 119-25.

Endell, "Möglichkeiten," 1898
Endell, August. "Möglichkeiten und Ziele einer neuen Architektur." *Deutsche Kunst und Dekoration,* vol. 1 (1897-98), pp. 141-53.

Endell, 1900
Endell, August. "Architektonische Erstlinge." *Die Kunst,* vol. 2 (1900), pp. 297-317.

Endres, Franz Carl. *Georg Hirth: Ein deutscher Publizist.* Munich, 1921.

Esswein, 1904
Esswein, Hermann. *Thomas Theodor Heine.* Moderne Illustrationen, no. 1. Munich, 1904.

Fanelli and Fanelli, 1976
Fanelli, Giovanni, and Rosalia Fanelli. *Il tessuto moderno: Disegno moda architettura, 1890-1940.* Florence, 1976.

Frankfurt, 1955
Frankfurt am Main, Museum für Kunsthandwerk. *Jugendstil.* 1955.

Frankfurt, 1974
Frankfurt am Main, Museum für Kunsthandwerk. *Neuerwerbungen: 1956-1974.* 1974.

Fred, 1901
Fred, W. "A Chapter on German Arts and Crafts with Special Reference to the Work of Hermann Obrist." *The Artist,* vol. 19 (1901), pp. 17-26.

Fuchs, 1902-3
Fuchs, Georg. "Die Wohnräume der Deutschen Abteilung." *Deutsche Kunst und Dekoration,* vol. 11 (1902-3), pp. 45-64.

Gasser, ed., 1977
Gasser, Manuel, ed. *München um 1900.* Bern, 1977.

Gmelin, "Kleinkunst," 1897-98
Gmelin, Leopold. "Die Kleinkunst auf der Kunstausstellung zu München 1897." *Kunst und Handwerk,* vol. 47 (1897-98), pp. 17-28, 50-58.

Gmelin, "Kunsthandwerk," 1897-98
Gmelin, Leopold. "Das Kunsthandwerk im Münchener Glaspalast 1898." *Kunst und Handwerk,* vol. 47 (1897-98), pp. 369-80, 405-29.

Gmelin, 1901-2
Gmelin, Leopold. "Die I. internationale Ausstellung für moderne dekorative Kunst in Turin 1902." *Kunst und Handwerk,* vol. 52 (1901-2), pp. 293-316, 325-342.

Graul, Richard, ed. *Die Krisis im Kunstgewerbe: Studien über die Wege und Ziele der modernen Richtung.* Leipzig, 1901.

Günther, 1971
Günther, Sonja. *Interieurs um 1900: Bernhard Pankok, Bruno Paul und Richard Riemerschmid als Mitarbeiter der Vereinigten Werkstätten für Kunst im Handwerk.* Munich, 1971.

Günther, 1982
Günther, Sonja. "Das Werk des Karikaturisten, Möbelentwerfers und Architekten Bruno Paul (1874-1968)." *Stadt,* vol. 29, no. 10 (Oct. 1982), pp. 18-45, 72.

Habich, 1903-4
Habich, Georg. "Ignatius Taschner." *Kunst und Handwerk,* vol. 54 (1903-4), pp. 1-18.

Habich, 1907
Habich, Georg. "Julius Diez." *Kunst und Handwerk,* vol. 57 (1906-7), pp. 225-41.

Haenel, 1906
Haenel, Erich. "Die Dritte Deutsche Kunstgewerbe-Ausstellung Dresden 1906." *Die Kunst,* vol. 14 (1906), pp. 393-511.

Haenel, Erich, and Heinrich Tscharmann, eds. *Die Wohnung der Neuzeit.* Leipzig, 1908.

Hamann and Hermand, 1967
Hamann, Richard, and Jost Hermand. *Stilkunst um 1900.* Berlin, 1967.

Hamburg, 1963
Hamburg, Museum für Kunst und Gewerbe. *Plakat- und Buchkunst um 1900.* Mar. 1-May 12, 1963.

Hamburg, 1968
Hamburg, Museum für Kunst und Gewerbe. *Jugendstil in Hamburg.* Sept. 13-Oct. 25, 1968.

Hamburg, Museum für Kunst und Gewerbe. *Jugendstil.* 1983.

Hermann, Jost. *Jugendstil: Ein Forschungsbericht 1918-1964.* Stuttgart, 1965.

Heskett, 1986
Heskett, John. *German Design 1870-1918.* New York, 1986.

Heyck, ed., 1907
Heyck, Eduard, ed. *Moderne Kultur: Ein Handbuch der Lebensbildung und des guten Geschmacks.* Vol. 1, *Grundbegriffe: Die Häuslichkeit.* Stuttgart, 1907.

Himmelheber, 1973
Himmelheber, Georg. *Die Kunst des deutschen Möbels.* Vol. 3, *Klassizismus, Historismus, Jugendstil.* Munich, 1973. 2nd. ed., rev. Heinrich Kreisel. 1983.

Hirth, ed., 1908
Hirth, Georg, ed. *Dreitausend Kunstblätter der Münchner "Jugend": Ausgewählt aus den Jahrgängen 1896-1908.* Munich, 1908.

Hoeber, 1913
Hoeber, Fritz. *Peter Behrens.* Munich, 1913.

Hofmann, 1898-99
Hofmann, Albert. "Das Kunstgewerbe auf der Berliner und auf der Münchner Kunstausstellung 1898." *Kunstgewerbeblatt,* n. s., vol. 10 (1898-99), pp. 41-57.

Hofstätter, 1968
Hofstätter, Hans H. *Jugendstil: Druckkunst.* Baden-Baden, 1968. 2nd. ed., 1973.

Hollmann, et al., 1980
Hollmann, Helga, et al. *Das frühe Plakat in Europa und den USA: Ein Bestandskatalog.* Vol. 3, *Deutschland.* Berlin, 1980.

Kadatz, 1977
Kadatz, Hans-Joachim. *Peter Behrens: Architekt, Maler, Grafiker und Formgestalter, 1868-1940.* Leipzig, 1977.

Kaiserslautern, 1966-67
Kaiserslautern, Pfalzgalerie. *Peter Behrens (1868-1940).* 1966-67.

Karlsruhe, 1978
Karlsruhe, Badisches Landesmuseum. *Jugendstil: Skulpturen, Möbel, Metallarbeiten, Glas, Textilien, Porzellan, Keramik.* 1978.

Koch, Alexander. *L'Exposition Internationale des arts décoratifs modernes à Turin, 1902.* Darmstadt, 1903.

Krefeld, 1898
Krefeld, Kaiser Wilhelm Museum. *Ausstellung künstlerischer Möbel und Geräte.* May-June 1898.

Krefeld, 1903
Krefeld, Kaiser Wilhelm Museum. *Otto Eckmann-Gedächtnis-Ausstellung.* Flier. Apr. 1903.

Krefeld, 1977-78
Krefeld, Kaiser Wilhelm Museum. *Otto Eckmann (1865-1902): Ein Hauptmeister des Jugendstils.* Nov. 6, 1977-Jan. 8, 1978.

Krefeld, 1984
Krefeld, Kaiser Wilhelm Museum. *Der westdeutsche Impuls 1900-14: Kunst und Umweltgestaltung im Industriegebiet; Von der Künstlerseide zur Industriefotografie.* 1984.

Kubly, 1969
Kubly, Vincent Frederick. "Thomas Theodor Heine (1867-1948): The Satirist as an Artist." Diss., University of Wisconsin, 1969.

Lampe-von Bennigsen, 1970
Lampe-von Bennigsen, Silvie. *Hermann Obrist: Erinnerungen.* Munich, 1970.

Lang, 1970
Lang, Lothar, ed. *Thomas Thedor Heine.* Klassiker der Karikatur, no. 1. Munich, 1970.

Lang, 1974
Lang, Lothar, ed. *Bruno Paul.* Klassiker der Karikatur, no. 2. Munich, 1974.

Linz, 1983
Linz, Stadtmuseum. *Wolfgang von Wersin (1882-1976): Gestaltung und Produktentwicklung.* Apr. 7-30, 1983.

Loubier, 1902
Loubier, Jean. "Professor Otto Eckmanns buchgewerbliche Thätigkeit." *Archiv für Buchgewerbe,* vol. 39 (1902), pp. 309-24.

Lux, 1908
Lux, Joseph August. *Das neue Kunstgewerbe in Deutschland.* Leipzig, 1908.

Madsen, 1955
Madsen, Stephan Tschudi. *Sources of Art Nouveau.* Trans. Ragnar Christophersen. New York, 1955.

Malkowsky, Georg, ed. *Die Pariser Weltausstellung in Wort und Bild.* Berlin, 1900.

Marx, Roger. *La Décoration et les industries d'art à l'Exposition Universelle de 1900.* Paris, 1901.

Masini, 1984
Masini, Lara-Vinca. *Art Nouveau.* Trans. Linda Fairbairn. London, 1984.

Mayr, "Illustrationsstil," 1901
Mayr, Karl. "Der neue Münchner Illustrationsstil und seine Hauptvertreter." *Die graphischen Künste,* vol. 24 (1901), pp. 113 ff.

Mayreder, 1912
Mayreder, Karl. "Hans von Berlepsch-Valendas und sein Wirken." *Zeitschrift des österreichischen Ingenieur- und Architekten-Vereines,* vol. 64 (1912), pp. 385-90, 401-6.

Meier-Graefe, 1898
Meier-Graefe, Julius. "Peter Behrens." *Dekorative Kunst,* vol. 1 (1898), pp. 70-74.

Meier-Graefe, 1900
Meier-Graefe, Julius. "Peter Behrens." *Dekorative Kunst,* vol. 5 (1900), pp. 2-4.

Melk-Haen, 1988
Melk-Haen, Christina. "Zwischen Jugendstil und Historismus: Hans E. v. Berlepsch-Valendas und die Debatte der Kunstreform um 1900." Diss., Eberhard-Karls-Universität, Tübingen, 1988.

Merkelbach, 1905
Reinhold Merkelbach, Grenzhausen und München: Nachdruck der Spezialpreisliste 1905. Intro. Beate Dry von Zezschwitz. Munich, 1981.

Meyer, 1905
Meyer, Alfred C. "Otto Eckmann." In *Gesammelte Reden und Aufsätze*, pp. 147-59. Berlin, 1905.

Milan, 1965
Milan, Galleria del Levante. *L'Avanguardia, Jugendstil: Hans Schmithals.* Milan, 1965.

Munich, Internationale Kunst-Ausstellung... "Secession." *Offizieller Katalog.* 1896.

Munich, 1897
Munich, Königlicher Glaspalast, VII. Internationale Kunstausstellung. *Offizieller Katalog.* June 1-Oct. 1897.

Munich, 1898
Munich, Königlicher Glaspalast, Münchner Jahres-Ausstellung. *Offizieller Katalog.* 1898.

Munich, Glaspalast, 1899
Munich, Königlicher Glaspalast, Münchner Jahres-Ausstellung. *Offizieller Katalog.* 1899.

Munich, "Secession," 1899
Munich, Internationale Kunst-Ausstellung... "Secession." *Offizieller Katalog.* 1899.

Munich, Königlicher Glaspalast, VIII. Internationale Kunstausstellung. *Illustrirter Katalog.* 1901.

Munich, 1958
Munich, Haus der Kunst. *München 1869-1958: Aufbruch zur modernen Kunst.* June 21-Oct. 5, 1958.

Munich, 1964
Munich, Haus der Kunst. *Secession: Europäische Kunst um die Jahrhundertwende.* Mar. 14-May 10, 1964.

Munich, *Hermann Obrist,* 1968
Munich, Museum Villa Stuck. *Hermann Obrist: Wegbereiter der Moderne.* 1968.

Munich, *Franz von Stuck,* 1968
Munich, Museum Villa Stuck. *Franz von Stuck.* 1968.

Munich, 1969-70
Munich, Villa Stuck. *Jugendstil Illustration in München.* Dec. 12, 1969-Mar. 15, 1970.

Munich, 1970
Munich, Museum Villa Stuck. *Pankok – Riemerschmid – Paul: Interieurs Münchner Architekten um 1900.* Apr. 11-June, 1970.

Munich, Stadtmuseum, 1972
Munich, Stadtmuseum. *Bayern: Kunst und Kultur.* June 9-Oct. 15, 1972.

Munich, Haus der Kunst, 1972
Munich, Haus der Kunst. *World Cultures and Modern Art.* June 16-Sept. 30, 1972. (Also publ. in a German ed.)

Munich, 1975-76
Munich, Stadtmuseum. *Plakate in München 1840-1940.* Oct. 16, 1975-Jan. 6, 1976. 2nd., rev. ed., 1978.

Munich, 1976
Munich, Stadtmuseum. *125 Jahre Bayerischer Kunstgewerbeverein.* July 7-Oct. 10, 1976.

Munich, 1977
Munich, Museum Villa Stuck. *August Endell: Der Architekt des Photoateliers Elvira 1871-1925.* Feb. 9-Mar. 24, 1977.

Munich, 1977-78
Munich, Haus der Kunst. *Simplicissimus: Eine satirische Zeitschrift, München 1896-1944.* Nov. 19, 1977-Jan. 15, 1978.

Munich, Villa Stuck, 1979
Munich, Museum Villa Stuck. *Silber des Jugendstils.* Apr. 25-June 24, 1979.

Munich, *Kandinsky,* 1982
Munich, Städtische Galerie im Lenbachhaus. *Kandinsky und München: Begegnungen und Wandlungen 1896-1914.* Aug. 18-Oct. 17, 1982.

Munich, 1985-86
Munich, Stadtmuseum. *Hof-Atelier Elvira, 1887-1928: Ästheten, Emanzen, Aristokraten.* Dec. 13, 1985-Mar. 2, 1986.

Münster, 1986
Münster, Westfälisches Landesmuseum für Kunst und Kulturgeschichte. *Bernhard Pankok: Malerei, Grafik, Design im Prisma des Jugendstils.* Sept. 14-Nov. 9, 1986.

Muthesius, "Neues Ornament," 1901
Muthesius, Hermann. "Neues Ornament und neue Kunst." *Die Kunst,* vol. 4 (1901), pp. 349-66.

Muthesius, 1904
Muthesius, Hermann. "Die Kunst Richard Riemerschmids." *Die Kunst,* vol. 10 (1904), pp. 249-83.

Muthesius, 1905
Muthesius, Hermann. *Das moderne Landhaus und seine innere Ausstattung.* Munich, 1905.

Muthesius, Hermann. *Kunstgewerbe und Architektur.* Jena, 1907. Repr., 1976.

Nerdinger, ed., 1982
Nerdinger, Winfried, ed. *Richard Riemerschmid: Vom Jugendstil zum Werkbund, Werke und Dokumente.* Munich, 1982.

New York, 1960
New York, The Museum of Modern Art. *Art Nouveau: Art and Design at the Turn of the Century.* June 6-Sept. 6, 1960.

New York, 1982
New York, The Solomon R. Guggenheim Museum. *Kandinsky in Munich: 1896-1914.* Jan. 22-Mar. 21, 1982.

Nickl, ed., 1984
Nickl, Peter, ed. *Adelbert Niemeyer: Die Arbeit am Gefäss.* Munich, 1984.

Niggl, 1980
Niggl, Reto. "Margarethe von Brauchitsch: Stil im Textil." *Antiquitäten-Zeitung,* no. 18 (1980), p. 399.

Niggl, 1984
Niggl, Reto. "Hermann Gradl d.Ä., Max Joseph Gradl, Hermann Gradl d.J." Sonderheft, *Antiquitäten-Zeitung,* no. 16 (1984). Munich, 1984.

Nuremberg, 1980
Nuremberg, Germanisches Nationalmuseum. *Peter Behrens und Nürnberg.* Sept. 20-Nov. 9, 1980.

Obrist, "Pourquoi," 1900
Obrist, Hermann. "Pourquoi écrire sur l'art?" *L'Art Décoratif,* vol. 17 (Feb. 1900), pp. 185-201.

Obrist, "Wozu," 1900
Obrist, Hermann. "Wozu über Kunst schreiben?" *Dekorative Kunst,* vol. 5 (1900), pp. 169-95.

Obrist, 1903
Obrist, Hermann. *Neue Möglichkeiten in der bildenden Kunst.* Leipzig, 1903.

Obrist, 1904
Obrist, Hermann. "Die Lehr- und Versuch-Ateliers für angewandte und freie Kunst." *Dekorative Kunst,* vol. 12 (1904), pp. 228-37.

Ostini, 1921
Ostini, Fritz von. *Fritz Erler.* Bielefeld, 1921.

Ottomeyer, 1988
Ottomeyer, Hans. *Jugendstil-Möbel: Katalog der Möbelsammlung des Münchner Stadtmuseums.* Munich, 1988.

Paris, 1900
Paris, Exposition Universelle 1900. *Official Catalogue: Exhibition of the German Empire.* 1900.

Paris, 1960-61
Paris, Musée National d'Art Moderne. *Les Sources du XXᵉ siècle: Les arts en Europe de 1884 à 1914.* 1960-61.

Pese, 1980
Pese, Claus. *Das Nürnberger Kunsthandwerk des Jugendstils.* Nürnberger-Werkstücke zur Stadt- und Landesgeschichte, ed. Rudolf Endres, Gerhard Hirschmann, and Gerhard Pfeiffer, vol. 30. Nuremberg, 1980.

Pevsner, Nikolaus. *Pioneers of Modern Design: From William Morris to Walter Gropius.* New York, 1949.

Pevsner, 1968
Pevsner, Nikolaus. *The Sources of Modern Architecture and Design.* London, 1968.

Popp, 1916
Popp, Joseph. *Bruno Paul.* Munich, 1916.

Prague, 1980
Prague, Uměleckoprůmyslové Muzeum. *Německá Secese; Jugendstil in Deutschland.* Sept. 16-Nov. 2, 1980.

Rammert, 1987
Rammert, Michaela. *Richard Riemerschmid: Möbel und Innenräume von 1895-1900.* Munich, 1987.

Rauecker, Bruno. *Das Kunstgewerbe in München.* Münchener Volkswirtschaftliche Studien, ed. Lujo Brentano and Walther Lotz. Stuttgart, 1911.

Rée, 1906
Rée, Paul Johannes. "Richard Riemerschmid." *Die Kunst,* vol. 14 (1906), pp. 265-303.

Reichel, 1974
Reichel, Klaus. "Vom Jugendstil zur Sachlich-

keit: August Endell (1871-1925)." Diss., Ruhr-Universität, Bochum, 1974.

Rheims, 1966

Rheims, Maurice. *The Flowering of Art Nouveau.* Trans. Patrick Evans. New York, 1966.

Rosner, 1898

Rosner, Karl. *Die dekorative Kunst im neunzehnten Jahrhundert.* Berlin, 1898.

Rosner, 1899

Rosner, Karl. *Das Deutsche Zimmer in neunzehnten Jahrhundert: Eine Darstellung desselben im Zeitalter des Klassizismus, der Biedermeierzeit, der rückblickenden Bestrebungen und der neuen Kunst.* Munich, 1899.

Sailer, Anton. *Franz von Stuck: Ein Lebensmärchen.* Munich, 1969.

St. Louis, *Descriptive Catalogue,* 1904

St. Louis, Louisiana Purchase Exhibition. *Descriptive Catalogue of the German Arts and Crafts.* 1904.

St. Louis, *Official Catalogue,* 1904

St. Louis, Louisiana Purchase Exhibition. *Official Catalogue of the Exhibition of the German Empire.* 1904.

Schack, 1971

Schack von Wittenau, Clementine. "Glas zwischen Kunsthandwerk und Industrie-Design: Studien über Herstellungsarten und Formtypen des deutschen Jugendstilglases." Diss., Universität zu Köln, Cologne, 1971.

Schack, 1976

Schack von Wittenau, Clementine. *Die Glaskunst: Ein Handbuch über Herstellung, Sammeln und Gebrauch des Hohlglases.* Munich, 1976.

Schaefer, 1971

Schaefer, Inge. "August Endell." *Werk,* vol. 58 (1971), pp. 402-8.

Schäll, 1980

Schäll, Ernst. "Friedrich Adler (1878-1942): Ein zu Unrecht vergessener Künstler des deutschen Jugendstils." *Alte und moderne Kunst,* vol. 25, no. 168 (1980), pp. 24-30.

Schäll, 1981

Schäll, Ernst. "Friedrich Adler (1878-1942): Ein Künstler aus Laupheim." *Schwäbische Heimat,* 32nd. year, no. 1 (Jan.-Mar. 1981), pp. 46-61.

Scheffler, "Niemeyer," 1907

Scheffler, Karl "Adalbert [sic] Niemeyer." *Die Kunst,* vol. 16 (1907), pp. 481-504.

Schindler, 1972

Schindler, Herbert. *Monografie des Plakats: Entwicklung, Stil, Design.* Munich, 1972.

Schlee, 1984

Schlee, Ernst. *Scherrebeker Bildteppiche.* Kunst in Schleswig-Holstein, ed. Gerhard Wietek, vol. 26. Neumünster, 1984.

Schleswig, 1959

Schleswig, Schleswig-Holsteinisches Landesmuseum, Schloss Gottorf. *Bildteppiche der Webschule in Scherrebek, 1896-1902.* June 7-July 26, 1959.

Schmoll, ed., 1972

Schmoll gen. Eisenwerth, Josef Adolf, ed. *Das Phänomen Franz von Stuck: Kritiken, Essays, Interviews 1968-1972.* Munich, 1972.

Schmoll, 1977

Schmoll gen. Eisenwerth, Helga. "Die Münchner Debschitz-Schule: Lehr- und Versuchs-Ateliers für angewandte und freie Kunst, Hermann Obrist und Wilhelm von Debschitz, München, 1902-14 (1920)." In *Kunstschul-Reform 1900-1933,* ed. H. M. Wingler, pp. 68-82. Berlin, 1977.

Schmutzler, 1962

Schmutzler, Robert. *Art Nouveau.* New York, 1962.

Schneck, Adolf G. *Neue Möbel vom Jugendstil bis heute.* Munich, 1962.

Schroeter, 1988

Schroeter, Christina. "Fritz Erler und sein künstlerisches Wirken." Diss., Johann Wolfgang von Goethe Universität, Frankfurt am Main, 1988.

Schultze-Naumburg, Paul. *Hausbau: Einführende Gedanken zu den Kulturarbeiten.* 2nd ed. *Kulturarbeiten,* vol. 1. Munich, 1904.

Schultze-Naumburg, Paul. *Häusliche Kunstpflege.* Jena, 1910.

Schumacher, et al., 1906

Schumacher, Fritz, et al. *Das deutsche Kunstgewerbe 1906: III. Deutsche Kunstgewerbe-Ausstellung Dresden 1906.* Munich, 1906.

Schumann, 1899

Schumann, Paul. "Die Deutsche Kunst-Ausstellung zu Dresden von Mai-Oktober 1899, A: Moderne Zimmer-Ausstattung." *Deutsche Kunst und Dekoration,* vol. 4 (1899), pp. 493-525.

Seling, ed., 1959

Seling, Helmut, ed. *Jugendstil: Der Weg ins 20. Jahrhundert.* Heidelberg, 1959.

Selle, 1974

Selle, Gert. *Jugendstil und Kunst-Industrie: Zur Ökonomie und Ästhetik des Kunstgewerbes um 1900.* Ravensburg, 1974.

Simmen, 1982

Simmen, Jeannot. *Zeichnungen und Druckgraphik von Otto Eckmann: Der Bestand in der Kunstbibliothek Berlin.* Berlin, 1982.

Singer, 1898

Singer, Hans W. "Über Keramik von Schmuz-Baudiss." *Deutsche Kunst und Dekoration,* vol. 2 (1898), pp. 205-11.

Spielmann, 1965

Spielmann, Heinz, ed. *Der Jugendstil in Hamburg.* Bilderhefte des Museums für Kunst und Gewerbe, no. 7. Hamburg, 1965.

Spielmann, 1977

Hamburg, Museum für Kunst und Gewerbe. *Räume und Meisterwerke der Jugendstil-Sammlung.* Ed. Heinz Spielmann. 1977.

Spielmann, 1979

Hamburg, Museum für Kunst und Gewerbe. *Die Jugendstil-Sammlung.* Vol. 1, *Künstler A-F.* Ed. Heinz Spielmann, et al. 1979.

Stuttgart, 1973

Stuttgart, Württembergisches Landesmuseum, Altes Schloss. *Bernhard Pankok, 1872-1943: Kunsthandwerk – Malerei – Graphik – Architektur – Bühnenausstattungen.* May 24-July 29, 1973.

Stuttgart, 1980

Stuttgart, Württembergisches Landesmuseum. *Art Nouveau: Textil-Dekor um 1900.* July 10-Aug. 31, 1980.

Stüwe, 1978

Stüwe [von Dücker], Elisabeth. *Der Simplicissimus-Karikaturist Thomas Theodor Heine als Maler: Aspekte seiner Malerei.* Frankfurt am Main, 1978.

Suckale-Redlefsen, 1975

Suckale-Redlefsen, Gude. "Plakate in München, 1840-1940." *Novum Gebrauchsgraphik,* vol. 46 (Dec. 1975), pp. 44-45.

Thoma and Heilmeyer, 1921

Thoma, Ludwig, and Alexander Heilmeyer, eds. *Ignatius Taschner.* Munich, 1921.

Turin, 1902

Turin, Esposizione Internazionale. *Katalog der deutschen Abteilung.* Munich, 1902.

Uecker, 1978

Uecker, Wolf. *Lampen und Leuchter, Lampes et Bougeoirs, Lamps and Candlesticks: art nouveau, art deco.* Herrsching, 1978.

Unwin, 1922

Unwin, Raymond. "Memoir on H. E. Berlepsch-Valendas." *Garden Cities and Town-Planning* (Mar. 1922), pp. 44-45.

Voss, 1973

Voss, Heinrich. *Franz von Stuck, 1863-1928.* Munich, 1973.

Warlich, 1908

Warlich, Hermann. *Wohnung und Hausrat: Beispiele neuzeitlicher Wohnräume und ihrer Ausstattung.* Munich, 1908.

Weiss, 1979

Weiss, Peg. *Kandinsky in Munich: The Formative Jugendstil Years.* Princeton, 1979.

Weiss, "Kandinsky in Munich," 1982

Weiss, Peg. "Kandinsky in Munich: Encounters and Transformations." See New York, 1982.

Weiss, "Kandinsky und München," 1982

Weiss, Peg. "Kandinsky und München: Begegnungen und Wandlungen." See Munich, *Kandinsky,* 1982.

Wersin, 1962

Wersin, Wolfgang von. *Vom Adel der Form zum reinen Raum.* Vienna, 1962.

Westheim, 1907

Westheim, Paul. "Deutsche Plakatkünstler der Gegenwart," *Buch- und Kunstdruck,* vol. 7 (1907), pp. 224-29.

H. Wichmann, 1978

Wichmann, Hans. *Aufbruch zum neuen Wohnen: Deutsche Werkstätten und WK-Verband; ihr Beitrag zur Kultur unseres Jahrhunderts.* Basel, 1978.

H. Wichmann, 1985

Wichmann, Hans. *Industrial Design, Unikate,*

Serienerzeugnisse: Die Neue Sammlung, ein neuer Museumstyp des 20. Jahrhunderts. Munich, 1985.

S. Wichmann, 1977
Wichmann, Siegfried. *Jugendstil: Art Nouveau.* Munich, 1977.

S. Wichmann, 1980
Wichmann, Siegfried. *Japonismus: Ostasien – Europa; Begegnungen in der Kunst des 19. und 20. Jahrhunderts.* Herrsching, 1980.

S. Wichmann, 1984
Wichmann, Siegfried. *Jugendstil Art Nouveau: Floral and Functional Forms.* Trans. Michael Heron. Boston, 1984.

S. Wichmann, *Jugendstil Floral,* 1984
Wichmann, Siegfried. *Jugendstil Floral Funktional.* Herrsching, 1984.

Windsor, 1981
Windsor, Alan. *Peter Behrens: Architect and Designer.* New York, 1981.

Woeckel, 1968
Woeckel, Gerhard P. *Jugendstilsammlung.* Kassel, 1968.

Ziegert, 1985
Ziegert, Beate. "The Debschitz School Munich 1902–1914." Master's thesis, Syracuse University, 1985.

Ziegert, 1986
Ziegert, Beate. "The Debschitz School Munich: 1902–1914." *Design Issues,* vol. 3, no. 1 (Spring 1986), pp. 28–41.

Zimmermann, 1900
Zimmermann, Ernst. "Prof. Otto Eckmann, I: Die Jahre künstlerischer Entwickelung." *Deutsche Kunst und Dekoration,* vol. 6 (1900), pp. 305–13.

Zurich, 1952
Zurich, Kunstgewerbemuseum. *Um 1900, Art Nouveau und Jugendstil: Kunst und Kunstgewerbe aus Europa und Amerika zur Zeit der Stilwende.* June 28–Sept. 28, 1952.

Zurich, 1967
Zurich, Kunsthaus: *Neue Kunst in der Schweiz zu Beginn unseres Jahrhunderts.* Aug. 19–Sept. 24, 1967.

Zurich, 1975
Zurich, Kunstgewerbemuseum. *Objekte des Jugendstils.* 1975.

Index